Between the Bookends
with
Ted Malone
VOLUME FIVE

Between the Bookends with Ted Malone

VOLUME FIVE

✯ ✯ ✯ ✯ ✯ ✯ ✯ ✯ ✯ ✯

BOOKMARK PRESS
CAMDEN, NEW JERSEY

Copyright 1942
F. Alden Russell

First Printing ....November, 1942
Second Printing ..December, 1942
Third Printing ....July, 1943
Fourth Printing ..September, 1943
Fifth Printing ....April, 1944

Original Illustration by RUTH KAHL

WHEN I mentioned to Bubbles that we were going to name this book *Between the Bookends*, she looked up, puzzled, and inquired how in the world anyone could name a book—*Between the Bookends?* Surprised at her reaction, I demanded, "And why not? How in the world could anyone name a little girl—*Bubbles?*" She said she had often wondered that one, too. Whereupon I decided the time had come to talk of cabbages and kings . . . or rather poetry . . . books . . . and little girls and the curious names of things.

So if you will excuse me, I would like to use a page or two to explain to Bubbles what this book is all about and how it came to have such an extraordinary name.

Between the Bookends . . . Bubbles . . . is not just a radio program . . . or a department in a magazine, as you might imagine. It is not just a clearinghouse for new poetry, although over a hundred thousand poems a year are sent to us for consideration by poets all over America. It is all these things and something much more important than any of them. Have you ever noticed a pair of bookends on our library table, Bubbles? Maybe a volume of Dickens stands between them . . . *A Tale of Two Cities* . . . maybe Omar Khayyam. You can almost hear the music of the temple bells . . . the musicians in the Persian garden. You can hear the hoarse cries of the shopkeepers along the narrow streets . . . yet it's only Omar Khayyam standing quietly between the bookends. They are a gateway to all the romance . . . all the knowledge . . . all the laughter . . . all the hope . . . all the everything worth keeping since the beginning of time. Maybe it sounds like a game . . . maybe it is . . . but I promise you it is a very delightful one—a game of endless adventures through the gateway Between the Bookends.

But this is only a book of poetry . . . you are thinking . . . why should it have this name? Wait until you start in reading it. You'll find this isn't just one single book . . . but dozens of books . . . books of mystery stories . . . philosophy . . . biographies . . . cook books . . . garden books . . . diaries . . . doctors' books . . . and a dozen more. That is the enchanting thing about poetry . . . it can fill a hundred books . . . on a hundred different subjects . . . because it can be interpreted a thousand different ways.

But let me tell you something more about this book, and then you will understand better what I mean. I call this one *V Volume* . . . *Volume Five* . . . *Between the Bookends*. And you might think that that is simply because this is our fifth book . . . the others being *The American Album of Poetry*, the *Scrapbook*, *American Pilgrimage*, and *Pack Up Your Troubles*. But a happy coincidence gives this an added importance. Certain symbols in our alphabet have come to have great significance in our way of life. *E*, for example, stands for *excellence* . . . and now the letter *V* has come to mean *victory* in the broadest terms in which it has ever been interpreted. More than *superior strength* . . . *triumph in arms* . . . it means *victory in peace* as well as *victory in war*. *V for Victory* is a song of triumph for all civilization. But wait a minute . . . these are just abstract terms, names, like *democracy* . . . *republic* . . . *indivisible we stand* . . . *liberty and justice for all* . . . *the four freedoms* . . . and their meanings may not be any clearer to you, Bubbles, than they were to me until I discovered something. 'Names are things' . . . and life is just the game of learning what these 'name things' really are . . . and what they do . . . and learning how to use them. And now comes the important part, reading the thousands of poems, week in and week out, I have discovered that the poets have found a way to translate these abstract terms . . . *freedom* . . . *hope* . . . *liberty* . . . into simple human experiences. *Freedom,* as a word in a book, is only seven important little letters, but going to church on Sunday . . . dressed in nice clean clothes . . . buying anything you choose at the store . . . writing books saying anything you believe . . . those are freedoms more important than the Seven Wonders of the World.

The Constitution of these United States, as a document in a museum or a half dozen pages in a history book, is nothing more than a great many words in grammatical sequence. But when you think of the peasant families struggling to harvest the crops for the feudal lords . . . the dauntless warriors who fought King John until they forced him to lay down his sword and take up a pen to sign the Magna Charta . . . the Pilgrims starting out on their perilous journey in their tiny sailing ship . . . the courageous Colonists building new homes in the New World . . . going out to battle defending these homes . . . many of them dying to protect their families and to give their children a chance to think and say what they believe. Then when you realize that all those words in that Constitution in the book are really the story of all this, though none of these things are even mentioned . . . when you understand that they grew out of the lives of all these people, although most of them are forgotten . . . you may begin to wonder if your life will ever be a part of it . . . you may begin to wonder if it's a part of you. I've mentioned the Constitution, Bubbles, only because most people, whether they realize it or not, think of it as the name of something kept in Washington. Just as they think of *life* as the name of something going on downtown; or *fun* the name of something everybody else has more of than they do. And that's all wrong because, as you once told me, laughter is most fun when you're the one who's laughing. That's just as true of all these other words . . . *hope* . . . *faith* . . . *courage* . . . they are only words until some magic can translate them into life.

Poetry can do this. If you want to know the hungers of people, the simple wishes they share with their neighbors, the dreams they have . . . read poetry. If you want to know what freedom means . . . read the poems of homes . . . of little children . . . of love . . . of work. If you want to know why men and women work faithfully all their lives, what they march into battle and death to defend . . . read their poetry. Read the simple verses written in their letters . . . the boisterous boasts they publish in their papers . . . the prayers they whisper . . . and the solemn stories they tell in the lyric meters of poetry. During this past year, Bubbles, I have read thousands and thousands of poems written by thousands of men and women . . . homemakers . . . boys and girls in school . . . soldiers in the Far East, and in England, India, Egypt . . . business men . . . government officers . . . poems translating into stories and songs the hunger . . . the need . . . the courage . . . the laughter . . . of a people striving for this thing called *victory* in the great adventure of living. And I have selected from all these the stories . . . the songs . . . the poems that I believe best tell what people want out of life . . . their work and games . . . gardens . . . letters . . . philosophies . . . their idea of *victory* in the adventure of living. I have gathered all these Between the Bookends and built this fifth book . . . our *V Book* . . . of America . . . by America . . . and for America.

You are America, Bubbles . . . you and Verlia and Happy . . . and all the boys and girls and men and women in our neighborhood . . . and all the other neighborhoods. That's all America is . . . that's simple, isn't it? Everything is just that simple when you make it a part of your own life. . . . but then it becomes important too, because there isn't anything more important than us . . . is there? Poetry is important for that same reason . . . it's simple, because it's all about us . . . it's important, because it's a part of us. It *is* a game, after all, isn't it . . . Bubbles . . . and as we read the book together, I think maybe you will find it a most delightful game that we *can* name after that enchanting gateway . . . "Between the Bookends."

Acknowledgment

For the privilege of using poems in this book, our thanks are due first to each individual author who has graciously consented to have them reprinted. In every case where it was possible, we have searched out the book or magazine in which the poems have previously appeared, and because it is our hope that you will want to read more poems by each of these authors, we are listing as many such sources as we are able to find . . .

First the magazines which are always a rich mine of modern poetry . . . our thanks to . . . America, American Magazine, American National Catholic Weekly, American Poetry Magazine, Atlantic Monthly, Better Homes & Gardens, Christian Science Monitor, Columbia, Commonweal, Cornwall House, Cosmopolitan, Current Opinion, Driftwind, Farm Journal and Farmer's Wife, Good Housekeeping, Harper's Monthly, Household Magazine, Kaleidograph, Kansas Industrialist, Ladies' Home Journal, Los Angeles School Journal, Music in Miniature, Needlecraft, Ohio Schools, Parent-Teacher Magazine, Pasque Petals, Pictorial Review, Poesy, Poet Lore, Poetry Caravan, Poetry Presents, Poetry Society of Southern California, Poetry World, Quest, Relief Society Magazine, Rotarian, St. Anthony Messenger, St. Nicholas, Saturday Evening Post, Script, Shards, Silhouette, Spokane Spokesman Review, Street and Smith's Publications, Sunset Magazine, Talaria, The American Mercury, The Ave Maria, The Better Home, The Brides' Magazine, The Catholic Woman's World, The Christian Century, The Coast, The Congress Lantern, The Dream Shop, The Gypsy, The New Yorker, The Saturday Review of Literature, The Singing Quill, The Southern Literary Messenger,

The Standard Review of Literature, The Step Ladder, Verse Craft, Vers Libre, Wings.

Then the newspapers whose columns have contributed to these pages . . . Columbus Citizen, Columbus Dispatch, Daily Missourian, Denver Post, Evening Sun, Indianapolis Star, Lansing Journal, New York Herald Tribune, New York Journal-American, New York Sun, New York Times, Oregon Journal, Providence Sunday Journal, Toronto Saturday Night, Washington Evening Star, Washington-Post and Nixson Denton's Column in the Cincinnati Times-Star, and Lee Shippey's Column in the Los Angeles Times.

And to the following . . . Samuel J. Allard for permission to reprint his selection from "Scimitar and Song"; D. Appleton & Co. for permission to reprint Violet Alleyn Storey's poems from "Tea in an Old House"; Banner Press for poems by James E. Warren, Jr., from "This Side of Babylon"; Morton Meade Cheney for Ethel B. Cheney's poems from "New Language"; Circle Publishing Co. for Kathryn Kay's poems from "With Tongue in Cheek"; John B. Cruise for his poem from "Green Altars"; Edwin and Betsy Davis for Jeannette Sewell Davis' poems from "Day and Night"; Stephen Daye Press for Mabel Posegate's poems from "Once When Arcturus Shone"; Dodd Mead & Co. for Adelaide Love's poems from "The Crystal Flute," and also John Richard Moreland's quatrain from "Stevenson's Home Book of Quotations"; Dorrance & Co., Inc., for Mary White Slater's poems from "The Child Book"; E. P. Dutton & Co., Inc., for Helen Welshimer's poems from "Singing Drums"; Henry Harrison for Eunice Mildred Lon Coske's poems from "Coal Dust and Crystals," and Dudley B. Madden's poem from "The Hermit's Peak and Other Poems"; House of Field, Inc., for Erica May Brooks' poem from "Into Space"; Bruce Humphries, Inc., for Isabel Fiske Conant's poems from "Orange Feather"; Ruth Inscho for her poem from "Songs from the Canyon Country"; Klein-Heimbinder Co. for Florence Hamilton's poems from "A Moment's Monument"; Liveright for Irene Wilde's poems from "Fire Against the Sky"; MacMillan Co. for Anderson M. Scruggs' poem from "Ritual for Myself," and Mary Carolyn Davies' poems from "Youth Riding"; Metropolitan Press for Ethel Romig Fuller's poems from "Kitchen Sonnets"; John Richard Moreland for his poems from "The Moon Mender" and "What of the Night"; Mosher Press for Sydney King Russell's poems from "Lost Warrior"; Barton Rees Pogue for his poem from "Wayside Windows"; Harriet Seymour Popowski for her poems from "Twenty Christmases"; Anna M. Priestly for her poem from " Bright Spires"; G. P. Putnam's Sons for Lulu Chittenden's poem from "My Heart Goes Home", Gertrude Ryder Bennett's poems from "Etched in Words", and Virginia Taylor McCormick's poem from "Winter Apples"; Cecile Houghton Stury for the poem from "Patter of Rain"; George Sully & Co. for B. Y. Williams' poems from "House of Happiness"; Talaria for Annette Patton Cornell's poem from "The Forbidden Woman'"; The English Club of Cornell College for William L. Stidger's poem from "Rainbow-Born is Beauty"; The Wings Press for Louise Liebhardt's poem from "Love is a Thistle"; Yale University Press for Karle Wilson Baker's poem from "Burning Bush" . . . and a host more books, written and unwritten, published and unpublished which are represented here in word and spirit, but were not included by title or published because to include them all would be a book in itself.

Of course since all the poems in the book are a part of "Between the Bookends" let me say again as I did in our "Album" and "Scrapbook" it is my privilege to acknowledge Herbert Mayes, Editor of Good Housekeeping Magazine, and Phillips Carlin, Program Director of the Blue Network, Inc., for their inestimable aid in guiding "Between the Bookends" to what I immodestly describe as its eminent place in both the publishing and broadcasting fields.

Lastly, let me thank those unsung workers in song who kept at me until this book was started and then kept at *it* until it was done . . . the ladies—God bless them!—who did the work: Joan Riesbeck, who had all the ideas . . . and made all the mistakes; Harriet Lundgaard, who corrected all the mistakes . . . and caused all the troubles; Gwen Alden, who smoothed out the troubles . . . and mixed up the book; Verlia, who straightened out the book . . . and drove me . . . home . . . So, since home is where I like to be when I read a book . . . this looks like a good place to start in with the index.

Sectional Index

In the Beginning Was the Word	14
The Road is Marked . . . You Can't Miss It	32
According to the Almanac	50
Any Similarity to Persons Living or Dead	70
With This Ring I Thee Wed	96
Run, Postman, Run	112
Little Pitchers Have Big Ears	126
An Apple a Day Keeps the Doctor	146
I Beg Your Pardon	160
I Solemnly Swear to Do My Duty	174
Sugar and Spice to Taste	196
And They Came Out of Our Own Garden	208
Dear Diary	228
Once in the Dear Dead Days Beyond Recall	246
Please Do Feed the Animals	268
From a Purely Philosophical Standpoint	286
The Mystery Deepens	306
To Make a Long Story Short	332

THE EMINENT GUEST

Here let me be alone with poetry
Tonight. Today was too much. Let me be
Intoxicated with the ecstasy
Of imagination; something wide, free,
Something perfect, something to bury pain,
Something greater than disappointment or
The cause of disappointment. Let the rain
Fall then, if it must, let any door
Close, if it can. Once I have been alone
With poetry the silences will tell
Where Heaven is and where the unbeknown
Of God and beauty waits: where true thoughts dwell
Unborn and where there's something greater than
The small things that can happen to a man.

C. Faye Bennett.

In the Beginning Was the Word

"Yet out of his joy . . . was born his sorrow . . . the apples were so good that Fall . . .

ADAM WAS HAPPIER THAN WE

We look on Autumn's glory:
Its scarlet and its gold,
With gladness that is tempered.
Far-seeing eyes behold

The interval to follow
With blustering and snow.
The heart of man is wistful;
He does not crave it so.

When Adam first saw Autumn,
In its felicity,
The seasons that he numbered
Were three.

MABEL POSEGATE.

"Begging all pardons, I've always doubted Solomon's wisdom . . . since I heard he had seven hundred wives . . .

MOTHERHOOD

Oh it would take a Solomon
  In wisdom to decide
What judgment should be meted out
  To these who stand beside
My chair. She snatched his hat and ran—
  He made her trip and fall—
She was at fault when it began,
  And yet she broke her doll
In falling. How am I to judge?
What rule shall I employ?
I am that tearful little girl!
I am that sober boy!

EDITH CHERRINGTON.

"Those little white lies . . . in a great big way . . .

ANANIAS

Prevarication was his first resort,
   The refuge of a swift and subtle mind
Keyed to the cunning of the sly retort;
   Yet he could tell the truth when so inclined,
Which was but seldom. He was one to weave
   Amazing tales that sought to glorify
His own bravado, and at once deceive
   A score of minds that failed to pierce the lie.

The simple love of truth for its own sake
   Was never bred in him. The fact that white
Was always white and never black, that two
   And two, however reckoned, could not make
More than their sum or less, he never knew
   Who dared to think two wrongs could make a right.

SYDNEY KING RUSSELL.

"Whatever the answer . . . there's no question but what all ladies are the salt of the earth . . .

QUESTIONS ON LOT'S WIFE

Oftentimes I picture Lot's wife,
Salt statue on the plain
Of Sodom, choked eyes toward the city
Drenched in burning rain.

Later did the sheep and oxen
Stand and lick her form?
Did she harden in oven-desert
Or melt in eastern storm?

Did Lot entreat a late forgiveness,
Owning his part of fault?
And since her day have tears of women
Stung with surplus salt?

MILDRED SHACKLETT.

"Lots of wives should be wives of Lot . . . and, adding a grain of salt . . . so what?

SUBSTITUTE

I should be pillared salt, who swore
Never to take this long a look
Backward over the roads we took,
Wanting a joy that is no more.

Yet from these eyes designed for sleeping,
Watching the passing lovely thing,
Or laughing, crueler salt can spring
Than statuary, in slow weeping.

ELAINE V. EMANS.

"I knew an old man who always read each verse in the Bible twice . . . he said it was clearer the third time that way . . . Read this poem four times . . .

OH ABRAHAM

Oh, Abraham, beloved of God,
Yours was a trial, indeed,
But God was gracious, Abraham,
He gave you back your seed.

Oh, Abraham, you were so sure,
Your faith so undefiled,
If through such testing I endure,
Will He preserve my child?

Will He exempt from awful blight
My sacrifice to war,
That through a black and crucial night
Of agony, I bore?

Oh, Abraham, brave Abraham,
Sad mothers everywhere
Would know the secret of your faith
That God may hear their prayer.

CECILE BONHAM.

"You're not anticipating any other likeness to the gentleman . . . I hope . . . There's something very tempting about this . . . nevertheless I doubt if it would be a great trial after all . . .

WHEN I AM OLD AND FULL OF YEARS

When I am old, like Job, and full of years,
Oh, bring no somber-colored shawl, my Dears,
To mantle my stooped shoulders from the cold,
Thinking, "This neutral gray becomes the old."
Come not with scarf of muted lavender,
And whisper, "Pastel shades are best for her,"
But, rather, bring a gypsy scarf of plaid
As vibrant as the thrilling years I've had.
Give me a housecoat, warm, tomato red,
To touch with flame my silver-sprinkled head.
I crave no pale, thin cups for twilight tea,
But I would love a bright blue pot pourri
To bid my soul, by rainbow ribbons drawn,
Swing down the Sunset Trail to meet the Dawn.

JULIA CLAY BARRON WEBB.

" 'And God said, Let us make man in our image, after our likeness: and let them have dominion . . . over all the earth' . . .

NAZARETH'S BOY

Was He a boy like other boys . . . I wonder?
   Trudging the fields and hills of Galilee?
Flinging Himself, when tired, at full length under
   Some ancient sycamore, or olive tree?

Did He build tall dream towers in that out-yonder
   Rimming blue waves? Did white ships, bound for sea,
Beckon? And tempests thrill Him with sharp thunder?
   Was He a boy like any boy . . . like me?

JESSIE WILMORE MURTON.

"1 A . . .

YOUNG FISHERMAN ON THE GULF

He was golden from the sun, and tall and strong.
His eyes, sea-blue, were crinkled round
From looking into shining distances,
And they were steadfast eyes, as lighthouses
On the rocky shores.
His smile was quick and sweet upon small children
And stray dogs. One knew that faith was in his soul
And courage in his heart, while with content
He labored at his daily tasks.
I think that had he lived in Nazareth
And had my Lord come by, He would have chosen
This young fisherman to follow Him,
And he would have gone with gladness
And that same steadfastness in his sea-blue eyes.

EDITH TATUM.

"It's a curious commentary on our social structure . . . that it really is about as difficult for a girl to be as bad as a boy . . . as for a boy to be as nice as a girl . . .

RETURN

The prodigal daughter came home;
   She had traveled too far and too fast,
She had wasted her substance and eaten of husks
   Ere she came to herself at last.

Her mother kissed her—and wept,
   Her father was sad and stern;
There was no ring and robe, and no joyful feast
   For the wandering one's return.

The neighborhood looked askance
   And gossiped of what she had done—
For no one believed that the parable meant
   The daughter as well as the son.

GERTRUDE PERRY STANTON.

" 'Oh, come, come, come, come, come, to the church in the wildwood' .."

SUNDAY NIGHT SERVICE

In this still place, and musty-sweet,
The neighbors meet together
To thank the Lord for growing wheat,
And perfect haying weather.

All cherry-stained the hands that turn
The hymnbook's yellow pages,
And sun-burned men, clear-eyed and stern,
Chant out the Rock of Ages.

The pews reflect the sunset cloud,
A truce to fear and doubting—
And over heads devoutly bowed,
Young lovers' eyes are shouting.

LOUISE LOUNSBURY.

"Moment miracle . . .

"AND THIS I ASK—"

The "Now I lay me's" floated in
Rare eloquence, that once more sin
Be pardoned, shamed the sunset's glow.
And clouds grew thick with thanks. Below
Earth held up hands for Heaven to fill.

God leaned against His window-sill
In pensive brooding. . . . Through the noise
A sob cut clearly. Then a boy's:
"If Rags should die before I wake,
I pray Thee, Lord, his soul to take."

God's hand, past priest and pedagogue,
Reached out to heal a small boy's dog.

MAYHOWARD AUSTIN MCEACHERN.

" *'The Lord is my shepherd . . . I shall not want'* . . .

KNITTED SHAWL

She said when we asked her: "Why, nothing, dears, at all.
Perhaps a large-print Bible or a little knitted shawl."

We begged her, "Oh, remember!" Because she used to tell
Of all that we should bring her when our grown world
      went well—

Gardens full of roses and trips to carry her
Where lovely halls of statues and ancient temples were

(Gay feet and restless, that never could run free,
Because of our hands clinging to hand and breast and knee!)

Cobweb-patterned laces and yellow, starry rings
And clinking silver bracelets and silken underthings!

But we who could recall her, so young and tired and gay
With long, wild, girlish longings for things she could not
      say—

All that we could bring her forever now at all
Was just a large-print Bible and a little knitted shawl.

                              Margaret Widdemer.

" *'Here we go around the mulberry bush . . . so early in the morning'* . . .

FOR A LITTLE GIRL

We took a pail and walking hand in hand,
We picked blueberries in the pasture-land.
And from each handful she had eaten one
Blue globule, honey-sweet with dew and sun.
And as I stooped to kiss her small stained mouth,
She said, "Look, Mother, there toward the South
Is stretched a band of deeper, bluest blue.
I guess God keeps a patch of berries, too."

O God, let her pick berries once again,
And make mud-pies; run bare-foot in the rain;
To sew ineptly for a heavenly doll,
To keep a pony in a golden stall;
Let her begin where she left off ... at seven,
Continuing all childish joys in Heaven!

EUNICE MILDRED LONCOSKE.

"Alpha to Omega . . . the long and short of it . . .

HEAVEN'S BOUNDARY

How vast is Heaven?—Its space can fit
The boundary you give to it;
So broad—it takes in all things true:
So narrow—it can hold but you.

JOHN RICHARD MORELAND.

" 'And the scales fell from her eyes . . . and they were opened' . . .

BLIND CHILD

When first I spoke His name,
  You begged of me;
"Oh, let me touch His face!
  Then I shall see
Just how He looks. He must
  Be beautiful!"
Your little hand reached out
  In the strange lull
Before I said: "He's there—
  Wherever we go.
But fingers cannot touch, eyes see
  Him, even so.
He must be felt by each
  With heart and mind."
You smiled. "Why, then, for Him,
  There are no blind!"

VIOLET ALLEYN STOREY.

" 'And the Lord said, It is not good that man should be alone; I will make him a helpmate for him' . . .

WOMAN'S SACRAMENT

Men were His last companions at the table
At that sad meal, within the upper room,
Striving to do the utmost they were able
To lift the shadow of His coming doom.

Men broke with Him the bread of consecration
And drained with Him the sacramental cup—
Through men He also suffered condemnation;
By them the cruel cross was lifted up.

The women He had taught and treated kindly,
Who had sat daily at the Master's feet,
Gathered in little groups and waited blindly,
As they had waited in the learner's seat.

For them there was no promise of tomorrow,
No hope to carry with them through the years,
Upon their tongues the acid bread of sorrow,
And, on their lips, the bitter wine of tears.

But, on the morning of the Resurrection,
Women were first to reach the open tomb,
First with the evidence of their affection,
First to put off the clinging shroud of gloom.

ANNA M. PRIESTLEY

"Or would they all be calling for a drink of water!

QUESTION BEFORE THE HOUSE

If God took the tops off the houses tonight,
Would He find them, all through with their playing—
The children, I mean—being sent STRAIGHT to bed,
Or, most of them, FOLDED, for praying?

MAYHOWARD AUSTIN MCEACHERN.

"Where were his friends? ... Where were his friends? ... Where are his friends today? ..."

PONTIUS PILATE SPEAKS

I hoped to hear, through calls importunate,
   But yet another sound as moments passed,
A sudden clamor at the outer gate
   To tell me that his friends had come at last.

Where were they all? Why, only days before,
   They hailed him with hosannas and with palms.
Where was the palsied man who walked once more?
   The beggar given sight instead of alms?

Where were the ones who saw their children blest?
   The erstwhile lepers free to roam at will?
The dead called back as if but waked from rest?
   The hungry thousands fed upon the hill?

Aye, even as he heard the taunting jeers
   On that dark morning of a darker day,
Peter was wasting precious time in tears
   And faithless Judas went the coward's way.

I was a ruler sent from other lands.
   I worshipped other gods. Though I could see
No fault in Him, I did but wash my hands
   To put aside responsibility.

And yet my heart was heavy. Had there been
   Even a few to shout for his release,
I could have told the gentle Nazarene—
   "I find you guiltless. Go your way in peace."

So put not, overmuch, the blame on me—
   You who at Easter kneel again to pray,
For, more than by my indecision, He
   Was crucified by those who stayed away.

                      MABEL FREER LOVERIDGE.

"And thus we inherit the Kingdom of Heaven . . .

BEATITUDES

We live by faith—though never a prayer we say.
We trust the earth to roll from night to day,
The tides of grass to break in foaming flowers,
The fountain trees to rise in cool green showers.

We live by beauty—though no song we sing.
Our nostrils know the ecstasy of spring,
Warm whiffs of rain on lilacs cold as snow—
Our eyes know hills at dawn and sunset glow.

We live by love—though never our love we meet.
Home, comrades, children, work and play are sweet,
Books, firelight, dogs; a window to the moon
And stars rose-white in midnight's black lagoon.

We live by hope—though loved and lovers die—
That death brings wakening to another sky,
And when our shining beads of day are said,
Like children we fall trustfully to bed.

Mary White Slater.

Life, like a dome of many-coloured glass,
Stains the white radiance of eternity.

Percy Bysshe Shelley.

" 'No place is so dear to my childhood . . . as the little brown church in the vale' . . .

IN CHURCH

It does not seem so very long ago
Since I watched them every Sunday night;
She was younger then, and he, I know,
Not more than three, a truly lovely sight!
Before the sermon ended he would curl
Up close to Grandma, blue eyes closed in sleep;
In summer she would gently fan and swirl
A song book just to cool his slumbers deep.

Today I watched them—he is now a man
So tall that she must tiptoe very high
To whisper things, and he leans all he can
To hear her words, and smiles to catch her eye,
And deftly turns the page for her to sing,
And helps her with her coat and everything.

Helen Loomis Linham.

Earth's crammed with heaven,
And every common bush afire with God;
And only he who sees takes off his shoes—
The rest sit round it and pluck blackberries.

Elizabeth Barrett Browning.

"Well, let's see . . . you sit over there . . . and you may sit over there . . . and you there . . . and . . . Judas, do you want to sit down there at the corner . . .

THE LAST SUPPER

Perhaps at first they talked of little things
At supper-time that evening in the spring—
The upper room was dim with candle-shine
As Jesus sat with twelve, remembering.
Then quietly He said, "There is one here
Whose kiss will bring betrayal by and by."
They did not look at Judas curiously,
But each man murmured, "Master, is it I?"

Each one looked inward, frightened lest he find
A shoddy place where he had dreamed of steel.
None placed the guilt on any other guest
Who had partaken of that gracious meal . . .
When there are hungry on my little street,
When I see tears or hear a heart's hurt cry
Because some one has failed to keep high faith,
May I, too, murmur, "Master, is it I?"

Helen Welshimer.

" 'Our Father, who art in Heaven' ..."

PRAYER

>Prayer
>Is an
>Amulet
>Worn in our hearts
>For peace.
>
>>EDITH HASKELL TAPPAN.

>Heaven gives almonds
>To those who have no teeth. That's nuts to crack.
>
>>HENRY WADSWORTH LONGFELLOW.

" 'For Thine is the Kingdom ... and the Power ... and the Glory ... Amen' ..."

MY FATHER AND I

>In those days Sabbath mornings
>Meant a long, long ride to town,
>Something to learn for Sabbath school,
>Going up the hills and down.
>Whenever I say, "Our Father ..."
>I better understand,
>For the memory of a morning
>With Father by the hand ....
>That prayer seemed such a heavy chore
>For one small girl; but I
>Leaned against Father's shoulder
>As the little hills leaned on the sky. ...
>I thought the words more lovely
>On the long, long road to town,
>Watching the far horizon,
>Going up the hills and down ....
>And I think I said it better
>And trusted it more, when I
>Leaned against Father's shoulder
>As the little hills leaned on the sky. ...
>
>>KATHRINE H. WILLIAMS.

"Could this be that famous little bird that tells . . . everybody . . . everything . . ."

TELLING THE NEWS

It dropped from out my tallest tree,
So poignant and so sharp,
Like Paganini's violin
Or David's little harp.

A song of all the sorrow
Men know through bitter years,
Or Mary kneeling by the cross
Smiling through her tears.

Then fluting, musical and clear,
A silver scale of seven,
It rose in glory on the breeze
And burst the door of heaven.

Peter let fall his golden keys,
Old Aaron dropped his rod,
To hear a little bird from earth
Telling the news to God.

VIRGINIA TAYLOR MCCORMICK.

" 'As it was in the beginning . . . is now and ever shall be' . . ."

QUIET PURITANS

Praise God from whom all blessings flow
"And for Priscilla here below,"
John Alden softly sang, well-versed
In love. His psalm reached Heaven first . . .

St. Peter laughed, and rumbled on;
"You *did* speak for yourself, old John!"
Meanwhile the lovers kept their look,
And thumbs, upon the same hymnbook.

ISABEL FISKE CONANT.

"I've sometimes wondered this too . . . but all the Wise Men brought were gifts of gold and frankincense and myrrh . . .

SHARING

I never saw a picture
   Where Jesus held a toy,
But don't you think His father
   Would make one for his Boy?

A sheep that's carved from cedar,
   A ball that He could bound,
A wagon always handy
   As anything around.

Of all the trucks and engines
   About my room you see
I'd gladly give Him several
   If He would play with me.

CECILE HOUGHTON STURY.

"Just put it to soak . . . it'll be all right . . .

WASHERWOMAN'S PRAYER

Lord, I can't pray the words the preachers pray;
   All that I know is clothes and soap and dirt;
But here I bring this badly laundered day.
   It won't come clean—just like the mister's shirt.

I soaked it in my tears, Lord, rubbed each cuff
   Against the hard board of experience;
But all that I could do was not enough—
   The spots still show across my neighbor's fence.

You gave me all I needed—a whole sky
   Of cloudy soapsuds and Your heaven's own
Bottle of bluing, and, to whip it dry,
   Upon this day Your choicest winds have blown;
But there it hangs still streaked with sin and sorrow.
Lord, could I try another day tomorrow?

HELEN FRAZEE-BOWER.

"The Bible has always seemed to me to begin at Christmas and end at Easter . . . and never to have had a Fall . . . at all . . .

SUMMER OF ST. LUKE

The linden berried long ago,
    And narrow leaves of sycamore
Drifted like flakes of yellow snow,
    To heap a mound before the door.

Yet on the edge of rigid cold,
    A little summer has come back,
The small flower of the marigold
    Has bloomed despite the almanac.

After the languid leaf is mold
    Cattle lie on the southward hill,
After the podded weed is old,
    Weather is warm and sweet and still.

CARRIE CHASE SHERIDAN.

" 'In the beginning was the word' . . . and now and always . . .

IT IS STILL GOD'S WORLD

Though men may desecrate the world with blood,
They cannot hurt the throbbing heart of earth.
The winds shall blow, and waking leaf and bud
Each spring eternally shall come to birth.
The rains shall fall, the stars light heaven's door,
And birds wing back to some safe nesting place.
The river weave its song against the shore;
Children be born . . . a credit to the race!
It is God's world . . . it shall be always so.
Though men play God, the green arms of the grass
Shall fold them close to make a field . . . bestow
Obscurity. This, too, shall come to pass!
For men are tenants, and a pound of sod
Is all they are! The world belongs to God!

EUNICE MILDRED LONCOSKE.

The Road is Marked ... You Can't Miss It

"Long ago . . . a little boy sat on a wharf . . . in Genoa . . . and gazed out to sea . . .

YOUNG MARINER

He is a tiny seaman,
   And the boat has a three-inch sail,
And beyond the pads of the lily
   Lies a fathomless ocean trail.

There are far-distant lands to discover
   And ventures to quicken the heart,
And solemn indeed is this sailor,
   And he weighs his anchor to start.

The pool casts up the reflection
   Of eyes in whose depths there gleams
The hope of a future uncharted,
   The faith of a little boy's dreams.

LOIS SNELLING.

Two voices are there: one is of the sea,
One of the mountains; each a mighty voice.

WILLIAM WORDSWORTH.

"After mountains . . . there is peace in one's eyes . . .

TIMBER LINE

The valley sleeps and the faint stars shine.
It is close to heaven at timber line.
The slow winds bite and the thin airs freeze
And the great white owl can sleep if he please.
The grey rat skulks and the snowshoe hare
Must stop in his tracks to cower and stare.
The marten, sleek in his coat's brown sable,
Dines upon roots with a rock for a table.

Slim green elves, while the young moon waxes,
Chip off silence with their silver axes.

DOROTHY MOORE GARRISON.

"And if I'd been a boy . . . I might have joined the Foreign Legion . . . to forget . . ."

THE WANDERER

Today I felt so very bad
I left my mother and my dad,
My sisters Mary, Rose and Sue,
And everyone I ever knew—
For since we've got that brand new brother
They all forget me—even mother.

I walked a hundred miles away
To show them all how long I'd stay
And let them see how sad they'd be
If anyone should kidnap me.

The world grew cool—the world grew dark—
And everybody left the park.
"Time to go home," the watchman said,
"The swans and ducks have gone to bed,
And every little girl alive
Should be at home by half past five."

It seemed a hundred years or two
Since I'd seen anyone I knew,
So I went hurrying home to see
If anyone remembered me.

And there the house stood just the same,
The same old street, the same old name,
The same old dog, the same old cat,
The same old door, the same old mat,
The same old table set for tea,
And no one even noticed me—
The same old tea-pot on the tray—
And no one knew I'd been away.

MARY WHITE SLATER.

"Sailing time . . . all ashore that's going ashore!

WORDS FOR A DAUGHTER

Though you have shut me out, your eyes
Betray some wound your speech denies.
You need not fear. I shall remain
Outside. That baffled look of pain
I shall not see, for I must learn
To mask my pity and concern.
And I am proud that you have shown
Courage to face your world alone.

Only remember this: when there
Are times when you have need to share
Your problems, I shall always be
Waiting for you to come to me—
Eager to help you on your way,
Or blunt the sharp edge of dismay.
Your need of me, if you but knew,
Is nothing to my need of you!

ELIZABETH GREY STEWART.

Vessels large may venture more,
But little boats should keep near shore.

BENJAMIN FRANKLIN.

"And we stayed the night in San Francisco . . . or was it Los Angeles?"

OUTMANEUVERED

When folks say, "Tell us about the trip,"
  And Mother beats Father to it,
He listens for something to contradict;
  But she never lets him do it.

Before any definite statement
  Her recollections dim.
"Exactly how was it, dear?" she asks,
  And then she contradicts him!

EVANTHA CALDWELL.

*"A fellow might eventually be able to make up his mind, if it **weren't** for so many delays on the high road . . . and detours on the low . . .*

THERE WERE TWO ROADS

There were two roads that he could take,
One road was joy and one heartbreak.

The right road led up, up a hill,
Where silence lived and stars stood still.

The other twisted, turned down, down
Where there was laughter in the town.

"If there be one who ever tried
These roads," he begged, "help me decide!"

But no one stopped to tell him how,
So he stands as you see him now—

With one hand pointing up, up, up,
To heartbreak in a starry cup,

And one hand pointing down, down, down,
To lighted laughter in the town.

The passers-by all stop and stare
And whisper, "What's he doing there?—

"A stupid sign post not to know
Where he, himself, would like to go!"

Irene McDermott.

How much a dunce that has been sent to roam
Excels a dunce that has been kept at home!

William Cowper.

"Yes, she has her ticket . . . but she won't voyage far on that . . . it isn't paid for . . .

LIFE HISTORY

She sent no sails from port, yet life has been
One constant hope her ships would soon come in.

Gail Brook Burket.

"Around the corner . . . and under a tree . . .

HEAVEN ISN'T ONE PLACE

Heaven isn't one place—
There are lots of them.
Mary knew enchantment
Once in Bethlehem.
After forty winters
Israel's roaming band
Found that Heaven waited
In a Promised Land.
Heaven isn't one thing,
It may be a song
Running down the twilight,
Never over-long.

When a weary woman
Sought a garment's hem
On an Eastern highway,
Thinking it might stem
Weakness she had suffered,
Paradise was there—
Sometimes it is firelight
On a woman's hair.
I have tried forgetting
Little days with you.
Heavens never leave us—
Have you learned that, too?

Helen Welshimer.

"And sometimes . . . traveling backwards is the quickest way to get somewhere . . .

LILLIPUT

We talk of childhood, while the winter dusk
Is blent to evening and the fire dims
Forgotten in the grate. The burnished horse,
Poised for prancing at the andiron's tip,
Begins to breathe beneath its flickering brass,
By shadow-magic stirred to molten life.

You rap your pipe against the mantelshelf,
Spilling a rosy comet to the hearth;
Then fill and light and toss the charring match
Into the grate.

          "There whisked across my mind
Just now a shred of memory," you begin,
"So meaningless, it's hardly worth my chase
Behind the wind of time, to capture it.
Something about brass horses . . . I was five . . ."
And so, remembering, you build a tale.

Between your groping words I hear the clink
And chatter of a teatime long ago;
The room is fragrant with the vague perfume
Of ladies; and, oblivious to the guests,
A solemn little boy with stockinged knees
Sprawls on the carpet here, before the fire,
Chin on his knuckles, eyes immense with thoughts
About enchanted horses, sheathed in gold . . .

Your story ends; the silence bids me speak;
Yet I can find no utterance but love's;
For all my heart is your dominion now—
Even that inmost, Lilliputian town
Whose gates admit no charger but a child's.

                                  VIRGINIA FRENCH.

"Have you ever noticed how the rhythm of a train's wheels seems to make words . . . songs . . . The other night on the Santa Fé . . . I heard . . .

PRAIRIE SONG

The moon rides high with the wind tonight,
   Rides high with the prairie wind;
And it has for its road a western way
That goes from the night to a newborn day,
And it has for its road a starlit way,
   As it rides with the wind tonight.

The tall grass bends to the wind tonight,
   Bends low to the prairie wind;
And it has for its song a plaintive cry
That calls to the moon as it rides on high,
And it has for its song a lonely cry,
   As it bends to the wind tonight.

A heart rides high with the wind tonight,
   Rides high with the prairie wind;
But it has for its song a plaintive cry
That calls to its love as the moon rides by,
And it has for its song a lonely cry,
   As it rides with the wind tonight.

CHARLA M. BACKLUND.

"We did our duty as travelers . . . hunted up all the Sights . . . waited for hours to catch a glimpse of Personages . . . went to look at all the Masterpieces . . . . . . Most of the time it was wonderful . . . but once in a while . . . when our shoes began to feel tight . . . the Sights seemed overrated . . . the Personages looked just like anybody . . . and . . . oh, some of those Masterpieces . . . !

YES SURREALISM

Salvidor Dali must paint in a sally,
Or else his eruptions come purely from folly,
But his horrid concoctions don't end in the alley—
They are sold to some other dumb dodo like Dali.

JOHNNY MCKINNEY.

"Sometimes people don't really care about going on a trip . . . they like to plan . . . to think of where they would go . . . what they might wear . . . but the trip is so much trouble . . . it's so much easier to stay at home . . . And yet it is nice to go . . . if only to send cards home . . . 'having a wonderful time . . .'

SUNDAY SERVICE

They tell me I've no longer need to go
To church, come Sabbath morn; that, now the Lord
Has time and station on the radio,
The old can sit at home and hear the Word.
So in my best black silk, I draw a chair
Up to the carven case . . . A famed quartet,
Or soloist, sings; someone leads in prayer;
The preaching's wonderful—and yet—and yet—

There are no children after Sunday School;
No choir for looking at; no ushers, as
They smilingly show folks to pews and pass
The plates . . . and afterward, no vestibule
For talk, or chance to shake the pastor's hand,
And say, "Your sermon, Brother, was just grand."

ETHEL ROMIG FULLER.

"I asked him about Venice . . . and all he said was . . . that he saw a dead cat floating in the Grand Canal . . .

SPIRIT

Here comes one who went through life a seeker,
   But, having found, comes back to try if he
Can catch again the joy of not quite knowing
   And hoping for what seems about to be.

For since he was above all things a seeker,
   He knows now that he never wishes to find;
And being secure, he longs for the old wonder
   Of the uncertainty he left behind.

LOUISE DRISCOLL.

"Dear Friends at Home . . . There is so much to tell . . . that I don't know where to begin . . .

LETTER TO MANY

Companions, in this verse of little music
I write to you as I could never write
And seal and thrust into a box, content
That you should know the weather here was cloudy;
Or that I liked this town, disliked another;
Or how I climbed up Skiddaw (as John Keats
Had done); or what I heard of babbling pipes
Deep in the Trossachs—the expected things,
The all-conventional.

        Now I shall say
Britain is what you dream and something more;
It is a land piled high of story books;
Green meadows and white sheep; tumultuous bells
That chime in sermons; towers that must have made
Imprisonment glorious; rivers of great name;
And rusty heather turning to purple now;
Bookstalls in crooked streets; and curious maps
Behind a dingy glass; abbeys that crumbled
To rosy stone like some forgotten monks
Fallen to sleep upon their weary knees
Because their prayers had been too long; and walls
Crested with flowers in centuries of sand
The wind had lifted there for gardens brighter
Than Van Gogh could have painted. Things more real:
Bacon and marmalade and toast and tea:
And red-cheeked English boys with cricket bats;
The sunshine flooding over Soutra Hill;
And buttered scones; and Edinburgh at night . . .
Till you might think I had a mind washed bare
Of my old self and everything I knew.

But these, as I have said, are only books
Wherein I read. And I, the reader, must
Turn all their fairy pages with my fingers
Still warm from yours, feel with a heart recalling
Another list—and a more lovely one—
Of things I shall not name. You know them, too.

And here in England I am only part
Of that One City, see and tremble with Her.
And here I am as calm as small brown houses
That slumber in West End among old trees;
Gay as the flowered yards in Morningside;
And sad as the first yellowed leaves of autumn
Blown lingeringly down the roads in Druid Hills.

YORK, ENGLAND, JULY, 1938.
JAMES E. WARREN, JR.

The use of travelling is to regulate imagination by reality.
SAMUEL JOHNSON.

'Wherever I may wander . . .'

TRANQUILLITY

It should not be too difficult to find
The long way back, O Heart, if we but turn
Down the dim road that we have left behind,
And cross an old stile where the maples burn
Like lifted torches on the smoky air—
It cannot be so very far from there . . .

And we may find again that lost delight;
A field's dark furrows bronzed with evening sun,
May see the first star shyly come in sight,
The first lamp lighted when the day is done,
May hear a lonely cricket sing a song
That we once knew, and have not heard for long.

Surely there still is peace in sky and ground—
O Heart, if we but search, it can be found.
GRACE NOLL CROWELL.

"Shipboard romance . . .

DIVERGENCE

You take the high road
   Leading to fame,
But I'll take the by-road,
The one I call my road,
   Having no name.

In ivoried tower
   You shall hold sway,
But I'll find a bower
Where summer leaves shower
   And children play.

Up in your sky-way
   You shall ride far,
But Love pointed my way,
A humble, sweet, shy way—
   Mapped by a star!

HELEN DARBY BERNING.

"We started off in opposite directions . . . but we're both still in the same boat . . .

REMINDER

It is not easy to remember why
We took our roads so casually apart
With only sun and stars to reckon by
Who might have fondly lingered, heart to heart.
You on the high road, I upon the low,
Eager to greet the merriest of days,
Careless of how the winds of time must blow,
We flipped a coin and kissed, and went our ways.

The gypsy in his roving understands
What calls him forth in quest of pastures new,
Yet still I think we might have joined our hands
And found one joyous road, instead of two.
It is not easy to remember why
We failed to walk together, you and I.

SYDNEY KING RUSSELL.

"There are some sights guidebooks cannot anticipate . . .

AS I WALKED INTO LONDON TOWN

As I came down to London Town
Upon a traveled road and long,
I met a maid in a lurid gown
Who sang a mirthless song.

I scanned Cheapside for Guildhall's tower,
And searched for Richard's gold-paved street;
Between each cobble sprang a flower
With crimson sap replete.

High overhead were monstrous birds
That dipped and circled in the air.
For things I saw I had no words;
I sought a house of prayer.

St. Paul's alone within a ring
Of fire, did not fall.
I marked an angel's burnished wing
Outlined above its wall.

As I walked into London Town,
Besides the Thames, and near its shore,
There came a blood-besplattered clown,
Who vanished through a door.

I let him pass. The Channel lay
In folds of fog and bitter smoke.
I watched men drag debris away,
And cover something with a cloak.

MABEL POSEGATE.

All places that the eye of heaven visits
Are to the wise man ports and happy havens.

WILLIAM SHAKESPEARE.

"Journey's end . . .

EPITAPH FOR A LOST ADVENTURER

Say that
He loved the lovely
Waywardness of water;
Say that he loved
The glamour of old ships
Better than man loves wife or daughter,
Or a woman's lips.

Say that
The morning light upon the sea
Was lovelier than Lilith's golden hair,
And starlight lost in waves' immensity
More fair than Eve was fair.

Say that
The lace at a breaker's emerald seam
Enticed him more than lace at Delilah's throat,
And tell how he preferred the strident scream
Of a gull to the skylark's note.

Say that
He rests where he longed to be:
Home is the sailor—
At the bottom of the sea.
Take down his epitaph,
Etch it in sand—
When the tide goes out
He will understand.

MARION DOYLE.

"I've read so much about Paris and Constantinople and Shanghai . . . that there can't be many people who could understand far cities as I do . . . but I've never seen any . . .

THE LITTLE ROAD

When I was young a little road
   Called loud and merrily:
"Ho, leave your musty books and come
   Adventuring with me."

44

I bade the little road begone;
   No time to play had I;
And running on before the wind,
   It waved a gay goodbye.

But often now at twilight,
   My books upon my knee,
I wonder what the little road
   Might have found for me.

MINNIE CASE HOPKINS.

"If I only were rich . . . I'd go to Illinois . . .

EVEN IN DREAMS

Even in dreams I have no money,
But arrive in Chicago
With a dollar and eighty-five cents.

IRMA WASSALL.

" 'Something there is that does not love a wall . . .'

THE CALL

Did you light a candle for me that night?
   (And I never came.)
A candle! When stars were burning so bright,
   Burning me with their flame!
Did you draw the curtains, and shut the door
   To keep out the wind?
The wind was calling as never before—
   How could I stay behind!

There was peace and comfort and love, I know,
   In that room for me.
But something stronger than love made me go.
   It will always be!
For my soul has a need that no love can fill;
   There's a call I must follow for good or for ill,
Though it lead to the top of the farthest hill,
   To the deepest sea.

ELIZABETH VIRGINIA RAPLEE.

"All roads lead to Home . . ."

FREEDOM

Though all the gates are open
And roads beyond are free,
I let you go
Because I know
Each one leads back to me.

ALICIA KAY SMITH.

I will follow thee
To the last gasp with truth and loyalty.

WILLIAM SHAKESPEARE.

"You'll never know how blue the Mediterranean is . . . until you've seen it . . ."

QUERY

They said that there was madness
In moonlight's silver touch,
And warned him against wandering
In it, overmuch:

For he would climb the tallest hill
On any summer night
To see a misty valley drenched
In the moon's white light;

And he would trudge the wintriest road
Of valley or of plain
Just to see one lone tree drip
Bright moon-crystal rain.

They said that there was madness!
I wonder how *they* knew—
Who never walked abroad at night—
Just why this was true!

JESSIE WILMORE MURTON.

"Dear Anne ... Having wonderful time ... don't you wish you were here ..."

TRAVELERS

Anne can boast about her travels;
I'm entranced, while she unravels,
Magically,
Themes ... of strange adventure met;
A gate turned gold as sun is set;
Storms at sea.
But one night I went to heaven
Round about the hour eleven,
So they said.
I, without a chart to guide me;
No one called, who stood beside me ...
"Rocks ahead!"
Finally, an angel white-capped
Answered with a bundle blue-wrapped
To my "Why?"
Now my heart the question's turning ...
Who's been farther in her journeying,
Anne, or I?

MABEL TUTTLE CRAIG.

" 'Pilgrim's Progress' ..."

THE DESOLATE COUNTRY

Wit's End is a desolate country
Where, over briar and stone,
Most of us wander at some time
And always wander alone;

Where, at the ultimate boundary,
After bleak miles have been trod,
Many have found the gateway
With the single inscription: God.

ADELAIDE LOVE.

According to the Almanac

"January 1 . . . Into each year some rain may fall . . . but we always hope for a clear sunrise . . .

THRESHOLD

The slow routine of peace begins with dawn,
The clatter of a truck, a first bird call
Breaking the ordered silences of dark—
Familiar things, habitual and small.

As mind drifts back from clouded wells of sleep,
The eye perceives time's record on the blinds
In bands of gold. The mirror floats in light,
Within the room the web of day unwinds.

KATHERINE VAN DER VEER.

"Even in a February heart . . . 'if winter comes' . . .

CHANGELING

In winter I'm a woman old and slow;
I bank my heart as ashes bank the fire,
And blanche the buds of every live desire
And chill their roots with thoughts as bleak as snow.

    And then I love slow rain,
    And soft gray knitting yarns,
    And garments dull and plain
    As lonely rain-washed barns.

But when peony buds, wine-red, prick through
The sodden mold to life, renewed and bright,
My heart awakes as from a sleep at night,
And all the meanings of my life renew.

    And then I love young trees,
    And laughing winds and grass,
    And throw—when no one sees—
    Gay kisses as you pass.

FLORENCE HARTMAN TOWNSEND.

" 'Beware the Ides of March' . . . especially if March comes in like a lamb . . . because it's a long lamb that has no turning . . .

THE RACE

The wind and I had a race today,
Across the town and over the way.
The wind won out, and, for his prize
Took my hat before my eyes!

But he, contrite, as it sailed thru the streets,
Left some roses in my cheeks.
HELEN BICKEL.

Often do the spirits
Of great events stride on before the events,
And in today already walks tomorrow.
SAMUEL TAYLOR COLERIDGE.

"A red-letter day on the calendar . . . when, suddenly, you could smell violets in the cold wind along the Avenue . . . and it was Spring in the city . . .

CITY WIND

This wind which walks the city streets with me,
The smoke and grime so gray upon its face,
Knows well the intricate and lovely lace
Of spider weaving, and each day may see
Still beauty carved in stone or tapestry
Of dust and sun in some wall-centered space.
When evening comes it may seek out a place
Of vibrant light or darkened mystery.

But does this dull, sophisticated thing
Remember still the free, mad way to go
Across a mountain top or how to swing
From larch to spruce and bend a tall pine low?
Does it remember and when street lamps flower
Climb longingly to some tall city tower?
GILEAN DOUGLAS.

"Now is the time to start Spring cleaning . . . throw out those wintry old regrets . . . bring in some gay plans from the garden . . . rearrange the dreams in your hope chest . . . and go shopping for a new . . . you know what . . .

WOMAN IN SPRING

I am so very glad to be
A woman when the redbud tree
Flickers with flame before the leaf
In blossoms, delicate and brief;
Or when the tulips brightly stand
Like sturdy children in a land
So lately desolate of youth.
A man is wary of the truth
That flowers in ecstatic things;
When beauty like a rush of wings
Stirs the rare ether of his heart
He dare not let the frail tear start,
Or bare a rapture unconfessed
Within his stoutly tweeded breast.
But I, a woman, I may wear
Sprigs of lilac in my hair,
Let worship kindle in my face
Openly without disgrace.
I may throw my free arms wide
To all the mist of bloom outside
And capture violets in my dress.
While he, in fear of spring excess,
Chooses another brown cravat,
I yield my stipend to possess
A purple flowerpot for a hat!

Isabelle Bryans Longfellow.

"Oh, to be in April . . .

MONDAY IN APRIL

Spring turns the tap
In April's washtub now,
And orange blossom buds,
Like new soap suds,
Foam up along each bough.

Aimée B. Andresen.

"Spring showers . . . may sour . . . and yet splash blossoms on an ivory tower . . .

RAIN AT MIDNIGHT

There is rain upon the wind tonight
   And wind upon the sea—
The world is rough and old tonight
   And black and cold to me.

There is dampness in the room tonight
   And shadows on the wall
But none of You is here tonight
   My shadow, that is all.

Oh I am small and cold tonight
   The world is far too wise—
And while it holds poor dreams tonight
   There are kingdoms in your eyes!

JULIA B. COHAN.

"It's wonderful . . . how some people get around . . .

FABLE FOR SPRING

The rambler rose that climbs our latticed bone
Remains unsatisfied, forever yearning
To mount on azure trellises, full blown,
In altitudes where braver light is burning.
Its racing veins of vertical desire
Are urged by valiant instinct to outrun
This six-foot frame of breath, and clamber higher
To satisfy their hunger for the sun.
The passive earth cannot restrain such zeal,
Nor fraying moth prevent its ultimate flower—
The seed of high desire will break the seal,
And climb and light in its appointed hour.

IRENE WILDE.

"May ... Time to set out plants ... each one a small, green hope ... for life ... and beauty ... and peace ...

GRACE BEFORE SUMMER

Winter has been cold and the winds rude;
But spring is here and I work in the sun and my shoulder
    leans to be hot.
How good to transplant seedlings in this unembattled spot,
And if we shall live to see the bloom, how good!

WITTER BYNNER.

"Mother, mother—may I swim? ... Yes, my darling son; hang your clothes on a hickory limb, but don't go near the ... oh, you might as well go on in ... it doesn't rhyme anyway ...

FIVE BARE BOYS

Five bare boys leap out of their pants.
They run in old male arrogance
Along the springboard, and they dive,
Rampant, shining, as alive
In the air as on the ground.
Each makes an arc of treble sound
And vanishes in silver bubbles.
A bird sings low; there are no troubles
In all the world; the world stands still.

But up the boys come, and they spill
Water and laughter, arch their tails.
Five small hard and happy males,
They gleam naked, blare like horns,
Sharp and beautiful as thorns.
They drown the bird out, rankle white,
Five slender barbs of appetite,
And the universe can spin
On its handsome way again.

ROBERT P. TRISTRAM COFFIN.

"Do you suppose they have May in Heaven . . . and do the angels have head colds . . . and are there dandelions to match the golden streets . . .?"

BELOVED

The years have brought us very close, beloved;
I feel when other avenues of air
Are open to my free and earth-purged spirit,
Yours will be there.

If there are sweet birds in the dim hereafter,
Among the perfumed boughs of deathless spring,
I shall be needing you to name them for me—
The birds that sing.

I shall not fare apart from you, beloved,
Let us go now and look upon the stars.
If I am summoned hence, dear one, remember,
Souls own no bars.

MABEL POSEGATE.

"June . . . There's going to be a storm today . . . a little bird told me . . ."

THE WEATHERCOCK

Up on the roof where the breezes are scurrying,
   Cock of the neighborhood, cock of the world,
Round goes the weatherbird, round, never worrying,
   Jaunty, no matter which way he is whirled.

Bright in the sun on his belfry or cupola,
   Calmly audacious, he takes the long view;
And you would think that he cares not a whoopola
   What sort of weather he's bringing to you.

But when the heavens grow cloudy and threatening,
   Weathercock gallantly faces the siege,
Rides at his post through a terrible wettening,
   All in the spirit of *noblesse oblige*.

JULIA ANNE ROGERS.

"The barometer's still going down ... Maybe this will clear the air ... because I really am sorry, darling ... I didn't mean a word of it ..."

SUMMER STORM

Noon is the sullen weight of lead,
When—sudden redemption—strikes the rain.
The gilded horse on the weathervane
Nuzzles the east with outstretched head.

The wind and the rain drive home their store
To freshen the bone-dry day, and pass,
Wave upon wave, through pliant grass,
To die on, who knows, what summer shore?

Prophecy-tall, the white church stands,
Tapered to heaven and clean of dust:
God's finger raised from the moth and rust
To salvation of souls and thirsting lands.

EUGENIE CARVER

"July ... The year rolls round ... good weather and bad ... even this shall pass away ..."

CRICKET IN A CYCLONE

I heard a crane scream,
And a hound-dog bark;
The tree tops shook,
And the sky grew dark—
I heard a child cry,
And a mother call;
I saw a house crumble
Wall upon wall . . .
I saw a black cricket
On a slim grass blade,
Swinging in the windstorm,
Queerly unafraid.
I stared at the sky,
And held my breath . . .
While the cricket sang,
Unheard by Death.

ROSA ZAGNONI MARINONI

" 'Shall I compare thee to a Summer's day' . . ."

LATE SUMMER DUSK

Everybody thought, of course, the day was over,
For rain in gusts had whipped the afternoon.
Once only had the sick sun broken cover,
Sallow and shrunken, like a watered moon.
Lightning shuddered blue, the clouds closed surly,
Thunder cursed the world, and the dusk dropped early.

But suddenly, in the west, the cloud-pall shifted,
And half of the sun, a jubilant large eye,
Looked out upon the sullen world and lifted
A long flight of javelins to the darkened sky.
Midway, on the treetops, the light fell yellow,
With a splendor as of laughter full and mellow.

Out of the houses the people ran and wondered,
Asking and peering and pointing at the light
Where the last glance of day had laughed and sundered
The twilight of men from the down-coming night.
For below, on the earth, the dusk still doubted,
While the glory on the treetops shone and shouted.

When I am old, and my day is at the finish,
All that you shared with me I shall recall.
Although other joys in the darkness may diminish,
This one will not be dark. It will be tall
To catch, in the dusk, all the flying graces
Of the last light of memory on the high places.

Quincy Guy Burris.

Dost thou love life? Then do not squander time, for that is the stuff life is made of.

Benjamin Franklin.

"I see by the stars ... Mars ... Venus ... Aldeberan ... he's going to do great things ... that boy ..."

COMPENSATION

His mother taught him stars, her eager son;
They paced the garden path each magic night
And tried to count the pinpoints one by one,
Till falling worlds put figuring to flight.
Her placements were uncertain, and the names;
But she knew legends, and she told them right,
And he was well content with guessing games.

He never feared the dark, because God chalked
Such fathomless enchantment on its slate
As lessons never offered. Thus he walked
To knowledge, having night to compensate
For days of misadventure, and the whim
That Mother stood at heaven's garden gate,
Selecting stars and tossing them to him.

JOHN GALLINARI WHIDDING.

"August ... and the sun is setting on the Summer ... Sunset is a weary hour ... but the sun also rises ..."

FARMER'S TWILIGHT

He leans against the topmost board
And folds his arms. His body sags,
Empty of strength his years have poured,
Sixty of them, on land that drags
Him toward it. Almost he looks, at times,
A ridge in the sparse alfalfa field;
But when his one boy's namesake climbs
Beside him, now is he revealed—
A something more than fields suggest
(He turns to answer the childish fun)
More like that graying glimmer in the west,
More like tomorrow's sun.

MARGARET J. E. BROWN.

"Watch for the beginning of an eclipse ..."

END OF SUMMER

The end of Summer comes so very gently—
  It is a murmured song, a wistful sigh;
The shadows deepen under every hedgerow;
  The very breeze is hushed as it drifts by!

The garden dreams of youth and love and springtime;
  The butterflies are flower souls reborn;
There is no room on earth for flaming passion,
  For jealousy or bitterness or scorn.

The end of Summer comes with haunting sweetness,
  With memory to take ambition's place—
For though the dawn has lost its burning wonder,
  The dusk has gained tranquillity and grace.
And we who read Life's book pause for a moment,
  Before we turn the last enchanted page,
And lift our eyes and scan the veiled horizon
  And whisper, "This, at last, is middle age!"

MARGARET E. SANGSTER.

At Christmas I no more desire a rose
Than wish a snow in May's new-fangled mirth;
But like of each thing that in season grows.

WILLIAM SHAKESPEARE.

"Can you fold your tent like an Arab?"

DUSK

The night
Settles about
Like a wise mother hen,
Gathering in all the noises
Of earth.

HARRIET SEYMOUR POPOWSKI.

"September morn . . .

AURORA

The sun arose and blushed a charming red,
For dawn had pulled the covers off his bed.

CLAUDE GEORGE WILSON.

"And September evening . . .

THE OLD FARM SLEEPS

The cows in the stanchions, motherly brown,
Brindle and Roan, have given down
Their riches in musical milky swirls.
The tow-haired boys and the calico girls
Rest foam-heaped pails at the peeled birch bars
And linger to wish on the early stars.

The youngest, latching the coop's slab door,
Peers up at the perch and down at the floor:
At the rooster arching his red-toothed comb,
At the velvety chickens all clucked home
Safe in their circular feather beds
Under ruffled heads tucked in to their heads.

Sorrel and Dapple with harness-bands off
Roll over twice as they turn from the trough;
And now from the stable come whinnied thanks
For oat-filled mangers and curried flanks . . .
The firefly lanterns over the bog
Swing to the steady chug of a frog.

A whittled thin moon runs aground on the hill;
And the leaf-green fiddlers are suddenly still,
Under the gables near straw-tick beds
Where the pillows are printed with tousled heads.
The slippered motherly darkness creeps
Within and without . . . The old farm sleeps.

IRENE STANLEY.

"Grandmother used to say . . . 'There's blood on the moon tonight' . . .

DISCOVERED

The moon was a robber
With a mask on his eyes.
He peeked above the ocean
To take us by surprise.
We stared and he stared
And not a word he said,
But I think he was embarrassed . . .
Oh, his face was red!

Dorothy Burnham Eaton.

A calendar, a calendar! look in the almanack; find out moonshine.

William Shakespeare.

"Get the harvest in . . . before it is too late . . .

SOME OTHER TIME

How pleasantly the firelight leaped and shone
That Autumn afternoon upon my book!
My little son stood near. "Oh, mother, look,
See how the yellow leaves are blowing down!
I wish you'd walk out in the woods with me
And scuff the swishy leaves along the grass
And find red mittens on the sassafras!"
"Some other time," I answered, absently.

Once more October days are here, my son!
Do you remember how you used to run
Beneath the maples, reaching for a stray
Gold leaf before the wind blew it away?
Oh, do you know the grass with gold is spread
And in the woods the sassafras is red?

Mary Ferguson Legler.

"These are special Mondays along about now ... our washday linen never is whiter ... bleached with October's bright blue weather ...

RECORDS FROM A CLOTHES-LINE

At bed-time we went out and brought the clothes in from the line;
They bore the scents of Autumn dusk, as old kegs smell of wine.
The ripened sweet of apple trees, the blue grapes' subtle tang
Were in the clean and dewy folds that we had left to hang.
The wind had blown the hearty smoke of bonfires through their weft,
Blent with the garden musk of flowers the early frost had left;
We folded them with slow delight, and caught the rich perfume
Of melons ripened with the corn, which filled the evening room.
We smoothed the soft and pliant sheets, and felt the hands of Night
Who passed and brushed them gently with fingers cool and white.
And from the colored pile of towels rose scent of mint and sage,
The faint, sweet records of the pool, like thoughts upon a page—
At bed-time we went out and got the clothes to fold away,
But we had brought in billowed heaps the whole bright Autumn day.

AGNES L. PORTER.

Men are April when they woo, December when they wed: maids are May when they are maids, but the sky changes when they are wives.

WILLIAM SHAKESPEARE.

"Time to bank the flower beds with leaves . . . as you would bank a memory . . . or a fire that will burn again . . . come Spring . . ."

OCTOBER EVENING

The dusk is stabbed with glancing spears of rain;
Mist, from the meadows rising, idly drifts;
Trees murmur legends; and a lone bird lifts
A single voice, one pure, hushed note of pain.
The leaves have fallen, in a golden stain
Sudden as sunlight through the fraying rifts
Of cloud. A pale moon flowers. Dim light sifts
Blurred silver on the pool. I watched it wane;
I heard the rain drums waken, heard them beat
Upon the water, saw the darkness hold
The moving shapes of swans, in still retreat,
Stranger than dreaming, like a tale once told,
Haunting the mind, or like the slow defeat
Of love remembered, when the heart is old.

FAITH BALDWIN.

"November . . . the year is dying . . . but there is beauty . . . even in death . . ."

AUTUMN

If the Autumn of life is half as lovely
   As the Autumn of earth, I shall not grieve
For the vanished days of a rapturous Spring,
   Nor beg for one moment of reprieve.

I have loved the snows of hawthorn and plum
   That rivaled the frost flakes' mystic designs,
But what of a world in crimson and gold
   With wild grapes spilling their purple wines!

And if Winter should come? I am content
   To leave my life in the hands of a god
Whose mind could conceive the Autumn of earth
   And star it with asters and goldenrod.

MARION DOYLE.

"Open season for trouble-shooting . . . forget about the day the neighbors broke your lawnmower . . . and ask them over . . .

FIRESIDE WEATHER

This is fireside weather
   Now November's here.
Maple trees are thinning,
   Downy flakes appear,
Sharp winds that tingle;
   Warmth and cheer inside—
Chairs drawn together,
   Cushioned deep and wide.

Time to get acquainted,
   Time for books and friends,
Embroideries and patchwork,
   Firelight that blends—
Gentle talk and laughter,
   Cups of steaming tea,
Sandwiches and cookies
   When there's company.

Thoughts that run like magic,
   Great adventures planned
Over tiny teacups.
   Hearts that understand
Travel far together.
   When the frosts begin.
This is fireside weather—
   Come and walk right in!

                INEZ CULVER CORBIN.

"The nights are long now . . . clear and cold . . . sleep well . . .

THE TOWN WATCH

The people of the village lie
abed. No house has light.
Cordially the moon and I
go on our rounds through night.

The white frost creaks beneath my tread,
and white as frost her glow
shines radiantly overhead,
as we together go.

For she around the world, and I
around the town must keep
the watch by night that men may lie
securely down to sleep.

If she to lovers is a friend,
applauding from above,
my tact is also known to lend
a surety to love.

If she to poets is the muse
and theme, I too can be
put into rhyme: Let none abuse
the watching moon and me.
KEITH THOMAS.

There's not a breathing of the common wind
That will forget thee.
WILLIAM WORDSWORTH.

"Winter in New York is cold and bleak ... but somehow ... it always makes my heart beat faster ...

WIND IN THE CITY

Do you remember Athens in its glory—
And Carthage, stranger, when it first was built?
And all the towns the years remember—Troy,
Or a hundred not so proudly recollected?
Here is another city marked for honor,
In storied stone another man-made world—
Granite and gleaming marble, feldspar, flint:
Stone is the city's flesh as steel its bone;
So have we built with flesh and bone and pride,
And out of our youth we've shaped a city's youth.

Our city, young enough to face a sun
Whose light can find no secrets of decay,
Pillars the sky with towering evidence
Of our supreme efficiency. The wind
Assaults our citadels and screams with rage,
A bitter, wild resentment in our streets,
Forever wailing.

                       But we like a wind,
Even a wind that masquerades too boldly,
Crying wild havoc, like the voice of time,
And prophesying dust and weeds in dust.
We like to see it test our strength and prove
How strong we are, how strongly we have built.
This is a wind like that which helped to scatter
Ashes of Athens and the dust of Troy,
Or helped the Romans with their bitter sowing
On plains of Carthage, when their seed was salt.

When there's a wind to cry the somber warning,
To voice the wisdom of all cities lost
Too long ago for this year's memory—
We have no need to raise our voices, too.
Let the mad wind grow hoarse with dark foreboding
And leave us free to walk with heads as high
And proud and fearless as the loftiest towers
In this tall town we built just yesterday.

Danger there is—and fear and doubt and winter:
Perhaps it is as well that now the wind
Still challenges with omens of disaster
To spur us at our self-appointed task.
Today may be the end. Today may bring
Destruction. Watch us, wind, we keep on building
For the future. We are not afraid.

HARRIET LUNDGAARD.

"December . . . shop early for Christmas . . . picnic indoors by your own fireplace . . . and watch, outdoors, for the Star . . .

FROST IN THE NIGHT

Now while the moon's thin ghost still haunts the hill,
Let us creep softly forth without a sound,
Chiding our very breath that it be still
And not betray us to the watchful hound;
For there is that within the darkness hid
Which has not yet been seen by any dawn,
From whose bright eye the old and wrinkled lid
Of night draws back to find the wizard gone,
And nothing of his magic left, alas,
To prove so still a thing was not a dream
Except a shard of crystal in the grass,
A silver reed abandoned by a stream,
And nothing more to tell at what a cost
Beauty was purchased from the secret frost.

ELIZABETH-ELLEN LONG.

See, Winter comes to rule the varied year.
JAMES THOMSON.

"Deep winter . . . the shortest days in the year . . . lengthening a little as the New Year approaches . . . like a promise . . .

INVADER

Winter-time, that old invader
  Drove into our town last night,
Wrote commands upon my window,
  Signed his signature in white.

Farms and meadows, lanes and gardens
  Knew that battle was no use
So in silence they surrendered
  To a snow-incrusted truce.

GERTRUDE RYDER BENNETT.

Any Similarity to Persons Living or Dead

"East is East ... and West is West ... and never—well, sometimes ... maybe ..."

STARSHINE AND SAWDUST

He was one with the wind and stars,
She was akin to the sod,
He found the heart of the Universe
And knew that he talked with God.

She could knit while a rainbow dipped
Its head in her apple tree,
Yet the Imps of Love had welded them—
Earth and a melody.

BLYTHE CLEAVE BRETZ.

Small habits, well pursued betimes,
May reach the dignity of crimes.

HANNAH MORE.

"Portrait of a lady ... a real lady ... who worked in the fields ... and fought prairie fires ... and poured tea from a battered tin kettle ..."

PIONEER WOMAN

She left behind her all that she had known
   Of comfort and of ease,
White house, green blinds, smooth walks of stone,
   Cool springs and tall old trees.

She came to live upon a grassy plain
   And hot winds burned her face,
She must have longed to hear the sound of rain,
   To see a garden's grace.

And yet she lent a graciousness and charm
   To the cabin made of sod,
And all the while, through hardship and alarm,
   Kept firm her faith in God.

MAY FRINK CONVERSE.

"Everybody says she never was like other girls . . . didn't care about beaux and parties . . . she always had her nose in a book . . ."

STRANGE COMFORTING

Her father and her husband were stern men,
To them all life was only meat and drink,
And when sometimes she stood and tried to think
Of what life ought to mean, tears came, and then
She pressed her side, for always next her heart
She wore some love-words written, not to her,
But to some woman dead, whose pulses were
Long still, and yet they made her own to start.

Oh, pitiful, of all that I have heard,
That one soul's longing should have come to this,
For lack of love and of a lover's kiss,
A clasp of hand and understanding word,
There should remain this one and only thing,
Another's love-words for her comforting.

KATHARINE WASHBURN HARDING.

"There's a horse-thief in everybody's family . . . somewhere . . . though I never heard of one in mine . . . Maybe our horse-thief hasn't started his career yet . . . maybe it's going to be . . . me . . ."

ANCESTORS

If resourcefulness is needed, think of Michael Rudolf
Who, accompanied by two henchmen and a coop of pullets,
Took a British craft in the War of Eighteen-Twelve
With gusto and a minimum exchange of bullets.

And if coolness is desired, consider Sarah Cope
Who, opening a clothes press where a thief was hid,
Said in her Quaker fashion: *Friend, all honest folk
Should be in bed, I'll light thee out!* And did.

ELEANOR GLENN WALLIS.

" 'Lives of great men all remind us' . . . the little boy next door may be President . . . someday . . .

FOUR-FOOT ORATORS

Golden Friday afternoons
    Were when our nation grew;
When boys spoke pieces at the school,
    The New World rooster crew.

Boys so freckled you could not
    Put a pinpoint down
Stood with Horatius at the bridge
    And saved the Roman town.

Boys with maps of Ireland
    All over their plain faces
Became old Rome's aristocrats
    And captains in white laces.

A boy who drove the brown cows home
    Was Spartacus defying
The Caesars, and a stub-nosed lad
    Was John of Gaunt a-dying

Son of Tom, the rail splitter,
    With patches at the knee
Commanded Moses from the bush
    To set a people free.

A plowboy turned to Regulus
    Felled Carthage with one breath;
A hired-man's son cried, "Give me
    Liberty or death!"

Henry Clays, John C. Calhouns,
    Websters four-foot high
Stood up to tyrants with the New
    World fire in their eye.

And these four-foot orators
Who acted out the great
Grew up and were the architects
Of our American state.

ROBERT P. TRISTRAM COFFIN.

"Friends, Romans, and countrymen, lend me your ears . . ."
"Four-score and seven years ago . . ."
"How well Horatius kept the bridge . . ."
"Ye call me chief, and ye do well . . ."
"Give me liberty or give me death . . ."
"*Carthago delenda est!*"

"*She always signed her name, 'Mrs. Albert Joseph Jackson Semple' . . . but they had a joint bank account . . .*"

EFFICIENCY EXPERT

Father was a man whose will would brook
No interference from his womenfolk;
While Mother, small and gentle, still believed
Her place was to agree when Father spoke.
He'd say, "I think I'll buy a car this spring."
She, mindful of the mortgage, would reply:
"How nice. Let's buy one just like Banker Brown's.
Why should we worry if the price is high?"
Then Father, shocked at her extravagance,
Would suddenly remember bills to pay;
The note they owed the bank would soon be due.
What made her want a new car, anyway?

At last the farm was paid for, stock and all,
And Father, mildly boastful, would declare,
"If I had listened to the womenfolks,
We'd never have had a single dime to spare."
But Mother, smiling, never let him know
That, even though he'd always had his say
In everything, as all good husbands should,
She'd managed right along to have her way.

JANE HARRIS.

"Not listed in 'Who's Who' . . . yet . . ."

CRACKER BOY

Deep are his eyes as the swamps of gray cypress,
Deep with the lore and the ways of the wild.
Lonely and far are the trails that he follows,
Trails traced by nature for her favored child.

Give him a gun and a hound bred to hunting,
Give him the sounds of the swamp in his ears,
Few are his needs who has Time in his pocket,
Trees for a temple and birds for his peers.

Give him some grits and a bait of white bacon,
Pone, and a few turnip greens in the Spring.
Life is a feast when there's Faith on the table,
Peace in the heart, and a star on a string.

ISABEL TUDEEN.

"Here is a poem . . . which bears as much exploring as a family tree . . . but be careful when you do . . . at the end you might find . . . yourself . . ."

ONE REBEL

She was an errant puritan
Descended from a knight
Who lost his tinseled epigram
When wisdom caused his flight.
He gave to her this heritage
And placed within her reach
A part of his unreasoning power
Primed with explosive speech.
And how can any one expect
Her vision to be calm,
For even David lived his life
Before he wrote a psalm!

GRACE M. LIPPINCOTT.

"Lost horizon . . .

HYBRID

Mismated his feet, one free, the other planted;
Foursquare his mind, his soul a little canted—
Life mocks him, knowing well his ache to wander,
Holding him here while his passionate thoughts flee yonder.

Desperate, he schools his heart to long resistance,
Home a dull word against the sparkling distance;
Type of the saint, even with sins twice-seven,
Serving earth well though hungering for his heaven!

NEETA MARQUIS.

Happy the man who sees a God employed
In all the good and ill that checker life.

WILLIAM COWPER.

"The best of all biographies begins with . . . 'Grandfather, tell about when you were a little boy' . . .

SEVENTY AND FIVE

Grandfather was past seventy when I was barely five.
I thought that he must surely be the greatest man alive,
For on a springtime afternoon, he'd take me by the hand
And together we'd go walking over acres of his land.

We were rather slow together, yet our paces seemed to fit,
For we'd walk and talk a little while and then we'd rest a bit.
I'd ask a thousand questions, and he'd patiently explain
And punctuate his sentences by pointing with his cane.

We'd sit beneath his favorite tree and hear the robins sing,
"The leaves are grown May tenth," he said, "or it's a backward spring."
The world was fresh and young then. I'm glad I was alive
When Grandfather was seventy, though I was only five.

SALIBELLE ROYSTER.

Old Father Time . . . made a typographical error . . .

LOVE STORY

Great-grandfather is very old,
Nearly a hundred years, I'm told.

Once, when nobody else was there,
I tiptoed up to the old man's chair.

He was whispering, sad and slow,
"Mary . . . dear Mary . . . I loved you so."

I left as quietly as I came,
Mary wasn't great-grandmother's name.

MILDRED GOFF.

"Yes . . . but she had the youngest . . . bluest . . . eyes . . .

SCULPTURED HANDS

Her hands were coarsened and rough
With nails worn down to the very quick,
But they sped lightly through a fluff
Of snowy flour, and golden loaves
Of fragrant bread stood row on row;
She patted the sloe-eyed heifer on its flanks
And put her wobbly calf on its feet;
The fractious cow stood still for her
At milking time; the wailing bleat
Of a lonesome lamb was stilled at a touch,
Old Dan and Nell reached and neighed
For a pat as she walked past their stalls.
Yes . . .
Her hands were coarse and greyed,
But when a heartache came our way,
We of the coddled bodies would
Take our soft white hands to be held
In hers that looked like splintered wood.

AGNES STEWART BECK.

"There is one really astonishing life story that has never appeared in print . . . not yet, anyway . . .

THREAT

If I should be telling what I know about John,
He wouldn't be passing and looking straight on,
Up-head, down the highway, or else at a tree
Or the mud, just in order to be not seeing me.

It's a secret, but some day, when my patience is gone,
And I see him, up-headed, to never let on
He is knowing Old Kate . . . *I will tell about John!*

NELLIE S. RICHARDSON.

Her house is all of Echo made
Where never dies the sound;
And as her brows the clouds invade,
Her feet do strike the ground.

BEN JONSON.

"Biographical footnote . . . there is a little of the poet in all of us . . . somewhere . . .

A BARD

Endearing phrases leaping to his tongue
   Choke and confuse him. Daily, at the sight
Of lovely girls whose beauty goes unsung
   He yearns to praise their bodies slim and white,
Their lips and bosoms and their graceful limbs,
   These are his own to sing did he but guess
Immortal ardor trembles in the hymns
   His heart has fashioned but can scarce express.

Forever silent and alone he goes
   Through lonely gardens of recurrent night,
Pausing to mark the wonder of the rose,
   Praying that time may close upon his sight
Lest he be caught forever in the snare
Of beauty greater than his heart may bear.

SYDNEY KING RUSSELL.

"Office hours ... nine to five ... but history is made at night ..."

YOUNG CLERK

His bargain serge is frayed with wear—
The polished sleeve reflects his day;
He writes all orders down with care,
Politely meek to earn his pay.

But—when at night he turns the key
Upon his work and tired good-byes:
He breathes again ... once more sets free
The prisoned stallion in his eyes.

Louise Liebhardt.

"Black sheep, black sheep ... have you any wool? ... yes, sir ... yes, sir ... and a good lot more than any white sheep you ever saw ...

ALIEN CHILD

Her hearth is always cleanly swept;
She smells of milk and fresh-baked bread;
Her house in shining order kept;
Her children warmly clothed and fed.

But one has known an avid drouth,
Whom she would shield from every pang.
Desire is sharp upon his mouth
For the dark foxgrape's wilding tang.

Now when the moon of madness swings
A mellow lantern on the hill,
He shuns the world of ordered things
And wanders through the woods at will.

He is not as the others are,
Darkly she thinks, but dares not speak.
The wild grape's stain's a bloody scar.
Across his cheek.

Myrtle G. Burger.

" 'There is no history . . . only biography' . . .

PINEY WOODS KINSHIP

Piney Woods Pap says when Lincoln was a lad,
A light-ud knot was all the lamp he had
To study old books that the neighbors lent
This readin'-hungry boy on learnin' bent.

Stretched by the pine fire, he'd work his sums,
With no forewarnin' of the roll of drums.
He studied and he read on the cabin floor—
And never was a free man any more!

EVANTHA CALDWELL.

His life was gentle, and the elements
So mix'd in him that Nature might stand up
And say to all the world, "This was a man!"

WILLIAM SHAKESPEARE.

"And if you think this is any exaggeration, you should attend a Teachers' Convention some year . . . or maybe it's better that neither of us ever knows . . .

STILL WATER

When Spanish music throbs its rhythmic call,
Haunting, seductive, out into the night,
I feel myself wearing a black lace shawl—
My hair piled high, in my black eyes a light
You've never seen there. Hands upon my hips
Or arching castanets above my head
Move to the music's beat. My unlearned lips
Are now the mobile mouth of passion—red
And warm and yielding. Sensuous ways
That no one ever taught me I know well.
And how I dance! And how my full skirt sways!
But now the music stops, breaking the spell,
And I become what all men see (the fools!)—
Another teacher from the public schools.

POLLY PRICE MADDEN.

"Have you heard the latest . . .

PRIVATE LIVES

Her maid tells my maid,
And my maid tells me,
And I lend half an ear
Philosophically,

Aware that in my life,
Should strange things occur,
My maid will tell her maid,
Her maid will tell her!

MAY RICHSTONE.

The feather, whence the pen
Was shaped that traced the lives of these good men,
Dropped from an Angel's wing.

WILLIAM WORDSWORTH.

"Hers was a quiet story . . . set down in words only once . . . 'Mary . . . born 1879 . . . died 1942 . . . beloved wife and mother' . . .

PORTRAIT OF MY MOTHER

My mother was not one who cared for flowers
As many did—she chose the hardy kind:
Perennials that stayed . . . but many hours
She tended vegetables, nor did she mind
The toil, for these meant sustenance to feed
The hungry mouths; these homely plants arrayed
In rows, to her, were beauty—were a creed
Of usefulness, a pledge that she had made.

Always she liked the elemental things—
The quaint old ways of doing work by hand;
She liked the fields—the song a wild bird sings,
Theirs was a language she could understand . . . .
She liked the tunes—the poems learned in youth,
And all her long life through she reverenced truth.

MARGARET E. BRUNER.

"Sometimes they write biographies . . . sometimes . . . 'lives and letters' . . . but once it was only a song . . . yet it was adequate . . .

CYNTHIE - ANN

Thet tune, it warn't called 'Cynthie-Ann',
Ner nothin' o' th' kind,
But the fust time thet I heered it
Hit jis' made me sorta blind
To all th' things aroun' me—
I could hear her start to sing,
Her trillin' voice like birdies
'Mongst th' willows in th' spring.

Hummin' like she used to
Days 'long about July
Whilst aputtin' up th' cherries
Fer th' winter's cherry pies.
And her merry laugh! I heered it
Jis' as plain as plain could be
Arunnin' through thet music
Jus' t' laugh ag'in fer me.

I could see her on the mount'in
An' hear her teasin' call—
(Like th' time we went to Gran-pap's
Durin' nuttin' time one fall)—
I closed my eyelids right up tight
T' keep th' likeness there—
Her cheeks flushed rosy from th' climb
And wind a-blowin' in her hair!

I'd like t' thank thet orchestry
Fer a-playin' thet refrain,
'Twas jis' like havin' Cynthie-Ann
Right here on earth again!
I'm gettin' childish-like, I guess,
Like o' folks git to be,
But—no matter what they call thet tune,
Hit's Cynthie-Ann to me!

Genevieve Atwood.

"There is no one so unsophisticated as someone who thinks she isn't . . .

A SHIRT TALE

We laughed at Grandma's romance when we read
How she had washed his shirt—how every thread
Was dear to her. His shirt—the handsome scout
Who whistled, sang—who rode, who put to rout
Their fears—this hero brave who led the train—
For they were dauntless pioneers. The plain
And canyon knew their West-turned feet. He tossed
It laughingly—bestowing favor—crossed
The wagon-tongue and tipped her face to his
So, for a breath, she thought—and hoped—his kiss
Would take her lips. All day, the story goes,
She hugged the shirt. They say she pressed her nose
Deep in the folds—and breathed the scent of sage
And dust, and campfire smoke—each smell a page
From his day's book—man odors, mingled, strong.
At night, by firelit wagons, shadowed long
Like galleon-sails against the stars, she scrubbed
The rough homespun. How lovingly she rubbed
Is duly told—the gentle pats—the care
She lavished, too. All this is charted there.
We laughed at her, and called her silly, young
(For she was scarce sixteen) that when she hung
It up to dry, the sleeves in shadow etched
She fancied it was he, with arms outstretched
To her. To-day I do not laugh, for I
Washed your shirt—and hung it up to dry.

ALICE MORREY BAILEY.

Enough, thank you . . . a small piece of lemon and a little sugar . . . to bring out the flavor in the tea . . . for me . . .

YOU DIDN'T KNOW

She has never told the story
Of her life:
She gave up a stage career
To be his wife.

When they told her he was flirting
With a blonde,
She but smiled, forgave, and grew
More deeply fond.

Friends gave sympathy and counselled
A divorce,
But she let infatuation
Take its course.

You have seen a gray-haired lady
Pouring tea
For the one she thought worth keeping—
Lucky me!
Eva Sparks Taylor.

Give me, next good, an understanding wife,
By nature wise, not learned much by art. . .
Sir Thomas Overbury.

" 'She is one of the town's most successful women' . . .

BIOGRAPHY

Here lie the subdivisions of her heart,
A city strangely made—its acres sown
With parks wherein old friendships had their start
And castles of adventure long outgrown.
Here stretch the tidy shops that she has made
In bitter victory—with steady hands.
Here was her cornerstone of Duty laid
And here her statue of Ambition stands.

Behold her conquest of these barren fields—
The swift accomplishment of urban ways—
And yet no single gleaming window yields
A warmth to solace deep her empty days
And here within these walls of steel and stone
She stands unloved, unwanted, and alone!
Virginia Scott Miner.

"Of the black sheep . . ."

AUTOBIOGRAPHY

Grandmother Davies made a red and white coverlet,
Letty Reed a sampler, cross-stitched 1795.
Mary Miller's linen sheets were skillfully handwoven,
And six chairs of needlepoint keep Sally Hughes alive.

But as for their great-granddaughter, Mary Willis Shuey,
She pieced no quilts, made no hooked rugs, her breads and
    jams don't matter,
The things they saved so carefully she used seven days a
    week,
She broke a Wedgwood bowl, cracked a yellow Lowestoft
    platter.

Count the hall-marked silver teaspoons, sort the Spode and
    pewter,
Sandwich glass and Sheffield servers, treasures of the past.
The last granddaughter added nothing to their heirlooms:
She made and saved some poems—not a single thing to last.

MARY WILLIS SHUEY.

" 'A joy forever' . . ."

THE POET

He crowded into life so much of living
That the few brief decades he existed physically
Could not contain him; and he spilled
A flood of crystal words from out his inmost self
Across the dam of death
So that they rush in unchecked torrent now
Down the narrow channel of the years
Causing to bloom rare fragrant flowers of thought
In thirsting minds of those who seek for beauty
Along the arid way.

ADRIAN F. NADER.

"Purls were her specialty . . . and the world was her oyster . . .

A PERSEVERING LITTLE OLD LADY

All day, in her armchair sitting,
Grandma keeps on knitting, knitting—
I'm sure, if God and time would let her,
She'd knit the universe a sweater.

CLAUDE GEORGE WILSON.

"I knew a chap once who saved all his money for a rainy day . . . and when it rained, bought himself an umbrella . . . but somebody stole it . . .

AUTOBIOGRAPHY

When I was young and lightly gay
And earning in a modest way,
My elders beckoned me aside
And told me youth must be denied.
They planted deep and dark in me
That age must have security!
And, oh, the trips I didn't take—
Refusing for the future's sake—
The nights I didn't light my fire,
The taxicabs I didn't hire!
I wanted to be lavish, free;
But age must have security.

And then when age was at the door,
Most thriftily provided for,
The great depression had begun—
The joke was on the careful one.
And so at last was firmly laid
The bogey of the Mauve Decade.
I learned, with unexpected glee,
There's no such thing, Security!
With every day a holiday,
I'm living in a big, new way—
Sedately, as becomes my years;
But had I known it—oh, my dears!

JULIET WILBOR TOMPKINS.

"Perhaps destiny is just another name for accident . . . but perhaps it isn't accident . . . that lilac leaves are shaped like hearts . . ."

MARY LOVED LILACS

Mary loved lilacs in long-ago Virginia
In Saint John's Parish on Mattapony River;
Loved them for the fragrance of fog in their blossoms—
      English fog.

Jemima and Joseph drove a Conestoga wagon
To frontier Kentucky. He took his axe and his
Bull-tongued plow; and she the walnut cradle
      And lilac roots.

Sarilda toiled the wilderness trail with her husband
To the muddy Missouri; planted a garden
Through ashes of council fires—lilacs, peonies,
      And damask roses.

Margaret followed Jim where the winds westward beckoned
Across the wild plains and the wolf-toothed Rockies;
Grubbed away sagebrush to stir in the red earth
      Seeds of home.

      Mary, Jemima, Sarilda, and Margaret—
Deeply your roots bound America together.
Give me faith to plant, by the trail of strange tomorrows,
      My lilacs!

                LULITA CRAWFORD PRITCHETT.

"'We are such stuff as dreams are made on . . . and our little life . . . is rounded with a sleep . . .'"

PORTRAIT

Her nimble fingers stitch the festive wear
Of all the village, and her needle plies
With neat precision through the silks and lace
Of party dresses; and in early springs
She bastes the filmy length of bridal veils.
Her brave pretending as she measures hems

In wedding gowns is all she'll ever know
Of love; but she is happy in her game
Of make-believe, and in her passive way
Is grateful for the meager crumbs her mind
Bestows upon her. Longings unfulfilled
Will never perish, and the wear of life
Can not unravel from her finished seams
The fragile threading of her secret dreams.

BILLY B. COOPER.

" 'I remember, I remember' . . . of course, it's impossible . . . but I do remember . . .

REFUGEE

I was born at midnight
  In an old log hut.
The panes were all out,
  And the door wouldn't shut.

There wasn't any bed,
  And there wasn't any bureau,
And the rain etched the ceiling
  In chiaroscuro.

There wasn't any stove,
  And there weren't any chairs.
There weren't any carpets,
  And there weren't any stairs.

The wind whistled through
  Chill and raw,
Whilst my mother bore me
  On a pallet of straw.

The rain kept leaking,
  And the midwife cried,
And my mother kissed me
  Before she died.

BEE FORSYTH WOLVERTON.

"Heredity maketh strange bedfellows . . .

BROTHERS

Bill always chose the hard way,
   And Joe, the easy road;
Seems Bill would tote his own pack,
   Likewise his brother's load.

Bill had no time for women,
   Joe danced his way along,
And if the piper must be paid,
   He'd settle for a song.

Bill crashed one blazing midnight
   While bombs screeched overhead,
But Joe died in a mansion
   The hard way—in bed.

BEULAH RIDGEWAY WINANS.

"Time never lay heavy on his hands . . . he improved the chiming hour . . .

RECONCILED

Calm-eyed the old clock-maker stands
And winds his clocks with practiced hands;
His sole companion—a dog;
His world—the pendulum, the cog,
The fine-coiled spring, the bird-like chime
That underlines the flight of Time!
He knows his knowledge cannot trace
The drama in an old clock's face;
He knows each day, each hour, each minute
Can hold all Hell or Heaven in it—
But reconciled, he makes and mends,
While fateful clocks become his friends!

PAULINE HAVARD.

" 'Not bread . . . but a stone' . . .

WAITRESS

This is no Hebe pampering a god,
   No Ganymede dispensing liquid fire,
Just Susie Brown (alike as pea in pod
   To all the other girls), who serves for hire.
Her uniform is gray, her collar white,
   Her manner semielegant, discreet,
Professionally trimmed to heed the slight
   Or major needs of those who run to eat.

No clue appears to her philosophy,
   Her loves and hates, her faith or disbelief.
In fact, she is a symbol meant to be
   Beyond the ready reach of joy or grief.
But when she smiles to put a child at ease,
She hints at hunger food cannot appease.

                                         ELIAS LIEBERMAN.

Secret, and self-contained, and solitary as an oyster.
                                         CHARLES DICKENS.

"There was an indefinable quality about her . . . and those who knew her say . . . that none of her biographers have caught it . . .

A CURIOUS LADY

A curious lady my sash often ties,
She does not seem wicked or wild,
But the strange little things that leap out of her eyes
Are enough to astonish a child.

They dance on my cheek bones until I am red,
They're mocking as oft as they're bland,
But sometimes they slide from the top of my head
And hold very gently my hand.

                                       JEANNETTE SEWELL DAVIS.

"It's perfectly proper to have a name for a thing, but how distressing to have Thing for a name . . ."

THE MISSES THING

The Misses Thing lived side by side
   In houses that were small.
They never had been married
   Or anything at all.

Miss Bessie Thing was short and plump;
   Miss Ellen, dark and tall.
They never drank or smoked or swore
   Or anything at all.

And since there were no Messrs. Thing
   Or any Thingsters small,
They hadn't any worries
   Or anything at all.

The Misses Thing both thought that spring
   Was just the same as fall.
There is no moral to this tale
   Or anything at all.

DOROTHY ANN BLANK.

" 'The pen is mightier than the sword' . . . they say . . . but some pens leak . . ."

PRAYER FOR POETS

Lord, pity all
Who, through death and worse,
Must dabble in meter
And potter with verse,

Who must take earth's sorrows
One at a time
And whittle them down
To a neat, small rhyme,

Who have ears to hear with
And eyes to see
And no stronger arm
Than a simile!

JOYCE MARSHALL.

"Here lies one . . . whose name is writ in water . . ."

TO A CERTAIN POET

She carries eternity
About her person,
As another would carry a compact,
Or small change in a purse.
Her mind is like a well,
With a living spring,
In which she lowers the bucket
From time to time,
Only to bring forth
A few blurred phrases
With green moss about them.
Some day . . . . . perhaps . . . . . the well
Will be crystal clear. In the meantime,
She waits behind a stone wall.
In a valley of hope.

HAZEL E. MELAMEDE.

"There is no epicure . . . in my eyes . . . superior to Happy . . . making mud pies . . . and yet . . ."

BASEMENT CAFETERIA

Fat, happy women chewing Chicken à la King;
Orchestra stricken with the rustle of spring;
Neat, nervous women gnawing toast and lettuce;
Dyspeptics dully wondering, "What does eating get us?"
Seven different vegetables suffering in steam;
Soup, stew, and codfish balls; two cents for cream;
Battered fruits and salad, puddings, cake, and pies,
Abject and swooning, shrink from greedy eyes.
Stolid and indifferent, mindless bite and munch,
Labor resolutely gluts the two-bit "Business Lunch."
With lumpy mashed potatoes, pale meat, and bread,
Peas, pie, and coffee, let them be fed.
Thick white cup and thick white platter;
Thin folks growing thinner, fat ones getting fatter;
Mouths smeared with mayonnaise; napkins scrubbing spoons;
Old smells, bold smells; persecuted tunes;
Scrape of knife and fork and glass; din of dirty dishes—
Ah, the lovely paucity of loaves and little fishes!

ANTOINETTE WILLSOD.

"But Uncle Jerry wasn't so dumb . . . he didn't have a nervous breakdown . . . or jump out of any building . . . and as for destiny . . . look at the space he has in this book . . . more than his more famous neighbors . . . for all their labors . . .

UNCLE JERRY

Poor Uncle Jerry,
Head in the clouds,
Never did take to common folks' ways.
"I been created,
Son," he would tell me,
"To fill a great destiny one o' these days."

Poor Uncle Jerry,
Sittin' and dreamin',
(How creditors plagued him, and Aunt Bessie too!)
Lived for tomorrow
For nearly eight decades,
Too proud to work like the rest of us do.

Poor Uncle Jerry—
Destiny passed him,
Weeds grew in his garden and holes in his pants;
They shoveled him under
One September morning
Before he had ever received his big chance.

ADRIAN F. NADER.

"And this our life . . . exempt from public haunt . . . finds . . . sermons in rolling stones . . . and moss on everything . . .

TIED

They let my brother go where fancy led;
They gave, to me, a little house to sweep.
"He's like his restless dad," they always said,
While I had hens to feed and bees to keep.
Through all the years I played a quiet part
In that small town with all its rigid bans;
While all my brother's letters hurt my heart
With talk of ships and roving caravans.

I braided mats and stitched the endless seams;
I washed the dishes, and I brushed the crumbs;
And no one knew that, in rebellious dreams,
I heard a temple bell and jungle drums.
They never thought, though it may well be true,
A daughter can be like her father, too.

MABEL FREER LOVERIDGE.

"The happiest days of anybody's life . . . can't be predicted . . . by an algebraic formula . . .

PLANKTON

One will be a warrior;
    One will be a priest;
One will deal in little cakes
    And ices for a feast;
One will venture underseas;
    One will sweep the sky;
But here in study-hall they frown
    O'er x-square minus y.

One will be a banker;
    One will drive a truck;
One will teach the ladies bridge;
    One will shovel muck;
One will cure the stomach-ache,
    While one is selling fudge;
But here they all through Hither Gaul
    With Caesar's legions trudge.

Soon, too soon, come wrinkles,
    Beards, and swelling girth;
Soon they don the liveries
    That placard men of earth;
Soon must come the need of gold,
    Restlessness and pain—
How they'll yearn to spatter ink
    In study-hall again!

HAROLD WILLARD GLEASON.

With This Ring I Thee Wed

"S. O. M. to J. T. K. . . . June 22, 1940 . . . with all my love . . .

FOR A NEW WEDDING RING

So small a thing to close a kingdom in,
Encircled in its fragile shining strength
Are fair eternal Aprils two may win
And bright dream roadways lie within its length.
Here is a vow said in a word of gold
That Time can never touch nor true heart doubt,
So slender on your finger and so bold
To close a kingdom in, a whole world out.

GLADYS MCKEE.

Marriage: a community consisting of a master, a mistress, and two slaves, making in all, two.

AMBROSE BIERCE.

"Proving that sturdier than brick and stone and steel . . . are what we say and how we feel . . .

A WEDDING PRAYER

God, give them length of days to live together
Upon this earth; and lend them grace, we pray
To keep in dignity and peace and splendor
This bright new house that they have built today.
Oh, always may the new rooms be encircled
By walls of love, and may the faith two hold,
Each in the other, grow with time's long passing.
We do not pray that they shall garner gold

From years to be . . . Far better to glean wisdom
Of understanding, and to draw so near
Each to the other that though storms may threaten
Their love will keep them guarded from all fear.
Oh teach them, God, on this their bridal morning
To walk love's path with fearless eyes, brave, gay;
To know that two who bear all things together
Will build a house that shall not pass away.

HELEN WELSHIMER.

"She was fair and nearly fifty . . . he was a grayish fifty-five . . . but at the wedding ceremony I heard a stranger say . . . 'What a lovely bride' . . .

BRIDES

A bride may hail from Halifax
Or London or New York
Or Wichita or Wagon Wheel
Or any country fork.

And she may wear a satin gown
Or crepe or calico,
A picture hat, a silken veil,
Or blossoms in a row.

She may be beautiful or not,
And flourish any grace,
But always, always she will have
Heaven in her face!

ISABELLE BRYANS LONGFELLOW.

Behold whiles she before the altar stands
Hearing the holy priest that to her speaks
And blesseth her with his two happy hands.

EDMUND SPENSER.

"Friendship . . . Courtship . . . Love . . . . Marriage . . . Ready . . . Aim . . . Fire . . .

SOFT CONQUEST

My thoughts were like an army ranged,
Prepared at any time to rout
Whatever siege the foes of peace
Might hurl against the mind's redoubt.

Impervious to friend and foe,
They stood unmoved by any fate
Until one silken day you came
And paused beside the outer gate.

With one white hand you swept aside
The sentries of the citadel;
Before the soft surge of your eyes
One after one the ramparts fell.

A conqueror, you entered in:
Now willing captives fawn and flex
Before the legions of your charm
That laid the subtle siege of sex.

ANDERSON M. SCRUGGS.

She who ne'er answers till a husband cools,
Or if she rules him, never shows she rules.

ALEXANDER POPE.

"Niagara Falls was never like this . . .

MARRIAGE

Back from the dusty church,
The words all said
And the strange kiss given,
We walked down the long lane of Fourteenth Street,
Our shoulders touching home-bound clerks
And shoppers, straggly shawls about their heads,
To the Hungarian restaurant where for weeks
You had courted me between the soup and steak.
Tonight
The mirrors all about the walls seemed only
To show your face to me, and mine to you.
Wherever I might look, I found your eyes,
You mine, and as we gazed,
We quite forgot that earth held other things
Until our friendly waiter, twinkling-eyes,
As happy as if he were himself the groom,
Came bustling back, a link from heaven to earth.

Four blocks of windy street,
Four flights of stairs,
And then we stood
Before your studio door.
You turned the key,
And groping in the dark, you found a candle
And pouring tallow in the little pool
Upon the mantelpiece, you stood it there
In its tall whiteness.
There was rain outside;
The skylight hummed and rattled with its coming.
A few faint sounds blew up from the loud distance;
The grunt of a Salvation Army's drum
Blent with the noise
Of women's voices, roughened by the night,
Singing from hearts the night has roughened, too,
And softened.

The street flung up its stones against our window,
But could not force the fortress of our thoughts—
Your thoughts of me and mine of you, old, new,
And riotous
And frightened.

We who had always been such open comrades
Now were half afraid
To touch each other's hands,
To see each other's faces in the dim
And holy dusk.

We thought of God. I prayed to Him,
As I had prayed when first you said, "I love you,"
The same quick, breathless, little broken prayer;
"God, oh, don't let us hurt each other ever!"
The portraits you have painted were about us,
A ghostly company of friends.
Life seemed all ends—
Ends of things finished, ends of things begun,

Ends, ends,
No safe and placid middles.
Because the silence choked from utterance
All other words, we talked of daily things:
Your order for a cartoon, and the story,
Long overdue, that I must mail tomorrow.
And then the silence
Laid its hands even on these commonplaces.

We looked at one another gravely,
Shy children that our mothers, Youth and Life,
Had brought to see each other and to play
Together.

Two startled children
Permitted by the gold ring on my hand
To stay and talk there in the dusk alone,
And for the first time not to think of clocks,
But, if we liked, watch night's dark bud bloom dawn.
The silence grew and filled the room's dark corners.

The candle on the table burned its life out,
And its flame died, and all the room was dark;
And on the skylight fell the black, loud rain;
And in the world there was no other sound
But your breathing
And the beating of my heart.
Then in the dark
You stumbled to me
And caught me by the shoulders
And laid your mouth on mine.
And all the hunger of our lives for life,
And all my hunger for you, yours for me,
Surged up in us. Love caught us as a storm
A ship, and beat upon us; joy
Rose like a tossing sea and swallowed us.

MARY CAROLYN DAVIES.

" 'What's to do about it? . . . Let's put out the lights' . . .

LOVE SONG

Hallow the room, curtain the bed,
Soften the light in the window's arc!
There is a bit of heaven, you said,
Here in the dark.

So let us dream for a little space,
Snuff out the world with its restless tide.
This is my realm, my ultimate place,
Close at your side!

MARGUERITE JANVRIN ADAMS.

"*Soldier's bride . . .*

PRAYER

God, try to make me big
and wise and strong enough
to love him in the way that suits Your plan;
and make these quickly passing moments long enough
to last us each a lifetime, if You can.
Don't make me weak after You once have made me brave
and taught me courage. Help me to take pride
that it was to my tiny singing heart You gave
his glorious love; that I was at his side
for one clear shining instant. Let me be content
to know his truest heart is mine, altho
his life must, of necessity, always be spent
away from me; and when You've made him go
give me the strength to keep his mem'ry ever fresh,
in spite of all the agony it brings
because You framed this soul of mine in silly flesh
that aches and writhes and longs for all the things
it is denied. I'm not the kind that moans and hunts
for some excuse to pester You with prayer,
but please, take time out from Your sparrows just this once
for me—You'll not be sorry, God, I swear.

KATHRYN KAY.

"And he probably thinks he's running after her . . .

DESIRABLE MALE

I won't live in a glass house . . .
Not ever, ever, ever,
For fear someone will see him
Who's clever, clever, clever!

I'll house him and I'll hide him;
I'll carpet every floor;
I'll slide my Queen Anne sofa
Across my painted door.

I'll feed him from my larder
And sleep him in my bed;
I'll warm his feet by firelight
And hold his cushioned head.

Never must they see him;
Never, never, never.
Never must he see them
Wearing out the weather,

Standing on my doorstep,
Hear their high heels clicking!
Little latch, hold fast, hold fast!
Little clock, keep ticking!

Kaye Huizing.

"Who is mere man to dispute this . . .

COMFORTING THOUGHT

It's true that they're illogical;
It's true their arguments are brittle;
It's true that women talk too much—
But then, they say so little!

May Richstone.

" 'Home is where the heart is' . . .

BRIDE'S HOUSE

The bride's house, frosted with moonlight,
Is white as a wedding cake;
Down the rolling driveway
Lacy shadows shake.

The bride's house, brave with newness,
Beckons happy years,
Grooms itself for laughter,
Braces itself for tears.

LIDA WILSON TURNER.

And truant husband should return, and say,
"My dear, I was the first who came away."

LORD BYRON.

"The marriage ceremony has a number of phrases in it . . . not mentioned at the church . . .

ETERNAL TRIANGLE

At first, she used to say, "My mother-in-*law*."
Placing the accent on the last, cold word,
As if, in such a forced affair, she saw
A matter, legal but a trifle absurd.
During the second year, it got to be—
"Dick's mother." After little Dick was born,
It turned to "Grandma Martin."—Gradually,
That same, once strange relationship was shorn
Of every small antagonism; at last,
Became a peaceful, kind, familiar thing—
Living renewal of my own dead past—
A safeguard against all old age might bring—
And when, to-day, she said—"Dick's-mother-and-mine,"
She set upon the words love's seal and sign.

VIOLET ALLEYN STOREY.

"And their income tax is small, too . . ."

RECOMPENSE

How truly wise perhaps it was
My dollars were so few,
For if my purse were full, then I
Would never know if you
Had married me for riches, or
Because my eyes were blue!

LOUISE SHAW.

"When double entry comes in the door . . . single blessedness flies out the window . . ."

"NO HELP WANTED"

Busy little bookkeeper
Toiling in my brain
Figuring out the profit
In loving you again.
Adding up the debits
Accountable to you
Deducting the credits
Where credits are due.
Busy little bookkeeper,
Crumple up that chart;
I just got the answer
By cable from my heart!

MILDRED BRESEE OSTERHOUT.

"Will it really be like this . . . oh, is it ever any different . . . would anybody ever want it?"

DOMESTICITY

I know I said we'd cut some ice
   In tails and ermine wraps;
But could these, dear, be half so nice
   As after-dinner naps?

We swore we'd never grow too old
   To cut a payday caper;
It's funny we were never told
   We'd rather read the paper.

ALBERT HORLINGS.

"The chorus girl and the playboy . . . penthouse serenade . . .

THE AWAKENING

She was demure and pensive
When they pledged their marriage vow.
He said, "My dear, my worldly goods
On thee, I now endow."

She WAS demure and pensive
But she soon changed, and how!
No longer is she pensive,
She's just ex-pensive now.

HALLIE PHILIPS.

All tragedies are finished by a death,
All comedies are ended by a marriage.

LORD BYRON.

"Once upon . . . there was a wedding supper . . . fifty anniversaries ago . . .

PRAYER AT EVENING'S END

Here in this quiet room tonight
Where blooms a soft and lovely light
On tapering waxen stems of white:

Here in this room of hushed content,
Of love warm and beneficent,
Let me be mindful we have spent

Some hours so good to live that we
Can face like kings the days to be!
Let me have vision *now* to see

The beauty of this thing we share!
The slow heart learns, to its despair,
No beauty waits for it to grow aware.

ADELAIDE LOVE.

"Clasp hands . . .

HALO FOR A HUSBAND

To those who say the world is round,
I leave the world they own
And turn the one that I have found
Like some queer, star-shaped stone
Upon a sweeter Genesis
I feel at last is mine,
With folds of early twilight hemmed
And yards of midnight stitched,
By morning's halo diademed
And sunlight's seams bewitched.
This is a world whose shape is held,
Is certain, and endures
Beyond all fact and history
Within my hand and yours.

GLADYS MCKEE.

"Bake me a cake . . . paint me a picture . . . build me a house . . . then make a poem . . .

DESIGN FOR ENCHANTMENT

Make me a poem wherein petals,
In falling, musically strike
The ground, and lovely laughter settles
A little while around us, like

A host of butterflies. Compose
Me lines in which the wind with all
A magic forest in it blows,
And stars are low, a poplar tall

Enough to touch them with its peak.
And after you have done with it
And told it to me, let us sit
Here in the firelight, and not speak.

ELAINE V. EMANS.

"The bride and groom do not get to come in together, but that is no reason why they should not get to . . ."

ABDICATION

From high upon the pedestal
Where you have placed me, Dear,
I'm holding out my arms to you . . .
It's very lonely here.

KATHERINE KELLY WOODLEY.

"And promise me you'll never be a model husband . . . ."

HAND HIM A HALO

Perhaps *your* bread on both sides has been buttered!
Perhaps *your* cake is eaten and you *have* it, too!
Perhaps *all* pearls have been the words *you've* uttered!
Perhaps *you've* never bitten *more* than you can chew!

Who gives a rap
For such a chap?

ADDISON H. HALLOCK.

"Do you take this man . . .? I do . . . I do . . ."

PATTERN FOR LOVE

I'll be all women to you, love,
Sophisticated, gay and wise,
Demure and docile as a dove,
A gypsy girl with dancing eyes,

I'll be all women, love, to you,
Exotic, clinging, fancy-free,
So you can stay at home and do
All your philandering with me!

MAY RICHSTONE.

"Kiss the bride . ."

TWO WORDS

At times a woman wonders if all this
Routine of household duties is worth while—
They march ahead of her in endless file!—
And if there isn't something she must miss
By staying home so much, by taking care
Of babies, by mending and by making
Beds, dishwashing—thankless tasks!—by baking . . .
(The days slip past with scarce an hour to spare
For reading, save for rimes from Mother Goose!
Her music is confined to lullabies,
Her clever hands to buttonholes and pies!)
When suddenly she's circled in a noose
Of strong warm arms; a deep voice says: *"My wife!"*
And then, once more, how blessed, how sweet is life!

ETHEL ROMIG FULLER.

"He who marries a man and woman . . . may give them counsel . . .

TO A YOUNG WIFE

Never feel woman-weakly, never doubt
You have a place in this, his difficult hour.
You have a task to wear the long months out,
A certainty of one elusive power:
You will have kept the nestlings of his dreams
In a warm, feathered place, safe from alarms
Until the storm subsides, and swollen streams
Of time and men have ebbed, and death disarms.
You will have forged new chains that cannot rust;
Wear them with dignity and courage, banding
The bright hope to your heart with deeper trust,
In a swift ecstasy of understanding.
Whatever comes to you of joy or pain,
This one sure knowledge surely will remain.

JOHN PAUL SEIBERLING.

"And those who see them married . . . may add a prayer . . .

THE MOTHER

The wedding march peals forth—I turn to see
   The bride come softly down the ribboned aisle
Arrayed in shimmering white, upon her father's arm,
   And on her face a faint and tremulous smile.
My baby once, who walks so regally and slow . . . .
   I hear her first glad footsteps in the long ago.

Beneath her lacy cap brown ringlets circle down . . . .
   So silken were her first thin wisps of hair,
So dimpled was that little form that now attains
   Full stature of sweet womanhood naively fair.
Gold flames reach up from tapers tall and white . . . .
   Once candles on a little cake meant sheer delight.

The altar is abloom with pale and fragrant flowers . . . .
   Her chubby hands would bring a little bright bouquet
When April spread her loveliness upon the fields.
   She stands now by his side, and his adoring way
Stirs gladness in my heart while firm vows make them one—
   May happiness attend my daughter and my son!

NELL GRIFFITH WILSON.

Is not marriage an open question, when it is alleged, from the beginning of the world, that such as are in the institution wish to get out, and such as are out wish to get in?

RALPH WALDO EMERSON.

Run, Postman, Run

"Dear Madam . . . What do you mean by using a canceled stamp . . . wrinkled too . . . why, for two cents I'd . . . I . . . I . . . mean three . . .

NOTE TO THE POSTMASTER

Postmaster, this gray, rumpled stamp
  Has not been canceled; it just lay
Within a small seersucker suit
  Before it reached my hands today.
Wedged in with marbles and a bit
  Of writing charcoal and a tile,
It felt the swiftly beating heart
  That guarded second base a while.
Brought to me on a grimy palm,
  It's not, I hope, too creased to use.
That dark, I think, is chocolate bud.
  It isn't canceled. Please excuse.

BARBARA A. JONES.

"Lost in the mails . . .

O, THE LONG WAITING FOR THE WANTED WORD

O, the long waiting for the wanted word;
The sleepless eyes heavy with unshed tears,
The steps beset by indeterminate fears,
O, the deep silence, O, the voice unheard,
That voice that all the night to being stirred;
O, the long torment and the doubt that slays,
The lonely journeying through crowded ways—
The hollow waiting for the waited word.

The impositions of the flesh and bone
May somehow be forgotten, but the brain
Sadly can recognize how joys remain
Indissuadably designed as if of stone.
All night upon the world the rain, the rain,
Never your voice—always the vast alone.

FLORENCE HAMILTON.

"You wouldn't believe what odd things postmen find in the mail box .."

LOVE LETTER

She stops for one more look, and then
Hesitates and looks again.
She touches it with ruby lips
And breathes a prayer, then quickly tips
The lid, and with the cunning of the fox
She slips her heart into the letter box.

CY LANCE.

And oft the pangs of absence to remove
By letters, soft interpreters of love.

MATTHEW PRIOR.

"Some letters are written to be taken on a trip . . . gay good wishes . . . places to be sure and see . . . things to do. Sometimes letters are left behind . . .

DESIGN FOR A LAST LETTER

Dearest:
　　If I'm not home in time for tea,
Put on the silver pot and light the fire,
Use the new Wedgwood cups you brought to me,
The slender spoons that once were heart's desire,
Turn on the radio and shed no tear,
Nor mourn the hours that passed when I was there,
Let the first inch of twilight banish fear
And keep this interlude serene and fair.
Still if your thoughts turn to me and to things
We did together, let them still be glad,
Consider my delight in choosing wings,
A golden harp and jewels I never had,
Or better still, if you are feeling blue,
Think of me planning where we next shall meet,
Deciding on a certain star, or hue
To grace a cottage on a golden street.

GLADYS MCKEE.

"Bills should be barred from the males . . ."

LETTERS

What joys are held in letters!
And what distracted hope;
A message that's concealed
In one small envelope!

FLORENCE M. BENNELL.

Jove and my stars be praised! Here is yet a postscript.

WILLIAM SHAKESPEARE.

"James . . . . . Somewhere in the Pacific . . . . . Care of San Francisco Postmaster" . . .

LETTER TO JIM

Dear Jim:
    Today old Henry came to see
If he might make a garden on our land
While you are gone—the bit of land where we
Had thought to build our house, had long since planned
Each airy, sunlit room with confidence,
The fanlight that would curve above the door,
The pansy border, the white picket fence.
How far away in those days seemed the war!

It isn't easy, Jim, to wait and wait—
We've sacrificed now for so many years—
Yet if by waiting we may help create
Security for other homes like ours
Where man and wife may work in love and pride,
Free to plan the years, to live their own
Lives, free to have their children, undenied,
    Then, dearest, you and I can wait!

Your Joan.

MARY FERGUSON LEGLER.

"Air Mail . . . Special Delivery . . .

GIFT

I wrapped my fancy in a cloud
Fleecy pink and white,
I tied it round with rainbow silk
And hid it in the night.

I took the sunbeams of the day
And wrote your name on brightly;
Bits of sky I took for seals
And sealed my love in tightly.

And then I tossed it to the wind
Who held it in a starling
And raced across the world with it—
I hope it reached you, darling.

MARY ELLEN BUCKINGHAM.

"If you want a boy, call Western Union . . .

LOST LEAVE

Dear Matthew:
I only saw your telegram just now,
  Six hours of leave for you and oh, my dear—
I must confess I spent them with a stranger
  Who so consumed my body, heart and mind,
That I am weak and breathless with great loving.
  And with the telling of this news to you,
My heart pleads your forgiveness and blessing,
  And hopes that in the kindness of your soul
You'll find that you can share a part of me
  To one I hold most dear in every way.
He weighs nine pounds, we named him Matthew James.
  My dear, your son was born at noon today.

ROENA BURGER.

"Dear Teacher ... I'm afraid I'm on a tangent ... everything seems to be going 'round and 'round ...

TO A LOVELY YOUNG LADY TEACHING GEOMETRY

Oh, Lady think me not obtuse
Because I cannot comprehend
The square of the hypotenuse,
And pray, when you bisect a plane,
Forgive me if my thoughts pretend
To follow yours, but jump the train.

For when I see you standing there
Before the board, it fags my mind
To ponder angles in a square;
Such things are hard upon my nerves—
How can you blame me if I find
It easier to think in curves?

ANDERSON M. SCRUGGS.

The red-letter days now become, to all intents and purposes, dead-letter days.

CHARLES LAMB.

"Oh, I say!

LETTER FROM LONDON

Noggins' Book Store,
                    December eleventh.
In answer to yours of the twenty-seventh,
We're sorry to say we've a bit of a mess
Back in the sixpence-book recess.
No great damage was done to the store,
Only a bomb went through the floor.
If you could call in a week or two,
There'll be some books on sale, a few.
Our thanks for your interest,
                    Respectfully,
Alfred Noggins and Company.

MARION LIPSCOMB MILLER.

"After all, three cents will carry anything you can express . . ."

A LETTER FOR YOU

I would send you, if I could,
A little corner of this wood;
A balsam tree with pale new tips
Mottled by sunlight that drips
Slanting through close dusk; a lake
Shaped like a lily pad. I'd break
Fern fronds from shady hollows, bind
A fluttering wind and send them signed
With bird's feet, moth wings, and good wishes
From porcupine and spotted fishes.

If I could, I'd send to you
Silver of the foggy dew,
Lacquered gold and sunset spills
Over dark, uneven hills,
Shadow of green bough that lies
Where slow moving water tries
To pull it from the shore. I'd wrap
Morning in leaves that overlap,
Tie it with wild grape tendrils, and
Let the wind put it in your hand.

But since I can do nothing better,
I send you an ordinary letter,
There is not much to tell, I write
Swift drowsy day, cool quiet night,
A swim in clear blue water, then
Morning, gold noon, and night again
I send my love. You cannot see
Fern gardens on a rock. Near me
A crooked path goes through the wood.
I would send it to you if I could.

LOUISE DRISCOLL.

"Marked 'Personal' . . .

LETTER OF CONDOLENCE

Grief, being private, must be borne alone,
And though I cannot share your sorrow, still
Your anguished tears are mingled with my own;
I walk unseen beside you—up the hill.

I can but hope that the pain within your breast
Will lose its sting, your loneliness will melt
When spring returns to meet the yearly test,
When on the pear the first white blow is dealt.

I shall not surfeit you with vapid words,
Claiming to know the answer to it all;
I only ask, so long as darkness girds
Your world, to let these shoulders ease the fall.

       JOHN ROBERT QUINN.

"Fragile . . . Picture Enclosed . . . Do Not Fold!

FROM SOMEWHERE IN THE PACIFIC

You mailed a snapshot from a foreign shore,
Where warplanes zoom, and death itself is faced.
On opening it I caught the smile you wore,
And knew that grimmest horrors hadn't erased
The boyish tenderness you always felt
For every living creature while with me,
And I rejoiced that carnage had not dealt
A blow to my son's innate charity.

Your men regard your orders when you call—
You stand erect, six feet in army clothes—
Yet you're the boy who grieved at a robin's fall,
And stooped to lift a crushed and trampled rose.
Your snapshot cleared the tenseness in my breast,
And so tonight I'll sleep in quiet rest.

       RACHEL LUMPKIN WYLY.

"Letter to a friend . . ."

VALUES

You will notice the rose a little more this year
And lights that flower at the close of day
In towns that nestle; each a small bouquet
In night's dark vase, as sleep and dreams draw near.
You will quicken more to the smell of baking bread
And burning leaves, bright in a neighbor's field,
The clean, sweet odors berry patches yield,
The earthy scent of pumpkins in a shed.
You will hearten more at the greeting of a friend,
The open talk within a marketplace,
The quick smile flashing from a stranger's face,
And gatherings, where songs and laughter blend.
The thoughts of these go very, very deep
When they are things that we must fight to keep.

GERALDINE ROSS.

"Letter home . . ."

HIGH FLIGHT

Oh, I have slipped the surly bonds of earth,
And danced the skies on laughter-silvered wings;
Sunward I've climbed and joined the tumbling mirth
Of sun-split clouds—and done a hundred things
You have not dreamed of—wheeled and soared and swung
High in the sunlit silence. Hov'ring there,
I've chased the shouting wind along and flung
My eager craft through footless halls of air.
Up, up the long delirious, burning blue
I've topped the wind-swept heights with easy grace,
Where never lark, or even eagle, flew;
And, while with silent, lifting mind I've trod
The high untrespassed sanctity of space,
Put out my hand, and touched the face of God.

JOHN GILLESPIE MAGEE, JR.

"But if it doesn't .... All is!!! ... and that rhymes too!

LETTER

A letter, with its story
On a square of rag,
Can make a cloud of glory
In the postman's bag.

When I hear the ringing,
Twice, of the bell,
I run, singing . . .
If it comes, all is well . . .

ISABEL FISKE CONANT.

"Hidden in a pocket in Oslo . . . sent by secret agents to a fishing schooner . . . carried to a rendezvous at sea with Allied ships . . . placed aboard a convoy . . . Iceland . . . Greenland . . . Newfoundland . . . Boston . . . Washington . . . addressed to a stamp collector . . .

A LETTER FROM NORWAY

Dear friend, remember we are not afraid;
   Though grief is ours, and hunger, humbled pride,
We are not lost or scattered or dismayed;
   We are not beaten—we are occupied.

Remember how our winters endless seemed—
   Those bitter months of twilight steeped in cold—
And then they passed; the midnight sunshine streamed
   Across the fjords and tipped the firs with gold.

Of this storm-ridden season, these dark days,
   It shall be written in our history
How cherished faith and quiet, ordered ways
   Were not abandoned in catastrophe,
How this ordeal but quickened and brought forth
   The patient, stubborn courage of the north!

MARGOT MANSEAU.

"Atlas . . .

NEW POSTMAN

The love, the grief, the hate of them—
How can he bear the weight of them?

ISABEL FISKE CONANT.

"I take my pen in hand . . . but the ink is dry . . . as the weather has been . . . as life itself is . . . sometimes . . .

A SOLDIER'S MOTHER WRITES TO A FRIEND

Dear Jane:

You say your peach trees bloomed this year,
And veiled with pink each orchard row,
You ask about my plum trees here—
Perhaps they bloomed, I do not know.

You say that the early grass is long,
And the first red poppies are beginning to show,
That the birds have returned with their old-time song—
Perhaps you are right, I do not know.

You remember my handsome youngster, Jim—
Oh, Jane, he was one of the first to go!
If ever I walk once more with him,
Then, spring will come—this much I know.

        Lovingly,
         Sue.

       MAURICE HILL.

"P. S. . . .

CHRISTMAS LETTER FROM MY SON

   Hickam Field, Honolulu, Hawaii, U.S.A.
(*Peace? . . . There is no peace, I said.*
Only the ashes of the dead.
Goodwill? . . . An earth of warring men,
Hands at each other's throats again!)

And then his letter came, from oversea . . .
Strength in his lines—and wings of hope, for me!

       December 7th, 1942.
Dear Mom:
 A year can be so very brief:
palm-shadows on the moon, a sunrise sea,
the Trade-cloud's pattern on a coral reef . . .
(to you who wait, a heart's eternity!)

      Perhaps, if I could make you understand
the childlike faith these Island people show:
their reverence for the "Flag" and for their "Land,"
in this far outpost archipelago . . .
if, somehow, I might bridge the sea-green space
and bring you close—to see with your own eyes
this happy melting-pot of every race,
you would be quick to sanction—realize
the smug and narrow 'brotherhood' we boast
was like a promise never put to test:
that, in our coward souls, we cherished most
the Kipling fallacy of "East . . . and West,"
      Out here . . . where trading schooners load their loot
with cargoes, colorful as South Seas' fruit:
pearl shell from the Paumotus, breadfruit-green
and angelfish of Island-rainbow sheen,
copra . . . and copra! and the burnished blues
of seas, cerulean as Gulf Stream hues . . .
where frangipani lifts its luscious breath
while song and laughter temporize with death . . .
where every landfall tempts the poet-pen—
and beauty, blighted, may not come again . . .
Out here! . . .
      But you are smiling, now, at me
and saying, "After all, the boy is young:
this is his first long voyage on the sea—
youth will be youth, its songs must still be sung!"
      Perhaps I'm older than you really guess,
War has a way of changing boy to man.
(War . . . and a year of homesick loneliness!)
A year is brief! A tropic Island span
of dreamy days and nights of deeper dream—
and former values are not what they seem . . .
      Now . . . I am pondering the price of Peace,
when we have won—as never men may doubt!
Will we, as leaders, guarantee surcease
from War's atrocity? . . .

                For not without
the future welfare of mankind at heart
will we maintain our power. And every race
must own His wisdom—choose the wiser part:
God's right is might. Hates flee before His face!
    You did not wish a preacher for a son—
but, if this thing keeps on, you may *have* one!
But, first—so great our tolerance is vexed!—
a sub-machine gun might be better text! . . .
And, rest assured, we'll fight for all we're worth,
each mother's son . . . till Peace redeems this earth!
*Meanwhile . . . your letters, your sustaining love
build us a rampart that you dream not of!*
    *This is not war, alone, of battlefield:
each one of you at home wears shining shield!* . . .
Our hero dead, out here—beneath white leis—
shall be avenged! . . .
                More ships upon your ways!
Give us the planes—the wings—that's all we ask!
Ours is the battlefront—but yours the task
to keep our courage—*Peace our battle cry!*
A lasting Peace . . . when war and hatred die.
    There will be other years when we may feast . . .
Goodwill the host, then, West . . . to wiser East.
    Keep Christmas! And keep Faith within your heart.
        (Another year, we may not be apart!)
    Your prayers, your letters . . . *till this war is won!*
        Chin up! . . .
                        Aloha, now . . .
                        Your Soldier Son.
P. S.:
    (*I'd risk the guardhouse—and the dog-house, too—
If I could spend this Christmas Day . . . with you!*)
                      BLANCHE DeGOOD LOFTON.

Little Pitchers Have Big Ears

"The wonderful thing about New Year Resolutions is that no one expects you to keep your promises anyway . . . and you don't . . . and she won't either . ."

IT'S A PROMISE!

May heaven help me not to bore
  My friends with talk of teething.
They've met such miracles before,
  Including even breathing.

They've seen their share of babes in bed,
  Some somnolent, some sprightly.
They've heard what Little Eustace said,
  And oh'd and ah'd politely.

So I'll be kind to kin and kith
  And mind my subject matter,
Unless they persecute me with
  Their own maternal chatter.

MARGARET FISHBACK.

"Unaccustomed as I am to public speaking . . .

YOUNG AMERICA—FIRST

Let abler poets sing the score
  Of grandeur limned on distant skies;
I sing of epic deeds no more:
  My tones are pitched to lullabies.

Let clearer voices cry the need
  Of kings and thrones beyond the sea;
Give them the staunch and holy creed,
  And leave the cradle song to me.

Yet who shall say their songs are best,
  My notes are vain, and dull my task?
One drowsy head against my breast
  Is all the audience I ask!

BILLIE MARIE CRABB.

"The sand in your eyes, darling . . . is not from the sandman . . . nor your sandbox . . . but from my hourglass which is forever empty . . .

LULLABY FOR A YOUNG MOTHER

Oh, hush, little sleepy-head, lie down to slumber;
   A day is so long for you to go through,
And hours with sixty whole minutes by number
   Are really too much for a wee one like you.

So bye-bye-bye . . . your mother will order
   A different kind of a day for you soon,
A day with small minutes all set in a border
   Of pansies and pinks and a little new moon.

The left-over minutes will not one be wasted;
   She'll buy them all up with a shiny new dime,
And onto her day she'll have the lot pasted
   For she has only half enough time.

EDNA BECKER.

"Incipient Superman . . . sounds like Presidential timber to me . . . like a Congressman at election time . . .

NURSE'S DAY OUT

He falls asleep exactly when
It's time to have his bottle. Then,
The moment that the sprout's been fed
And I have tucked him back in bed,
His eyes grow big as silver dollars,
And how the little demon hollers!

So loud he hollers, and so long,
You'd think that I had done him wrong.
So long he hollers, and so loud,
He'd keep a fire department cowed.
Nor does he close his little trap,
Or even contemplate a nap,
Until it's bottle time, and then
He promptly falls asleep again.

MARGARET FISHBACK.

" 'There was an old woman who lived in a shoe' . . .

DAYTIME STARLIGHT

I wanted Mrs. Mother to tell me, if she could,
Where the little stars are hiding in the day.
Do they turn themselves to blue,
Or whatever do they do,
When the sun comes up and chases them away?

And Mrs. Mother told me she didn't really know,
But she thought that when the sun begins to rise,
Little stars can find a way
To come down and spend the day
Putting starlight into everybody's eyes!

She kissed me when she told me,
And I know the story's true,
For way inside her own gray eyes
I saw the stars shine through!

DIXIE WILLSON.

Men must be taught as if you taught them not,
And things unknown proposed as things forgot.

ALEXANDER POPE.

" 'Man's work is from sun to sun' . . . *woman's work is from son to daughter* . . .

AT MIDNIGHT I REMEMBERED

Wakening at the touch of a wind-blown curtain,
Wakening to joy in the soft loneliness of moonlight,
I remembered that I must go down the hall
Past the small beds all sweet and warm with sleep,
Down the white resting stairway
To the front door,
And step out onto the cold,
Moon-shadowed porch
To bring in little, frozen
Galoshes!

MARY BRENNAN CLAPP.

"The reward a mother gets for sterilizing . . . is surprising . . .

SMALL GENTLEMEN PREFER MOMS

You single me from any crowd
    For your most ardent glances;
Your preference for me, rudely loud,
    Repels their kind advances.

The honor might be laid to love,
    But I've a strong suspicion:
To you I'm chiefly symbol of
    Fresh clothing and nutrition.

SUSIE LEE CUMMINGS.

Men are but children of a larger growth.
JOHN DRYDEN.

"The lease reads 'no cats or dogs allowed on these premises,' . . . but . . .

APARTMENT-HOUSE CROONING

Hush, my darling, sleep and grow;
    Be as quiet as a mouse;
You are not too young to know
    This is an apartment house.

Hush, my little darling, please!
    Mrs. Jones despises boys.
She has trained her Pekingese
    Not to make the slightest noise.

Mrs. Smith, who lives above,
    Tapped the floor, Oh, think of that!
Can't you be, my little love,
    Quiet as her Persian cat?

Dogs and cats and boys, my dear,
    Must in silence bear their woes.
Tenants only want to hear
    Sound effects—on radios!

JANE SAYRE.

"Boy, it's cold and snowy tonight . . . tomorrow I kin get my sled . . . 'n Billy 'n me'll build a snowman . . . but, gee, it's cold 'n dark 'n windy outside . . . good 'n warm here . . .

CONTENTMENT

Cozy little house, open fire a-glowing,
Father with his pipe, mother with her sewing,
Sister doing problems 'neath the hanging lamp,
Bill and Ned still talking 'bout their summer camp.

I just lay a-thinking, like a boy will do,
Munching on an apple, tapping with my shoe,
Nice to have a fam'ly on a frosty night,
Makes me feel important and ev'rything just right.

ROSALIE GARRETT PETERS.

"Silhouette of a fleeting moment . . . held motionless in flight by a poet's pen . . .

BOY RUNNING

You cleave the frail, immediate air
With time blown backward through your hair,
With ancient mornings and lost skies
Melted to wonder in your eyes
And all your swift, mysterious need
Streaming within you for your speed.

The moment trembles to the fleet
Faintest thunder of your feet,
And the day is struck apart
By what has flashed inside your heart,
By what has poured its urgent flood
Into the rivers of your blood
To make of you an unnamed thing
Tilted against the winds of spring.

* * * *

Mindless and timeless as the sun
You fling your body free—and run!

SARAH LITSEY.

"If we could do unto ourselves what we say unto others . . ."

CHILDREN'S WARD

We each said to our own child:
"Come now, be brave!
You're all of 3 (or 2 or 4)
You mustn't cry. You're much too big.
Chin up! Be good! And all . . . "
Then there were two other women
Besides me
Sobbing in the hall.
MARY LANIGAN HEALY.

All will be gay when noontide wakes anew
The buttercups, the little children's dower.
ROBERT BROWNING.

"It's much, much, much, much, much better . . . than kicking the gong around . . ."

BOY ETERNAL

Kicking a can to grade-school,
  Kicking a can to "High,"
Would he kick a can to college,
  Could he possibly pass one by?
He'll be kicking a can with abandon
  On the day he matriculates,
And slyly taking a wallop
  Behind the pearly gates.

Make him a member of Congress,
  Or head of the U. S. A.,
A real boy recalls the tinware
  He has mangled in his day;
Give him a desk in a law-firm,
  Let him boss a wild wheat-pool,
And he'll wish to God for the mornings
  He kicked a can to school!
BARTON REES POGUE.

"What more can happen to her . . . when she's four . . . whatever it is I'm sure it'll be great . . .

GRANDMAMA

Her hair is neatly parted!
Her rouge is on just right!
Her specks are tilted slightly
To help her troubled sight!

Her sewing is forgotten,
She lives in reverie . . .
Her dolly has a baby—
She's grandmama at three!

BETH CONLEY.

"In California they call it a Spanish-style cottage . . . in Cape Cod it's Colonial . . . in New York it's a penthouse . . . in Georgia a plantation . . . but . . .

YOU CAN ALWAYS TELL WHERE A FAMILY LIVES

You can always tell where a family lives
By the gay effect that the hallway gives.
There are hooks arranged in a nice straight row,
And the coats grow shorter and shorter, so
At the very first glance you can surmise
That the people vary in shape and size.
Hats that have streamers mean little girls,
With perky haircuts or ribboned curls.
A wagon and ball and bat reveal
That a boy lives there; and a slim, high heel
On an overshoe is a certain clew
That a grown-up sister's an inmate, too.
A doll that flopped with a broken neck,
A toy train bunched in a pleasant wreck . . .
The rooms may be still as a sleeping mouse
But you know there's a family in the house!

HELEN WELSHIMER.

"A dirty story . . . shame on you! . . .

I LIKE MUD

I like mud.
It makes good pies
'Cept when I splash
It in my eyes.

Mud shoes are fun,
But my mud hat wuzn't.
I like mud
But mummie doesn't.

MAREL SCHWARTZ.

"If we only had some ham . . . we'd have ham and eggs . . . if we only had some eggs . . .

A PERSONAL MATTER

It isn't so much that I mind the freckles
(Sometimes for days I forget that they're there);
But when You ordained it, "This one: Freckles,"
Lord, why didn't You add, "Red hair"?

Red hair and freckles belong together:
Like sleep and waking, like meat and drink,
Like love and kisses, like bell and wether,
Like roaring presses and printing ink.
Having the one without the other
(Having the one *I* have, I mean)
Is about as sad as having a brother
You'll never meet and you've never seen.

It isn't so much that I mind the freckles
(We all have burdens that we must bear);
But when You ordained it, "This one: Freckles,"
Lord, why *did* You withhold red hair?

PATRICIA MARTIN.

"'All day I did the little things ... The little things that do not show' ..."

MY MOTHER

I need my mother all the time;
When I come home at half-past three,
To tell her how I missed in sums,
And show her how I skinned my knee.
It doesn't hurt so awful much,
But then I like to hear
Her when she's kissed me lots of times,
Say, "Oh, my son, my little dear!"

I'm kind o' big for kisses, too,
But mothers are so fond of you!

I need my mother all the time,
To mend my clothes and help with kites;
To hold my hand at picture-shows,
When there are thrills and are no lights.

I'm kind o' big for holding hands,
But Mother, she just understands.

I need my mother all the time.
I go to bed, turn off the light,
And wait to hear the creak the stairs
Make, when she comes to say good-night.
She slips her arm beneath my head,
We hug each other awful tight,
And tell each other things before
She leaves me with a "Sh-h—good-night!"

I'm awful big for hugging, too,
But mothers are so fond of you!

ANNE ZUKER.

"And likewise when he falls in love ... but after they are married ..."

A LITTLE BOY OUT WALKING

A little boy, when he is three,
Out walking with his mother,
Will hold her hand for all to see
That she belongs exclusively
To him, and to no other.

A little boy, when he is eight,
Out walking with his mother,
When there's a boy upon a gate,
Will streak ahead and never wait,
As if he did not love her.
HELEN DAHLE.

Besides they always smell of bread and butter.
LORD BYRON.

"I wouldn't want to hurt your feelings, mother ... but you ain't heard nothing yet ..."

FIRST DAY AT SCHOOL

Today you talk of things of which I know
Only your telling—how you measure sand
Or clap to music till your fingers glow,
Or beat a drum with an unsteady hand.
Your speech is full of toys I have not seen,
A colored donkey, papers that you hook
Together to make pictures, books between
Whose painted covers I shall never look.
And I am glad for you that in this bright
New world you hold without me you have found
Wide eyes to turn upon the world of sight,
Keen ears to lean unto the world of sound.
And only in my hidden heart I say
That I begin to lose you from this day.
JESSIE CORRIGAN PEGIS.

"And a wee small spanking would be preferred no doubt . . . to a resounding SMACK! . . . But mommies are stern . . . and seldom learn . . .

MORE FITTING, I THINK

Sometimes Mummy speaks up cross to me
(She's slim and small . . .
Big voices shouldn't come from her
At all, at all!)

I wish she'd scold in smaller words,
Then I could see
How nice a scolding voice could sound
That's small, like me!

BERNIECE GRAHAM.

"My dear daughter . . . I take my pen in hand . . . that is, I was going to say . . . now let me see . . . on the other hand . . .

THE POET TO HIS DAUGHTER

What can the poet say to this small face
That looks up through the twilight at his own
And reaches with its dark eyes to erase
All he has ever thought or been or known?
What can he answer to her dreams, that speak
The timid, hopeful questions of the young:
Why am I here, so little and so meek?
Why have I freckles and a wiggly tongue?
Why do I laugh when we are having fun?
Why do you hug and kiss me when I cry?
Why do I rock my dolly in the sun
And look up quickly when a boy goes by?

What can I say to keep her unafraid,
Whom God and the girl I love and I have made?

THOMAS SUGRUE.

"You are Alice in Wonderland . . . and Bo Peep . . . and little Miss Muffet . . . and Red Riding Hood . . . all the stories and all the songs . . . all mine . . . and still unsung . . ."

A POET TO HIS DAUGHTER

Of you my daughter, let these words be said:
Dearer to me you are than any song
Of mine the world might praise when I am dead.
I, who have lived for poetry many a long
And arduous year—who strove the while to sing
In a world of toil, serenely and sincerely—
I place my art below no living thing
Save you—for only you I love more dearly.

What though my words should perish with my breath?
Little it matters, if your flesh and mind
Shall be my lovely mansion after death;
You are the words my thoughts could never find,
The sum of all the beauty, all the art
That strove to find a language in my heart.

ANDERSON M. SCRUGGS.

"City folks just clean house . . . go shopping . . . chase the neighbor's cat down the fire escape . . . call the Salvation Army to come get some toys . . . write a dozen letters home . . . nothing . . . nothing at all . . ."

THE SCHOOL BUS TAKES MY YOUNGEST

The school bus stopped a while ago and picked him up;
He climbed aboard as proud as Punch—and left his pup
And me disconsolate! Before, I always had
A baby left—a smaller girl, a younger lad—
But now the littlest one is gone, and all the place
Has suddenly become so still I cannot face
The empty house indoors. I'm glad for rake and hoe,
For pruning shears, for flowers to tend. I'd like to know
What city mothers do, without some garden tool
To comfort them on Baby's first long day at school.

HAZEL M. KERR.

" 'Still sits the schoolhouse by the road, . . . A ragged beggar sunning; . . . Around it still the sumachs grow . . . And blackberry-vines are running! . . .

COUNTRY SCHOOLHOUSE

It ought to be time for school to begin;
   But there isn't a soul in sight,
And the ramshackle schoolhouse on the hill
   Dreams in the mellow light.

There's no path now to the padlocked door,
   And no path now to the spring.
The playground is a riotous wild garden
   In late-summer flowering.

The black-eyed Susans have yellow lashes,
   And the chicory blossoms are blue,
Like the wide-awake eyes of the children
   The little schoolhouse once knew.

The building is old and full of chinks,
   And they may as well tear it down,
For the district now owns a fine new bus
   And hauls the "scholars" to town.

Nobody comes and nothing happens;
   But the dark and light eyes stare
Out of the tangle of the sunlit jungle
   With an expectant air.

HARVEY WAGNER FLINK.

Nought cared this body for wind or weather,
When youth and I lived in't together.

SAMUEL TAYLOR COLERIDGE.

"Turn back the universe and give me yesterday . . . I remember this very incident . . . it happened about three blocks from our house . . . her name was . . . and by the way . . . we won the game . . .

AT SIXTEEN

The street lamp held us in its circle glow
The way it draws gray moths around its light
In summer. It was time for you to go,
But still you stayed. I marvelled at the white
Befeathered flakes that tangled in your hair.
One crystal star got caught on up-curled lash;
And clung precariously, then melted there.
It looked so like a tear in its wild dash
Across your scarlet cheek, I knew a mad
Impulse to kiss its wetly coursing flight—
But caught myself in time, for if I had,
You might have vanished whitely with the night.

You hugged yourself and tap-danced on the street,
For it was cold. Your breath was little puffs
Of misty vapor. Both my hands and feet
Were numb, you pushed your hands inside your cuffs
To keep them warm. But it was getting late,
I had to make the plunge or never know:
Some mumbled words fell out about a date
For next week's game. You said you'd love to go:

And then the door to your house opened wide—
You laughed and guessed you'd have to go inside.

IRENE MCDERMOTT.

Behold the child, by Nature's kindly law,
Pleased with a rattle, tickled with a straw.

ALEXANDER POPE.

" 'Hold fast your dreams! . . . Let wish and magic work at will in you . . . Make believe!' . . ."

CONSOLATION

My small neighbor
Just turned three,
Calls, "Please come out
And play with me."

Despite grey hairs
Or what folks say,
I know I am but
Three today.

ANNE MURRY MOVIUS.

" 'And a little child shall lead them' . . ."

CRIPPLED CHILD

Her wistful gray eyes
Were shadowed with a stain
Of purple pansy petals
Crumpled in rain.

But the soul peering from them
Was brave and tall and fine—
O braver than yours!
O taller than mine!

ETHEL ROMIG FULLER.

"There's little left to say . . . after this . . . which says so much in such a very few words . . ."

A MOTHER PRAYS

I thank You, God, that I have known
A child's moist hand within my own,
And that my ears have heard the ring
Of tuneless songs that children sing.
I thank You for the warm delight
Of children's nearness in the night,
And for the unimagined bliss
Of healing heartbreak with a kiss.

GOLDIE CAPERS SMITH.

" 'It makes a lovely light' . .

PUPPY LOVE

You think he is too green to burn?
Too young to feel desire?
A sapling makes a splendid torch;
I've seen a forest fire!

ELOISE WADE HACKETT.

" 'A wise old owl lived in an oak; . . . The more he saw the less he spoke' . . .

GRANDFATHER SAID

To A Little Girl Who Asks *So Many* Questions

If I were as old as the moon
And wiser than Solomon,
No doubt I could answer your questions—
To the last amazing one.
Then I could translate the rune
Of rain, and shadows spun
Of sunlight would no longer be
A baffling mystery to me.
I could tell how many flakes
In any winter's snows,
And why the leaf of aspen shakes
When no wind blows,
And why one says that daylight *breaks*,
And where a lost thing goes;
What lies beyond, where the highroad bends,
And the very place where the rainbow ends.

Yes, the moon is so old, she knows
All the secrets of earth and heaven;
Why the petals differ on every rose,
Where the light of a burned-out candle goes . . .

If I were old as the moon, my dear—
But I'm only seventy-seven!

MARION DOYLE.

"Sit down, my son . . . the time has come when we should have a nice long talk . . . I have something that I should tell you . . . although it won't be easy . . .

THE WOMAN OF IT

My dear loved son
I picked a scoundrel for your father
My dear loved son
This much can never be undone
But, if it could, I still would rather
You grew as handsome as your father
My dear loved son.

MARCIA NICHOLS HOLDEN.

"Have you read any good books lately . . . like 'Mother Goose'?

CENTURY OF NO PROGRESS

Well, here you are.
Five years old and ready for life.
Or if you're not, it's not my fault.
I've tried hard enough.
I read Watson and stopped petting you.
I read Montessori and let you express yourself with clay.
I read Kugelmas and Tested Your Accomplishments.
I read Steffens and pretended I knew nothing.
I read Holt and scheduled you within an inch of your life.
I read Manin and left you strictly alone.
I read Barnes and watched your vitamins.
I read Clendenning and let you eat anything you pleased.
And so you're ready for life, little man,
And I think you're wonderful.
But when your grandmother looks at you she says,
"God in His Heaven," she says,
"He's the image of his father.
"The way his left ankle turns in,
"The nervous wink of his eye when he's excited . . .
"The way eating eggs sickens him . . . "

Ah, me.
Well, I did my best.

MARTHA LEE LORENZ.

"In the heart of a child . . ."

LOVE'S BOUNTY

All that I had I gave you, never dreaming
Of a return; for it was love I gave.
I gave as a star gives her beauty streaming
In deep of night to a dark western wave.
It was my spirit that I yielded to you,
Surrendering all things; and I asked no more
Than that my mystery none other knew
Should be the secret diadem you wore.

But love is richer than we ever know:
We lavish it, and love comes back to us
A thousandfold. How can I think it so?
How else? Our little child proclaims it thus.
For in him love returns, in flower and light,
More than I gave you in the glimmering night.

ARCHIBALD RUTLEDGE.

"But for our sacrifice of blood and tears . . . our children shall come into the light . . . and the land shall be bright . . ."

BITTER HERITAGE

How we have failed them, these children of ours,
Whose burdensome task through the years must be
To gather the shards of a broken peace
That was handed down whole to such as we.
Lightly we held it, and carelessly; now,
On Mammon's rough boulders it lies shattered there
Beyond our poor mending, awaiting their touch
Whose birthright of hope is reduced to despair.

So have we failed them, who dared to expect
A heritage that our hands have wrecked!

BILLIE MARIE CRABB.

An Apple a Day Keeps the Doctor

"Tall, dark, and handsome . ."

OCCUPATIONAL THERAPY

My doctor says that what it takes
To cure a lot of ills and aches
Is simply this: Just substitute
Your business with some new pursuit.

On his advice I've made a start
To cure a badly injured heart.
Old love, no more you'll hear me sob.
I'm working on another job.

SPRAGUE O. SMITH.

The miserable have no other medicine,
But only hope.

WILLIAM SHAKESPEARE.

"In going on a diet, madame . . . one never knows just where it will be most evident . . . but if you suffer from the lack . . . what comes off can be put back . ."

TECHNIQUE

There are other ways to tell;
Do not toll the somber bell;
Take whatever love may leave;
Crumbs forgotten, now retrieve;
Fashion them into a song,
Not too loud and not too long,
Brief the lyrics, soft the tune,
Like the gossamer of June;
Make the music blue and white;
Steal for notes the stars of night . . .
Hear the melody that comes
High above the muffled drums,
Singing of a love that lies
Dormant under star-swept skies.
Lost love should not mourn in black;
Dress it up and coax it back.

JESSIE FARNHAM.

"Would you ever suspect that there is a heartthrob hidden in this . . .?

ANATOMIST

Ventricles velocitate
  at merest sight of you,
Auricles appraisingly
  give approval, too—
Corpuscles capitulate
  in conquered fashion fast;
But medulla oblongata
  resists stubbornly
    'till
      last.

ALDONA BAUSER.

Joy and Temperance and Repose
Slam the door on the doctor's nose.

HENRY WADSWORTH LONGFELLOW.

"But there will come a time . . . and there will come a doctor . . . yet maybe that won't happen until the end of the book . . .

PORTRAIT

She lives on chocolates and romantic fiction,
  For dreams of knightly chivalry are hers,
Of tender vows proclaimed in faultless diction;
  The heroes of her novel she prefers,
Though overdrawn, to the unseemly creatures
  With whom she must engage in conversation
And find, alas, without redeeming features
  If she commune with people of her station.

Her husband meekly tiptoes through her life,
  A timid wraith. Her children look their ages.
But still the bookish fancies of a wife
  Fetter her to the never-ending pages
Devoured, along with countless chocolate creams
By one whose weight grows daily with her dreams.

SYDNEY KING RUSSELL.

"I wonder what it feels like on the morning after . . .

SPRING SATURNALIA

Yes, I am drunk, but not with wine,
I heard a skylark sing,
I found the first pale violet
Close to a woodland spring.

I heard a fluted note of joy
In the robin's melody
As he flew into the outstretched arms
Of the waiting apple tree.

And there are some who pity me
Because I stagger past:
But I have time to touch a star
And hold a moonbeam fast.

ELSIE-JEAN.

"Grief divided is made lighter . . .

PINEY-WOODS GRIEVING

Pap says a man can grieve clean through
And not know what's the matter nor what to do;
The why and the wherefore he don't question,
Jest takes a little sody for indigestion.

But a woman spies a heartbreak a mile away,
And she can tell it howdy any day;
She can call its daddy and its mammy's name
And tell anybody just who's to blame.

Except one grief that tears her heart—
Without a comeback—plum apart,
And reasonin' only makes it double—
Her man bewilderin' around in trouble!

EVANTHA CALDWELL.

"Purse your lips and say, 'ah!'" . .

ENGINE TROUBLE

Something's really very wrong with me.
(A cylinder is doubtless missing),
I simply CANNOT close my eyes and be
Single-minded when I'm kissing!

JILL CHRISTOPHER.

Did you ever have the measles, and if so, how many?
ARTEMUS WARD.

"Now, little girl, don't worry . . . it won't hurt a bit . . . that is, not much . . . It's just a vaccination, and after it's all over you'll be immune to everything . . . that is, almost . . .

SPRING WISDOM

I was never going to be like other women are,
   I was never going to weep for love,
I said that I would never even try to touch a star,
   Nor wonder what the moon was patterned of.

I would never let my pulse move madly at a name,
   I would never sit and gaze in space,
I said that I would never let my lips be scarred by flame,
   Nor cherish foolish hearts of paper lace.

Yet here am I who shunned the flock, resentful of the herds,
   Weeping for a love that hurried by,
Standing in the darkness I make lassos of low words,
   Hoping that my loops will touch the sky.

Someone just speaks a name: my heart is caught as in a snare,
   While endless staring holds no anodyne,
My fingers soothe my lips, I still can feel a burning there,
   And tenderly I kiss a valentine.

JESSIE FARNHAM.

" 'Yet when I cast mine eyes and see that brave vibration each way free' . . . word for word from the original . . .

HUSTLING WITH HERRICK

Whenas in shorts my Julia goes
Methinks indeed how clearly shows
What portions need the grace of clothes.

I ponder, when mine eyes must see
Her awkward jointure at the knee,
Comparative anatomy.

KEITH THOMAS.

"The owl said, 'who-o-o! . . . who-o-o!' . . . but the rest of us worms just prayed for apples . . .

PRAYER BY A VERY NEW DOCTOR

Lord, send me patients—now! today!
  So far, I haven't any . . .
They needn't all be "majors," Lord,
  There needn't be too many.

A tonsilectomy would do,
  One plain appendicitis,
Old Banker Brown's sciatica,
  Or Grandma Green's arthritis.

Affairs are in a jam, O Lord,
  Finances . . . well, chaotic!—
Please send me, in a hurry, Lord,
  Some very rich neurotic!

Or, lacking one nice, chronic case—
  Incurably systemic—
(The rent is due tomorrow, Lord!)
Please send an epidemic.

BLANCHE DeGOOD LOFTON.

"But he was such a nice doctor I just couldn't say no . . .

SONG OF FUTILITY

If your surgeon is gifted,
   Your face can be lifted—
Your eyebrows drawn high and thin.

But what price pain
When you cancel the gain
With the same old brain
Within?

ETHEL M. WEGERT.

"A page from life to be inserted in a doctor's book . . .

THE HEART IS A STRANGE THING

The heart is a strange thing;
   It has no eyes,
But it can see through black earth
   And beyond blue skies.

The heart has no hands,
   But, knowing love's touch,
All the hands of the world
   Cannot do as much.

The heart has no feet,
   But it can go
Swiftly to Heaven above,
   Or Hell below.

The heart is a strange thing;
   More strange than the head—
Sometimes it will live again
   After long dead.

MINNIE CASE HOPKINS.

"And the silly doctor says I'm dizzy . . . Now am I . . . or izzy?

OFFICE WOMAN SPEAKS

I'm like a whirling dervish or a wildly-spinning top:
I go around in circles and it seems I'll never stop.
Although I turn and dip and hum, I get nowhere at all,
And should I dash, I'd only butt my head against the wall.

I often wish my fate could be to roam the open range,
And like the wind I'd blow around in places far and strange.
I'd gladly give away my bed, my table, and my chair,
And sleep beneath a bramble-bush, with thistles in my hair.

MARVEL BARROW.

When from our better selves we have too long
Been parted by the hurrying world, and droop,
Sick of its business. . . .

WILLIAM WORDSWORTH.

"When the doctor listened . . . he asked my age . . . I told him . . . he turned pale . . . and put his stethoscope in a cage . . .

MY HEART

My heart is a tropic bird, in flaming flight! . . .
My heart is a brown bird, singing in the night.

My heart is a seething cauldron—molten flame,
Surging and restless, lifting to your name . . .
Leaping in ecstasy—consuming fire,
Mounting, resurgent, quick . . . at your desire!

My heart is a high blue lake, whose placid sheen
Mirrors the silence of the forest-green . . .
Ripples and pulses at your touch . . . is spent—
You in my bosom, knowing deep content.

My heart is a tropic bird, in flaming flight! . . .
My heart is a brown bird, singing in the night.

BLANCHE DEGOOD LOFTON.

"Just a game of blindman's buff . . ."

THESE ARE THE EYES . . .

These are the eyes and this the brow
That house the many-jeweled mind.
This is the mouth that shapes from thought
All that a word may bind.

These mortal hands, because of love,
Have lain like music on your throat,
And yet the music of the mind
Is delicate . . . remote.

Bright to your touch are brow and lips,
Lighted the eyes that your eyes see;
Hooded forever is the mind
That loves you best, and secretly.

SARAH LITSEY.

For there was never yet philosopher
That could endure the toothache patiently.

WILLIAM SHAKESPEARE.

*"Please, Doctor, not the same colored pills for this new trouble . . .
Have you something in a sky blue?"*

RED FOR MOURNING

Please show me something just a little brighter
Than this hat I am wearing—something gay,
With rainbow-colored ribbon or a feather,
Maybe . . . Oh, but that was yesterday
I wanted something small, severely brimmed,
In unobtrusive brown or midnight blue.
This red one here—so pert and impudent—
I'll try it on. Look, it's becoming, too!
It says if I have grief, I well can bear it.
Don't bother with a box. I think I'll wear it!

EVANTHA CALDWELL.

" 'Where art thou going my pretty maid . . .?'

PROTEST

I dwell where stately structures loom
And crowds go thronging by;
Where earth is sealed within a tomb
That rises to the sky.

My Town Ideal would be complete
With never a dome or steeple,
And cows would amble down the street
Arm-in-arm with the people.

MARVEL BARROW.

"My, my . . . wouldn't a chiropractor be surprised! . . .

SIMILITUDE

My heart and I are much alike,
  (Her dreams are just like mine)
Except, poor foolish little heart,
  She hasn't any spine.

The one we love, loves us no more,
  But if we chance to meet,
My spine keeps me quite straight and tall,
  While she just crumples at his feet.

HELEN HOOPER.

"In either case, the report would say . . . 'The operation was successful' . . .

COLD SHOWER

If she could take
  Herself apart,
The girl who claims
  She's lost her heart
Would often be surprised, instead,
To find she'd only lost her head!

W. E. FARBSTEIN.

"Could this be a third dimension . . . suffering from acute dissension?"

PURE IN HEART

My faith in you
is as a thing apart
from all the tumult in a world of flux
and vacillation, where love reconstructs
and readjusts itself at will. My heart,
in spite of all the pressure brought to bear
upon it, somehow, never stoops to doubt.
It stands immutable, while all about
is turbulence, and even when despair
seeps in, as it is wont to do at times,
and hope hangs low, its faith remains secure.
My head, however, is not quite so sure
and rears its skeptic self throughout my rhymes.

KATHRYN KAY.

"And yet . . . I wonder what would happen to them at the Mayo Clinic . . .

SURREALISTIC REACTION

Oh, thank you Mr. Currier,
And thank you Mr. Ives!

Your bathtub's never furry or
Your women shaped like fives.

You do not deal in parables
From nightmare-ridden dreams,
Or elongate our wearables
Then only paint the seams.

Your men are men. Unquakingly
They brave a roaring gale.
They drive a horse unbreakingly,
Or carve a conquered whale.

Your women never hurry or
Forget to smile as wives.
Oh, unsubconscious Currier,
Unintroverted Ives!

MAUDE BARNES MILLER.

"I don't think Jake will be there for quite a spell ... he hated stairs ... and they say the way is paved to ... well, no matter ... he'd just get fired ... How come Jake was born so tired?

CHARITY WARD

Patient:

My land, a body'd think I was a queen
the way they've waited on me, hand and foot;
it's good to rest from all the scrubbin' floors
and washin' clothes and choppin' kindlin' wood
and feedin' pigs and hoein' in the patch
(Jake's always ailin' and his back is weak.)
Wonder how he's makin' out—I baked some bread
and there's canned beans and taters in the bin—
men are so helpless when we ain't around.
There's a nurse with blue eyes; she looks just like
my baby woulda looked if she had lived
(the doctor said I worked too hard—before.)

Nurse:

God, she'll be with You soon—she doesn't know—
and please, God, not a harp! Her hands are gnarled;
they'll be too stiff and rough to play a harp.
Just let her sit near You and rest, or let
her care for some wee girl—one with blue eyes ...

And God, when Jake comes up, put him to work!

ESTHER WEAKLEY.

I do not love thee, Doctor Fell,
The reason why I cannot tell;
But this alone I know full well,
I do not love thee, Doctor Fell.

THOMAS BROWN.

"A doctor always likes a case with lots of symptoms . . . it's easier to understand . . . to treat . . . to cure . . . But maybe it's fun to be a patient . . . and ache a little and groan a lot . . . sympathy is a lovely pastime . . . Who wants a doctor anyway?

VERITY

You want a love to catalogue; a love to understand;
Better choose a peasant girl, true daughter of the land.
Oh, I could give you ecstasy; I could give you pain;
I could teach you how to love hill-tops in midnight rain;
I could keep you guessing; your heart would stay alive;
Time would never trouble you; ten or one or five;
You would never know me though; never understand
That my heart would wander free, despite your dark command.
You don't want that kind of life; you'd be afraid, I know.
Choose a girl to darn your socks, cook and clean and sew—
Find a girl whose mind is not cluttered up with verse—
Then be glad and thankful you did not do much worse.

VIRGINIA LAURA SMITH.

I Beg Your Pardon

"Courtesy is the act of doing the right thing, wholly because you want to do it ... Etiquette is the art of doing the proper thing for the sheer artistry of the act ..."

LADY IN A SPOT

Never when I sat with wide
    Eyes at a circus, heart afire
With thrills, did I think someday I'd
    Be walking the precarious wire.

Faltering as it swings and swerves
    Above a host of curious faces,
Balancing with tautened nerves,
    Taking bows with strained grimaces!

Well I know the delicate fear
    Lest the lovely lady fall
To disaster!—Ah, my dear,
    You would be the first of all

To reach the crumpled broken thing
    Upon the sawdust and with pity
Straighten the gauzy gown and bring
    To mind how young she was and pretty.

KATHLEEN SUTTON.

Habit with him was all the test of truth;
"It must be right: I've done it from my youth."

GEORGE CRABBE.

"Ardent love-making should be avoided in crowds ... the kiss reserved for an audience of no more than five ... the old-fashioned hug tolerated only in case of a slip ..."

AND SO RESTRAINT

There is something that restrains me
Makes me shun your fond embraces,
Because the way you hold me
Makes my slip hang down in places.

MARGERY PARVIS.

"But what if I didn't like your umbrella, Mr. Chamberlain? . . .

APPEASEMENT POLICY

Why do people criticise everything I wear?
The color of my costume, the way I do my hair?
While I myself am always nice—
It's peace I want at any price.
For when they ask, "Do you like my dress?"
Invariably I answer, "Yes."
How much happier I would be
If they'd as calmly lie to me.
MARY KEITH COX.

For courtesy wins woman all as well
As valor may.
ALFRED, LORD TENNYSON.

"A real lady always wears APPROPRIATE clothing for every occasion . . . but a real woman doesn't let it go at that . . .

LADY OF DESIGN

She knows rich fabrics—satin and brocade,
fine wool and lace to match the spider's art.
And she knows women—how their souls are stayed
by beauty in which they may play some part.

With artistry and triumph of fine line
she conjures nymph and saint, sly mynx and queen
and for the magic wand of her design
Medusa fades or Helen's charms are seen.

She wears blue like a banner that reveals
a dauntless spirit and the clear white fire
of diamonds is a live screen that conceals
her fears and sorrows burning on their pyre.

Hers is the truth that every woman knows:
Eden well lost to gain the charm of clothes.
ANNETTE PATTON CORNELL.

"A man might observe ... if given a voice ... and the question of hose or paint were his choice ... hose won't rub off leaving places all bare ... still you can't start a run in the paint anywhere ... so since the observers are all going ... or gone ... what difference, my dear, what you don with the dawn ... yawn ... yawn ..."

PARADOX IN SOX

Ann's hose are unseamed
   And spider-web thick,
For she would aspire to
   That bare-legged chic.

Sue's legs, lily-white,
   She dabs with some paint,
And pencils some seams
   On stockings that ain't.

Oh, puzzled am I,
   Now what shall I wear,
Leg paint to look covered,
   Or hose to look bare?

LENORE EVERSOLE FISHER.

"A child should speak when spoken to ... an adult should speak ... But there are times when neither ... no one ... nothing ... should be spoken ... golden times ..."

THE DREAMER

I'd like to build a house
Where I could see a river winding,
To plant a young tree,
Or watch a hawk,

Or lie and count blue stars,
Or climb a hill to sunsets blinding,
To ride black horses,
Or sketch with chalk.

I'd like to trace old paths
Through ferny woodlands, never minding
Wind or sudden rain.
Taste sweet cane stalk.

I'd like to read rare books—
Old ones with faded broken binding,
To sail a cat-boat.
'Neath pine trees walk.

I'd like to share all these
Dear dreams ... could I succeed in finding
Someone who had learned
When *not* to talk.
KATHERINE M. HADDEN.

"Shut, shut the door, good John!" fatigued, I said;
"Tie up the knocker! say I'm sick, I'm dead."
ALEXANDER POPE.

"In the subway it is quite correct for the cashier to squint at all embarrassed quarters ... bounce them ... bite them ... hold them up to the light ... then solemnly hand over five laughing nickels ...

CONVINCED

He told his love in silver bits
That shone like coins in sun,
But, having known the counterfeits,
I weighed them every one.

I bade my wary heart begin
To test their metal's gleam,
And when I found them genuine,
I bought a new white dream.
HAZEL HARPER HARRIS.

"Advice . . . to son . . .

FULFILLMENT

Stretched parallel to grass and sky
One afternoon,
I wished that I was then a man.
I was, too soon.

When I was grown, I sought that spot
To watch the moon.
I wished that night I could be wed.
I was, too soon.

As my old bones sink in the grass
This day in June,
I wish I could just stay right here.
I will, too soon.

CHARLOTTE WISE.

"If you'll promise not to tell anyone, I'll tell you what I heard . . . but don't ask me where I heard it . . . because I promised not to mention any names . . . bad taste . . .

NEVER TELL THE WHOLE OF IT

Do not show the bright design,
Nor the pattern of the arc
Wrought beyond the secret line
Of your thoughts. Let the quick spark
Light the darkness, point the way,
Build immortal beauty; lift
Reluctant will to meet the day—
Break in showers of white the drift,
Snowy, chill, that binds desire.

Never tell the whole of it;
Show, perhaps, the gleam of fire,
But never where the flame is lit.

MARY WILLIS SHELBURNE.

"If a lady grows weary of a burden she is carrying, it is quite proper that she set it down and rest it . . . and later pick it up without apology . . .

FEMININE MATHEMATICS

Thirty years old I am today
And ten years hence, I shall contrive,
In my inimitable way
To be no more than thirty-five.

All trace of logic disappears
In this arithmetic of mine,
But O they were delightful years—
The five years I was twenty-nine!

MAY RICHSTONE.

"A true confession is good for the soul . . . but that doesn't mean to write it out and sign it . . . you might want to change your story without having to plead temporary insanity . . .

FULL CONFESSION

My lord, I make this full confession now:
You have your rivals and forever will.
But, though I yield to them, I break no vow;
And you are best beloved and dearest still.
The stalwart wave within his blue embrace
Can sweep me into swift unreasoned bliss;
And, oh, upon my warm uplifted face
I love the passion of the rain's white kiss!

And I would risk my very soul, I think,
To walk alone at midnight with a star
Or meet him at the twilight's purple brink
And go where only leaves and shadows are.
I have my loves in sea and sky and wood;
But I have told you, as a woman should.

ADELAIDE LOVE.

"There is no hide-bound rule against family rows . . . that is one of the privileges of marriage. But the wise woman is one who does not win too often . . . else man may discover her superior knowledge and make her do the work . . .

PATIENCE, PATIENCE

A woman should not struggle so
   To outtalk her mate,
Because statistics clearly show
   That if she'll only wait,
She'll outlive him, most emphatically,
And have the last word automatically.

W. E. FARBSTEIN.

Manner is all in all, whate'er is writ,
The substitute for genius, sense and wit.

WILLIAM COWPER.

"It is never too late to invite a friend . . . some of the happiest occasions have been arranged after all the other plans had been made . . .

LATE LOVE

There is a loveliness upon her face
The others could not show, those girlhood friends
Who earlier put on their bridal lace
While she stood by. The years have made amends
And have released, for all her lonely waiting,
A greater glory, a more perfect hour.
Within her eyes the miracle of mating
Glistens more brightly; on her cheeks the flower
Of rapture unbelievable has bloomed.
And she who walked the lowlands of despair
In the dark valley of the early-doomed,
Stands on a height the others could not share,
Who did not watch their dearest dream grow dim,
And blaze forth like a sun on finding him!

ISABELLE BRYANS LONGFELLOW.

"In case the wedding is called off after the invitations have been sent out . . . well . . . you will probably find yourself as red-faced as the Indian who shot the arrow on page 301 . . .

INCENDIARY

You lit the flame
which feeds desire,
but you are not a good Boy Scout,
for Boy Scouts never leave a fire
until they've put the damn thing out!

KATHRYN KAY.

He scratch'd his ear, the infallible resource
To which embarrass'd people have recourse.

LORD BYRON.

" 'Martha, Martha, thou art careful and troubled about many things. But one thing is needful: and Mary hath chosen that good part, which shall not be taken away from her.'

THE SERVING MAID

The busy women of our little town
Hold themselves proud and even worldly wise.
They visit each small vice with swift disdain,
Nor dwell too long upon each dark surmise.

But they are blind to sunsets, cannot hear
A bird's clear call, and never, never see
The silvered symmetry of falling rain
Against the trembling foliage of a tree.

Only one small maid looks with seeing eyes—
She plays each day a very humble part;
But oh, at night she walks among the stars,
And gathers heavenly music to her heart.

ETHEL B. CHENEY.

"Not for all the rice in China . . ."

SELF-PRESERVATION

My neighbor's maid has left for good.
They always treat her, you see,
Like a member of the family,
And she stood it as long as she could!

MAY RICHSTONE.

"The Society for the Prevention of Cruelty to Animals has talked some of taking in children . . . but until it does, there is hope for Democracy . . ."

DOUBLE DUTY

Mothers who raise
A child by the book
Can, if sufficiently vexed,
Hasten results
By applying the book
As well as applying the text.

W. E. FARBSTEIN.

"Discretion is the better part of conversation . . ."

You are so economical of love
You do not even name it so.
For saying makes a thing defined
And definition is too much to know
And give for one whose mind
Hoards by denial the inner fruit,
Affirms aloud
Only the prudent rind.

RUTH CARROLL.

"There are a number of marriage ceremonies available . . . but be sure and select one that pleases both families . . . something that promises obedience from the bride and support from the groom . . .

AN OLD CUSTOM

Hand in hand,
The old book said—
Let the betrothed
Walk—
Before they are wed.

No parent or friend
Shall give them away.
For each to the other
They shall say—

"I take thee now
My Dear—to be,
In the presence of this
Company—
On into Eternity."

"In the presence of this
Company—
I take thee now
My Dear—to be."

Bless this simplicit
Unity.
Erica May Brooks.

Ye Gods! annihilate but space and time,
And make two lovers happy.
Alexander Pope.

"It has been definitely proven that there was a time in history when ladies' cheeks were naturally pink . . . Therefore, we need blush no more to make them so . . . unnaturally . . . Of course, if you know how to blush . . . the problem solves itself.

TO SUSAN, REGARDING FRECKLES

Dappled as the shade of leaves
On the bracken's ancient brown
Is the deer against the hill
Shyly coming down.

Dappled as the pebbles are
Where the sun and water dream
Is the noblest fish, the trout,
Swimming up the stream.

So if your fair skin should gain
Spots from sun, you need not be
Shamed by marks that Nature gives
Her select society.

Keith Thomas.

Wanting is—what?
Summer redundant,
Blueness abundant,
Where is the blot?

Robert Browning.

"He has just discovered Emily is not a post . . .

YOUNG MAN'S FANCY

He's grown polite and orderly
He's lost his rowdy ways.
He has become quite neat and clean—
I hope this complex stays.
He's now respectful to his sis,
Which is the strangest thing.
What can have caused this change in him?
Biology and Spring.

Thelma Ireland.

" 'The quality of mercy is not strained' . . ."

TWO YEARS OLD

He finds a pencil and marks on the walls.
He climbs on the piano, and then he falls.
He eats the garbage and plays in the ink.
He spills the milk he declines to drink.
He crawls in the coalbin and plays it's bed.
He refuses to bathe and cries instead.
In short, he wishes to do what he wishes.
He break your heart as well as your dishes.
But all is forgiven, all is bliss,
When he comes and gives you a large wet kiss.

NANCY MOORE.

"If you are not sure of your silver . . . always use the outside piece for each succeeding course . . . You will never have any trouble if everything has been put in its proper place . . . never any trouble . . . or any fun . . ."

SUNDAY SONG

At ninety-two she told the tale to me.
Dressed in crisp calico, hair crimped, she sat
And stroked the fuzzy-furred gray cat
That perched himself upon her kindly knee.
Indoors, contentment lay on everything.
Outside, the winter dusk came down, and hills
Turned purple-blue beyond her windowsills
Where pink begonias recalled the spring.

"The reason I have lived in peace?" She said—
"When I was nine, one Lord's Day in the fall,
I entered singing, 'Yankee Doodle!' In the hall,
My grandsire stood and gravely shook his head.
'Young lady, that is not a Sunday Song!'
Since then, I have kept all things where they belong!"

VIOLET ALLEYN STOREY.

I Solemnly Swear to Do My Duty

"The duty of children is to all unknowingly grant absolution to the earth . . . to forgive the stupidity . . . selfishness . . . ugliness of the world and rejoice in the new beginning . . .

MY COUNTRY 'TIS OF THEE

A band passed by the hovel where they dwelt
In squalor; and the old people turned away
Their faces, sullen though the music fell
Upon their hearts, as some forgotten lay
Which they had loved in childhood; and the song
They would not sing; their hearts had burned too long.

But there was one, a child, beside the road,
Who heard the music, and forgot the pang
Of want and hunger and the galling load
Of poverty; and fresh the sweet voice sang:
"My Country, 'tis of thee, sweet land of Liberty,
Of thee, I sing." She still was free!

DUDLEY B. MADDEN.

"The draft board will meet in the library . . . with the busts of Washington . . . Jefferson and Lincoln solemnly looking on . . .

APOSTROPHE TO YOUTH

You will not think that once this troubled world
Wished on the moon, roll-called the evening stars,
Charted the passage of a comet hurled
Through outer space. Now every creature wars.
No longer does the architecture of
A blade of grass intrigue our small mankind,
And all young lovers whisper of their love
In bitter haste. The sea of life is mined.

Grieve not alone for bruised and broken flesh,
Young cries of anguish scattered on the wind;
Mourn for unfinished dreams caught in the mesh
Of war's deceit. Now is all beauty thinned
To every essence, suitable for men
Who, grim past recognition, march again.

FRANCES DAVIS ADAMS-MOORE.

"Then what is the duty of a mother . . . who takes no oaths . . swears no allegiances . . . yet serves with loyalty unspoken?

THE MOTHER

She did not weep on bidding him good-bye.
It would have been a luxury to cry,
And few of those, she thought, lips faintly curled,
Are given to the mothers of the world.
She did not weep when he was out of sight,
Though in that poignant moment well she might,
Recalling how young he was—absurdly so—
Absurdly proud and glad he, too, could go.
Go. Her heart froze, her boy gone somewhere away,
Leaving—ironically—on her birthday.
But that was tear-producing, that would keep,
And she could weep when others were asleep.
And it was fitting really, in a way,
To do her greatest, hardest job this day.
And anyway, motherhood was sigh on sigh
From never-ending bidding sons good-bye;
Losing them to school, to work, or to wives,
To their own distant, suddenly separate lives.
This was a new job, difficult to learn;
But once learned and learned well, he would return.
Return. Why, she had things to do, to plan,
That might take longer than his absent span;
Some other time she'd think these foolish things,
When she had time for her rememberings.
Absurd things . . . how he looked when he was born;
His first long pants, how proudly they were worn;
Things that should make her want to laugh, not cry,
She'd save them for some midnight and then try.

Swiftly she went to a looking-glass and stood,
Made her lips smile to see if still they could,
And forcing them from the way they tried to go,
Dry-eyed she made them practise saying, "Hello."

ETHEL BARNETT DE VITO.

"I swear . . . something good will come of this! . . . In spite of all the swearing . . . you shall not be profane . . . in vain . . .

MOTHER FEELS A DRAFT

What a nuisance, what a bore—
Pajamas left upon the floor,
A collar here, a necktie there,
A slipper underneath a chair,
Magazines, a pipe, a book,
Clutter everywhere I look.
Disorder is you middle name,
And Mother doubtless is to blame.

However, son, the army'll do
A multitude of things for you.

Gone the comforting morning doze,
Up the minute the bugle blows,
Quarters orderly, bed just so,
Everything in an even row.

Boy, how wonderful when you come
Straight from under the sergeant's thumb!

LOUISE SHAW.

His *faith,* perhaps, in some nice tenets might
Be wrong; his *life,* I'm sure, was in the right.

ABRAHAM COWLEY.

"Thou hast Thy duty too, my Lord, . . . I have Thy word . . .

A SON AT SEA

O God, through tomorrow and the next day and the next,
    Watch o'er the sea!
  Let starlit nights prevail,
    I ask of Thee!
Be Master of the waves that toss the ship upon the deep,
And safely guard a little boy I used to rock to sleep!

MARGERY RUEBUSH SHANK.

"Duty is a word designed for others . . . than brothers . . . yet at the whisper 'lo, thou must' . . . because they trust . . . all youth replies . . .

TO MY BROTHER

I always thought war was a gallant march
   Of brave young drums and flags that strew bright air;
I had supposed there was victory arch
   Where parades were ended and I didn't care
So very much when I saw soldiers leave,
   Or aircraft wing a swift, courageous way;
I thought that they would always find reprieve
   From harm . . .

        But that was yesterday!
Now you are grown and you must join the ranks—
   The little boy whom I told stories to—
I have much deeper interest now in tanks
   And armaments and troop trains passing through.
I seem to understand it all much more
Since I have heard that you are going to war.

HELEN WELSHIMER.

"But work! . . . work! . . . work! . . . is the only antidote for pain! . . .

DUSTING

   By this small rite the heart may keep some peace
   Where fear and hate have built a taunting wall.
   The dustcloth's anesthesia gives release
   From harried earth's relentless battle call,
   Whose constant clamor rends the tired ear,
   Whose printed message jades the weary sight.
   Death seems less poignant when swift fingers clear
   The table boards to still, brown pools of light.
   So dust the dining room and dust the stairs,
   Bring to new whiteness old piano keys,
   Rub back the honey glow on aging chairs—
   Mute solace dwells in humble tasks! From these
   Will come new flesh for healing grief's deep sore
   And strength to glean the twisted fruits of war.

LOUISE RHOADS.

"Boys flying kites haul in their white-winged birds . . . but God Himself . . .

WE WHO WAIT

His plane is molten silver in the sun,
A shining silhouette against the blue.
When each day's weary length is almost run
And not a task is left for me to do,
Our rosary of time love sets apart
We string with bright new hours of ecstasy.
Yet prayer is never ending in my heart
That each day, God, You bring him home to me;
For only we, who each dawn watch them go
With brightly smiling lips—hearts cold with fear—
Yes, only we who wait can ever know
What it must mean to send the one most dear
Aloft; and then through endless hours to pray,
"God, bring him safely home again today."

MARY CHERRY PHELPS.

"There is nothing in a soldier's oath about his wife . . . she is divorced by Mars . . . she who was by day as near as life . . . is now by night as distant as the stars . . .

CROSSROADS

I have no claim upon you, now that war
Has stretched its arm between your love and me.
The dignity that each gold stripe stands for
Has set you from all lesser bondage free.

I stand apart from everything you are—
From everything you do and think and feel.
Our nights of sweet unrest seem dreams afar;
Your arms now hold the cruel night of steel.

O, dearest one, when will I know again
The passion of your mouth, no longer grim?
Or will war brand you with its hate and pain?
(Dear God, dear, gracious God, watch over him!)

RUTH BASSETT.

"There are so few things one can send along to camp ... there is so much now to be thrown away ..."

INCIDENT AFTER INDUCTION

I could bear the last good-byes
And the train whistle fading.
And I did not cry
When I found your pipe next day.
These things we had rehearsed so much.
"Letters, of course ..."
"A snapshot in your uniform ..."
We were so careful, too,
To enjoy each day as we lived it,
I was sure my heart could not break.
But today a stranger's
Little girl with yellow braids
Smiled, and unthinkingly
Brought back a dream we threw away
Long, long ago.

JANET GERARD.

Let Fortune empty all her quiver on me;
I have a soul that, like an ample shield,
Can take in all, and verge enough for more.

JOHN DRYDEN.

"Switch on! ... Contact ... Let her go! ..."

ANGELING UP

"Tune up the kite,"
He said with a grin.
"Goodbye all;
See you in Berlin."

White wings lift through a peacock sky,
Skimming a drift of nebulae
As a jaunty lad from the shores of Devon
Goes angeling up to the doors of heaven.

RUTH AVERITTE.

"Grandmothers like kittens . . . and all the little yarns of yesterday . . . but when a man must march away . . . she takes her big wool ball of brown or gray . . . and knits him mittens . . .

TROOP TRAIN FOR DOVER

Take the wool mittens with you and the cap.
I made them extra thick to shed the snow.
You'll want the muffler, too, the one you wrap
Over your shoulders with the ends tied so.

And here's your fountain pen. I guess that's all
That I've forgotten. You've no need to start
For some time yet. Your knapsack's in the hall,
And in the top of it you'll find my heart.

I thought perhaps some night when you are lonely,
And mitts and scarf cannot shut out the storm,
You might take out my heart (that loves you only),
To wear on yours and keep your own heart warm.

KAYE STARBIRD.

"All out . . . the papers said . . . and they were right . . . air wardens . . . defense factories . . . auxiliary police . . . boy scouts . . . messengers . . . Red Cross . . . day and night . . . nobody home . . . All out . . .

"NOW IS THE TIME FOR ALL GOOD MEN TO—"

Darling,
    There's a cold chop in the ice-box,
    and cake in the bread-box.
    I'm on duty this evening.
    I love you,
May.

Darling,
    So sweet.
    I had a big dinner.
    I'm on duty tonight.
    I love you,
Mike.

ANGELO LANE.

"There is no need for the word 'isolationist' in the dictionary any more . . . peace will have no space for that which has no place in war . . .

I'VE NEVER BEEN IN ENGLAND

I've never been in England
To walk the countryside.
The chalk-white cliffs of Dover
Are crumbling in the tide.

I've never been in England
To watch the changing guards
Or hear the flourish on the drums
Or stroll in castle yards.

I've never been in England
To climb the London Tower.
There isn't much that I can do
To ease her hour.

Dorset, Hampshire, Shillingstone
I'm sure I'll never see;
Yet every bomb that falls on them
Falls on me.

FLORENCE WIGHTMAN ROWLAND.

So nigh is grandeur to our dust,
So near is God to man,
When Duty whispers low, *Thou must,*
The youth replies, *I can.*

RALPH WALDO EMERSON.

"Q. E. D. . . .

SILENT NIGHT

The hymn may be abbreviated now.
To the bombed, if only it be silent
The night is blest.

DAY WARD.

181

*"Ultimate ... is such a long, long time to wait to learn the danger ...
who knows but ultimately we may find our fear a total stranger ...*

THE DANGER

The danger does not lie in bombs,
but what the fear of them will do to you.
The danger does not lie in death,
but what the fear of it will make of you.
The danger does not lie in tears—
not if these tears will bring a new resolve
to hold the torch of tolerance,
of love for ever-erring man aloft;
to hold the hope that we will learn—
despite the tragedy of our mistakes.
The danger does not lie in what
we give, but what we get and can forget.
The danger does not lie in war,
but what the war can ultimately bring.

FRANCESCA.

"They also serve who only sit and wait ...

The heart grows faint at many things,
Especially, the whir of wings.

The angered eagle, or the hawk
Quickens the rooster's lordly walk,

And lords of roosters raise their eyes
To greater terrors of the skies.

Running to cover, as they should,
They diligently knock on wood.

Or, hidden deep from sight and sound,
They sit, white-knuckled, under ground,

Knowing there'll be small comfort in
The sun and stars where roofs had been.

DALE FISHER.

"Sisters ... brothers ... mothers ... dads ... wives ... grandparents ... what shall the oaths of sweethearts be ... I solemnly ...

LOVERS IN WARTIME

Oh, make no pledge, that you may ask no pardon
When you must fail to keep it. Dream no dream.
Love me today—tomorrow may not come.
There were two lovers in a Paris garden....
Where are they now? Trust not in things that seem.
There were two sweethearts on a road to Rome,
Dreaming a peasant dream of tranquil life,
Of home and fat bambinos .... He is gone,
Having no wish to kill or to be killed.
Maidens in Holland, blind to coming strife;
Along the Thames, the Danube, wait alone
Women within whose hearts is laughter stilled.

Love me today. When dies the sound of drums,
Dream then tomorrow, sweet, and pray it comes.

ALMA ROBERTS GIORDAN.

*"Is it so brief ... so very brief ... this rendezvous we know? ...
What life is more than the waiting before and the glad, glad after ...
what shall we hold against the woe ... but dreams and laughter ...*

SOLDIER'S FAREWELL AT DAWN

Those few full hours in the swift spring night
  Made intimate the strangers which we were,
Let down with effervescent, quick delight
The barriers of sham, and shy pretense:
  With charming ease we happened to discover
The tragi-comics of coincidence.

How little one may know how much has gone
  Out of his head, or into his heart's pain
In all so brief a time: there in the dawn
I loved you while we laughed and parted, we,
  Whose unfamiliar hands will not again
Meet ever in such careless ecstasy.

FAY P. LECOMPTE.

"Total war ... men at camp ... on ships bound for other shores ... fighting on a dozen fronts ... brothers ... dads ... working at home ... wives ... sweethearts working too ... sometimes preoccupied ..."

CANTEEN WORKER

Have some homemade cookies, soldier?
Those chocolate ones are good.

(Oh Johnny across the Pacific—
You'd write me if you could?!)

A cup of coffee, sergeant?
Oh sure, the smile's thrown in.

(You were cocky too, when you left me,
With your twisted boyish grin.)

How about another sandwich?
Double decker with ham and cheese?

("We'll lick 'em", you said, "and I'll bring you
The emperor's palace keys!")

Soup, soldier? It's full of onions—
To make you strong, you know.

(O God, make Johnny careful
When he takes Tokyo!)

ESTHER BALDWIN YORK.

O Captain! my Captain! our fearful trip is done!
The ship has weathered every wreck,
The prize we sought is won.
The port is near, the bells I hear, the people all exulting.

WALT WHITMAN.

" *'It's always fair weather . . . when good fellows get together'* . . .

GOOD MEN

Comrades, these are great nights we have together,
Clicking our glasses on the battered table,
Laughing carefree with hearts light as a feather,
Strength in our bodies, hearty men and able.
We speak a million inspired words tonight,
Flinging them joyously to the wind and weather.
The glass has made our weary hearts grow light
On this fine night, when good men get together.
Tonight we have forgotten slopes we've plowed;
We have forgotten toil our hands have wrought;
We have forgotten sun and rain and cloud,
And we've forgotten battles we have fought.
We're filled with gay carousel and good cheer,
With all our troubles, debts, and deeds at rest;
We click our glasses with our comrades here
While life is in us and our hearts are blest.

JESSE STUART.

A glass is good, and a lass is good,
   And a pipe to smoke in cold weather;
The world is good, and the people are good,
   And we're all good fellows together.

JOHN O'KEEFE.

"The War Department regrets to inform you . . . and yet if it must be, it is good to know . . .

AFTER BATAAN

He lies with honor on him from the start,
The flag close-wrapped about his hushed, bright heart.

My scarf was white against his tawny throat,
My gloves were warm upon his sturdy hands,
When he went out from us with his keen youth
To the stark battle in the elder lands.

Now he will sleep beneath a jungle sky
Or rest beside the island's sinuous foam,
Who in sweet northern pastures used to lie
And look down on the dear red barns of home.

Yet there has been a brown bird, rocked with song,
Over those pastures, all this morning long!

EDNA MEAD.

"Grandmothers who lose their little boys in war may have a secret way . . . of reading the communique . . .

THE FALLEN WARRIOR

He rests among familiar things he loved—
His clothes awry, the stains of combat still
Upon his face. Evidence of frantic
Fight bestrews the battlefield—a broken lamp,
Debris of all kinds scattered on the floor.
And window shades that hang by merest shreds.
His weapons lie in reach of outstretched hand—
A battered saucepan with the lid for shield,
A pair of lethal-looking candlesticks,
And blocks he used to aim with deadly skill.

He rests among the things he loved—
The infant warrior, felled by sleep.

H. FORD OGLESBY.

"Grandfathers read the casualty lists . . . like all the rest . . . and light their pipes . . . and wait . . . and say . . . whatever is, is best . . .

GALLANT ONES

I think it would be good to die
In war time when the big guns roar
And other souls are passing on,
Abreast, behind, before.

For I, who am not very brave,
Would surely find a hand to hold,
And walking with the gallant ones
Would make a coward bold.

There would be nothing left to fear,
No deep and lonely night,
With heroes for companions
Advancing toward the light.

DOROTHY QUICK.

When I'm not thanked at all, I'm thanked enough:
I've done my duty, and I've done no more.

HENRY FIELDING.

"There is tragedy in total war . . . affecting all . . . Then what is a father's line of duty?

THE MAN OF IT

Big boys don't cry.
However painful their dismay be,
Big boys don't cry.
This is supposed to signify
A fellow is no mother's baby.
Except in secret sometimes maybe,
Big boys don't cry.

MARCIA NICHOLS HOLDEN.

"Can a mother do no more . . . than sew a gold star on a flag . . . she who has sewed so much before?

THE FOURTH COAT

The first was of velvet.
    That one I made.
It had silver buttons
    And three rows of braid.

The next was a tweed coat.
    He bought it himself
When he stood as tall
    As the top book shelf.

The third was a grey drab
    That no store had.
It was one his country
    Gives to a lad.

And with it he now wears
    A fourth so bright
That where he lies sleeping
    It kindles the night,

A coat made of honor
    And a task well done,
And honor is a shining thing,
    My son! O my son!

                              MYRTLE ADAMS.

New occasions teach new duties; Time makes ancient good
    uncouth;
They must upward still, and onward, who would keep
    abreast of Truth.
                            JAMES RUSSELL LOWELL.

"No matter what happens . . . the knitting must continue . . . stitches or lives may be dropped . . . but the knitting must go on . . . needles in the heart must be threaded with yarn . . . this is the pledge . . . the oath . . . the duty . . . knit on . . . and on . . . and on . . .

KEEP KNITTING

This is the color of all despair,
This gaunt, unholy, gangrenous gray.
("Enough for a helmet, airman's blue," they said.)
Who named it blue named it surely by day.
In the night I knit—but not for a gunner anymore.
They meant to be kind when they gave me the gray
For an airman. But sea-boot stockings would do, they're white.
("Wrap the wool in a towel, carefully") and not remember it takes
But a split-second for the grim unravelling,
Not remember the sea is colder even than earth—cold as snowflakes.
Remember, least of all, that one artillery lieutenant has no need
Any more of any garment woman makes.

MARGARET EATON.

"What shall a sweetheart do?

"KILLED IN ACTION"

I read it in the paper—he is dead—
My lover of a summer-time ago!
I scanned the cold, hard lines—
Maybe they'd show
I had not read aright—but no! They said
That he had died last week!
I leaned my head
Against the window-pane and stared below
Into the street whose human ebb and flow
Mocked my stunned senses murmuring—"HE IS DEAD!"

You know your name was graven on my heart
No matter who might seem to take your place—
Always I dreamed—somehow—somewhere—
Those radiant days in which we rushed apart
Would come again and I would see your face—instead—
I read it in the papers—YOU ARE DEAD!

Esther Griffin White.

On Fame's eternal camping-ground
   Their silent tents are spread,
And Glory guards with solemn round
   The bivouac of the dead.

Theodore O'Hara.

" '*I pledge allegiance to the flag and to the Republic for which it stands*' . . .

INNER LOOKING

More peaceful hills than our hills
Were never anywhere,
Nor greener springs nor carolings
More richly on the air.
Bright velvet flowerings grass the slopes,
While emeralds grace the boughs.
The air is sweet with bridal hopes
Where birds exchange their vows.

And man can love a curving view
Framed by his window sills,
Until his heart grows tranquil, too,
With looking at the hills.
And many a man like my man,
Until the sick world mends,
Though far afield has in him sealed
The hills that he defends.

Virginia Brasier.

" 'Sail on . . . sail on . . . sail on and on' . . ."

CONVOY

The magic spreads
Through a seacoast town—
Sh!
There's a convoy
Homeward bound.
And with but the whisper
Of hearts that beat,
The news is flashed
From street to street.
What ships?
What men?
Ah, who can know—
'Til the anchor's dropped
And they hurrying go—
Each to his own small world
And love;
Each to all that a man dreams of.

DOROTHY CURRAN.

" 'Home is the sailor . . . home from the sea . . . and the hunter home from the hill' . . . If only the pilot . . . if only the soldier . . . if only the tall, broad-shouldered marine . . ."

SONG

He knew that he was home at last,
  Home to the quiet of the breast,
  To the sleep of joy and rest.
He knew that all the past was past,
Unaltered love still held him fast,
  He was home, was home at last.

This is true, will ever be true
  While the world goes round the sun—
  Love still draws the wandering one.
This dream drew Odysseus home
From the wars, the fears, the foam:
  All return when the wars are done.

FLORENCE HAMILTON.

" 'When Johnny comes marching home again . . . Hurrah! . . . Hurrah!' . . .

THE HOUSE REJOICES

These are the walls that danced and sang
And this the floor whose laughter rang,
And the peaked roof and chimneypot
That chuckled and clapped their hands, God wot,
When you tossed your cap on the newel post
(With it contending it loved you most),
And you cried: "I'm hungry! When do we eat?"
Ah, but the sound of your voice was sweet
To bricks and mortar and wood and tile—
And to me, who had waited the longest while!

MAY CARLETON LORD.

And hie him home, at evening's close,
To sweet repast and calm repose.

THOMAS GRAY.

" 'We won't come back till it's over . . . over there' . . .

AND AFTER THIS

And after this, please God, let us emerge
Washed clean of hate! Forget this battle urge;
Our hearts shall sing anew when freed from fears,
Our youth, triumphant, meet the coming years
With tested strength, in grateful servitude
To hearth and homeland. All this pulchritude
Of ours, this teeming wealth of brawn and brain,
Shall spend its might for Peace nor war again!

Our sons shall love the soil, our daughters spin
The fabric of devotion. Let war bring
That higher understanding to each heart—
The joyful right to serve, and so impart
To generations waiting at Life's door,
The heritage of Peace; we ask no more!

FRANCISCO VALLEJO.

" 'They shall not have died in vain . . . This nation . . . of the people, by the people and for the people . . . shall not perish from this earth' . . .

THEY SHALL COME BACK

They shall come back—the old, forgotten things—
When war's colossal artifice is done:
The summers asleep in dreams, the vanished springs
Heedless of all save love and warmth and sun,
The quiet evenings by the quiet lakes,
Where peace suffuses through the tranquil mind
Like fragrances a night wind leaves or takes.
These shall return. The vexed once more shall find
The still, unharried innocence of dawn,
The solace of a woodland's seeking ways
Down silences men deemed forever gone.
The heart shall find, in these as other days,
After the last projectile's crazed release,
Its ancient, sunlit citadel of peace.

ANDERSON M. SCRUGGS.

This hand, to tyrants ever sworn the Foe,
For Freedom only deals the deadly blow;
Then sheathes in calm repose the vengeful blade,
For gentle peace in Freedom's hallowed shade.

JOHN QUINCY ADAMS.

"Peace . . . with Honor . . .

NOTE TO AMERICA

Let us meet whatever
Enemy advances
With the newly-sharpened,
The shining lances

Of our intellect—
For, hurled forth well,
They are more deadly
Than shot and shell.

ELAINE V. EMANS.

Sugar and Spice to Taste

"But unfortunately the conductor on the 8:15 A. M. commuters' train knows none of this . . . so it's eat and run . . . or else . . ."

BREAKFAST

Breakfast is more than a mere excuse
For gulping a glass of orange juice,
More than a swallow of amber brew
And a dash for a bus before you are through.
Breakfast is leisurely sitting down
To portions of yellow and gold and brown,
Russet and amber and tangerine,
As though in a blend from a rare cuisine—
Golden omelet, orange jam,
Henna-rust in a slice of ham,
Yellow cream on the steaming bowls
Of nut-brown cereal, cinnamon rolls,
Waffles of old-gold, or yellow cakes
Speckled with brown, or amber flakes,
Yellow chrysanthemums of sun
Splotching a white cloth, freshly done,
And faces lit with the same bright glow
Of morning, lingering, loath to go.

ISABELLE BRYANS LONGFELLOW.

Eat no onions nor garlic, for we are to utter sweet breath.

WILLIAM SHAKESPEARE.

"Take with a grain of salt . . ."

DRAW THE VEIL

If there's anything worse
　Than a waffle that's cold
Or mashed potatoes
　Three days old,
It's suddenly meeting
　A fat old hen
That you loved in high school
　In nineteen-ten.

W. E. FARBSTEIN.

"Note to a hot-cross baker: There are more things in a loaf of bread, Horatio, than are dreamed of in your philosophy . . .

WHEATEN INTERVAL

I never take flour from a bin
But on the instant my thoughts spin
By country roads to fields of grain—
Roads where soon the autumn rain
Will lay the dust—I sense a fleet
And earthy tang; I smell ripe wheat;
I hear a distant reaper's clack,
I see new straw heaped in a stack.
Then teams with bells come jangling down
From the ranches into town
Hauling heavy loads until
The harvests all are brought to mill . . .
As I knead my bread I ponder
On earth's fecundity, its wonder;
On the beauty and the power
In a sieve of wheaten flour.

ETHEL ROMIG FULLER.

"Some people live to cook . . . others cook to love . . .

SONG FOR A CHILD

My mother never said much
When she was baking pies.
Those who work in silence
Are seldom fond of lies.

My mother never gossiped
While she was rolling tarts.
She held that tasteful cooking
Was finest of the arts.

She sometimes made us doughnuts
When she had finished bread.
The rich sweet dough was like her thoughts;
The hole was what she said.

W. H. MCCREARY.

"Cast your cake upon the waters . . . R. S. V. P.

HUNGER

Dearest, do you like the apple cake
  I made for you?
'Twas such a complicated thing to bake,
  Yet fun to do!
You said so? Yes—but quite as if by rote.
  Please! One small lie
Would make the bit that's sticking in my throat
  Not half so dry.
RUTH L. F. BARNETT.

Indigestion is—that inward fate
Which makes all Styx through one small liver flow.
LORD BYRON.

"And the book says if you eat everything up clean . . . then when dinner is over . . . you get to kiss the cook . . .

JENNIFER JEAN

Jennifer Jean is learning to cook
Jennifer Jean gets grease on the book.

She stands on a stool to stir the batter
And licks her fingers (one taste won't matter).

There's flour on the floor and flour in her hair
And splobs of goo on the seat of the chair.

An egg lies down on the table to cry,
Before she finds it, the white will dry.

Sugar grates beneath her tread,
The salt-shaker tries to stand on its head.

Stay clear of the kitchen, for heaven's sake,
For six-year-old Jean is making a cake!
JANICE BLANCHARD.

"In my cupboard . . . enough boxes to make a bare skeleton . . .

ON CLEANING CUPBOARDS

Housecleaning time has come again.
I envy Mother Hubbard
Whose fame has thundered down the years—
Her nice, bare, empty cupboard.

MABEL GEORGE HAIG.

Cauliflower is nothing but cabbage with a college education.

MARK TWAIN.

*"Three squares a day make an endless round of dish washing . . .
but there are worse things than soap and water . . .*

DOING DISHES

Little daughter, doing dishes,
Think of water—
It is so gleaming clear, so green,
Child, remember it has seen
Meadows, and has run between
Ferns and roots of trees;
It has ministered to these.
Sing, dear, at your work,
Be proud!
The old dishpan holds a cloud,
Holds a snowbank from a mountain!
Turn a faucet,
You've a fountain!
You have rivers, you have oceans
Come to serve your whims, your notions.
And your fingers, dear, are fishes,
See them dart among the dishes!
There are flowers in the suds—
Forget-me-nots, crabapple buds.
What more could a maiden ask
Of a task?
Little daughter, doing dishes,
Think of water!

ETHEL ROMIG FULLER.

"Half a loaf is worse than none . . . if you're on a diet!

SURE THING

Does destiny really
Shape our ends?
It's one of life's
Profoundest riddles.
But there's certainly
No question, friends,
That bread and potatoes
Shape our middles!

W. E. FARBSTEIN.

Some hae meat and canna eat,
And some wad eat that want it;
But we hae meat, and we can eat,
And sae the Lord be thankit.

ROBERT BURNS.

"Cooking is a laboratory science . . . you know . . . and here is a scientific formula for a laboratory . . .

THE HEART OF HOME

This is the heart of home, this sunny room,
With painted cupboards and a spotless floor,
With shining pans, a yellow-handled broom,
A pot of red geraniums before
An open window; and aroma spun
Of garden breezes, soap, of simmering broth;
Of mingled ginger, cloves, and cinnamon
From spice cake turned out warm upon a cloth.

A sunny room, a cheery kettle song,
A woman, love, a hearthfire's radiance—
From these a man goes forth to labor, strong;
A child to play upon tiptoes a-dance.
Beneath a cottage roof, a palace dome,
A kitchen is the heart of any home.

ETHEL ROMIG FULLER.

"Labor-saving hint for housekeepers—a visit on time saves nine . . ."

ALONG ABOUT NOW

My love and I are edgy.
    We quibble when we dine.
He wants to see his relatives,
    I crave to visit mine.
It's this way every summer,
    And, while we're splitting hairs,
They all arrive at our house
    Before we get to theirs.

                      JANE SAYRE.

          Swinish gluttony
No'er looks to heav'n amidst his gorgeous feast,
But with besotted base ingratitude
Crams, and blasphemes his feeder.

                      JOHN MILTON

"Which came first . . . the chicken or the egg?

ODE TO A BREAKFAST EGG
(Sunny-Side-Up)

Sweet egg, reposing upon the nut-brown toast
    (Whose charred black robe was shed in my sink of white),
You are my gustatory Song of Songs,
    You are my visual 8:00 a.m. delight!
Relaxed, serene on your carbohydrate couch,
    Your round breast rises above your white frilled skirt
And tempts me . . . I stab its smooth and tender skin
    And watch your molten gold, your heart's blood, squirt . . .
At last you're mine! No one will steal you now!!
    (Yet consternation clouds a bit my bliss . . .
How can I ever gather you to myself
    When you are trickling over the plate like this??)
Oh lovely, murdered egg, which, but for me
    Might yet have been a chick, I have a yen
To know how aught as exquisite as thee
    Could come from Min, our dour speckled hen!

                      MADELINE SLADE.

"Flowers for my dinner table ... bachelor buttons ... and bleeding heart ...

I'LL BET A BUTTON

I wish that men would like my ballads
As much as my nut-Waldorf salads,
Or praise the highlights of my soul
As they do lobster casserole.
But no, it's not my soul that glitters,
My fame rests on banana fritters!

Men say that my *Bisquit Tortoni*
Will lead them into matrimony,
But I, myself? Just a brunette
Less tasty than my *Crepe Suzette*.
I wish that men would like my dancing
And find my cooking less entrancing.

But what's the use? I'll bet a button
That every man was born a glutton!

FRANCES ROCKWELL.

A little more than Kin, and less than kind.
SHAKESPEARE.

"A wife ... is a wife ... is a wife ...

OCCUPATION: HOUSEWIFE

After planning, marketing, cooking, after
Scouring the house from cellar to rafter,

After the dinner dishes are done
And the children disposed of, one by one,

After a day as domestic pearls,
We're supposed to turn into glamour girls,

Lovely and well worth a husband's wooing.
And it can't be done—and that's what we're doing!

MAY RICHSTONE.

"For dinner tonight . . . olives from the well-known branch . . .

APOLOGY WITHOUT WORDS

Table set with creamy linen,
   Ivory candles, silver sticks,
Crystal goblets, snowy roses . . . .
     (Will he come? It's nearly six!

There's contrition, if he knew,
In this table laid for two!)

Little muffins, hot and golden,
   Crisp without and soft within;
Amber tea that tinkles coolly;
   Yellow lemon, paper thin . . . .

(Will he recognize in these
Tangible apologies?)

Jellied chicken, subtly seasoned;
  Jade-green lettuce, clean and curly;
Tiny, crimson, peeled tomatoes;
  Fresh-pulled scallions, small and pearly;

Cucumbers with edges pinked;
  Little peas as sweet as spring;
Radishes like baby tulips—
  Oh, a salad for a king!

(Can he read what salad spells,
Hear the tale a muffin tells?)

When you pass your plate tonight,
  Darling, darling, are you guessing
It's my heart I'm serving you?
    (Will you have French or Russian dressing?)

LOUISE OWEN.

"One man's helpmeet is another man's poison . . ."

I WOULD NOT HAVE YOUR MEALS ON TIME

I would not have your meals on time,
Or dust behind the door,
But I'd have roses in the bowls,
And firelight on the floor.

I know I'd leave a lumpy place
If I should mend your socks;
I'd keep my nose well-powdered, though,
And plant some hollyhocks.

Quite probably your toast would burn,
Your eggs be over-fried—
I'd never wear a pair of heels
Run over on the side.

Instead of making budgets work
I'd write another rhyme.
Still—you might bring guests home with you
For dinner any time.

But life is made of serious things
Like bills and meals and rents,
So run along and find a girl
Who shows some commonsense.

Helen Welshimer.

"And singing in the wilderness . . ."

A GRACE

Bread
Is your hand upon my head;
Wine
Is your warm mouth pressed to mine.

Let us thank the gods who give
Bread and wine that we may live.

Mary Carolyn Davies.

"It's just a walk-up ... the windows don't keep out the summer heat or the Christmas cold ... but they're fine big windows ... and home is where you hang your heart ...

STAR FROM AN APARTMENT

A living room and a kitchenette
Are little enough to pay a debt
The world owes you; but add to these
A star above the elm trees,
That rise to the height of a Murphy bed—
And this is enough, when all is said.
For a star is everything you may wish,
From a golden coin to a silver fish
That swims in the aerial blue;
A peg to fasten your wishes to;
The tested yardstick which you try
To measure time and its wonders by.
Here is a star by which you can
Endure the sufferings of man,
Knowing this very star will shine
On later woes than yours and mine;
Knowing this very star will be
When stalwart ships that sail the sea
Have gone to final haven under
The tide, when the mighty cannon's thunder,
The torment and the children's cry
No longer are, and the blood is dry.
Here is a star on which to feed
In this our awful time of need.
Here is a star that is a prayer
Hanging above the elms there,
To be uttered by night from a Murphy bed—
This is enough, when all is said.

MYRTLE ADAMS.

Your fair discourse hath been as sugar,
Making the had way sweet and delectable.

WILLIAM SHAKESPEARE.

And They Came Out of Our Own Garden

"I eavesdropped on a subway during rush hour . . . going to Flatbush . . . so interesting I went past my station . . .

THE WISH

I gotta ask the boss for a vacation.
The doc said if I don't they'll stick a lily
In my hand. Ain't that a laugh? A vacation!
But if I was a duke's wife, and rich, Milly,

I'd strike for the country. Here's you and me.
We'd sell our souls for just a piece of earth
A-holdin' up a piece of sky, and those that has
Don't seem to appreciate their worth.

They wanta change, and so they growl and crab,
And nothin' suits them. O they get my pity
When they wanta leave their woods and flowers
For some old dirty, God-forsaken city.

Each evenin' I ankle up to Central Park,
And watch the spotted cow that's stationed there,
And pretend I'm in a field where daisies grow.
And there I lay content, with not a care.

You know, Mill, sometimes I get an ache
Down in my heart thinkin' of a farm.
To hear the wind sweep through a lotta pines,
And usin' robin's songs for an alarm

Instead of the El. When I was a kid
I used to look for tin-foil in the gutter
To sell, and buy an apple from Tony's cart.
And once down in the garbage and the clutter—

I found a flower. A little pink-blue flower
Half out and in of a battered red pot.
I watered it, and O my God, it grew!
I aint forgot! Never, never forgot!

EUNICE MILDRED LONCOSKE.

"Even geraniums in a window box . . . or a single rose in a vase . . . beside an old-fashioned rocker . . . even one small flower in a tall man's lapel . . .

SMALL GARDENS

No garden is too small to hold the sky—
   Here shadows lengthen, here the rain is cool,
Here all the winds find space to hurry by,
   With leagues of clouds reflected in a pool.

A yard-long path can treasure sunset light;
   One opening bud can spread the news of spring—
No garden is too small to hold the sight
   Of homing doves, or wild geese on the wing.

Here is a world where patient branches bend
   To shield my soul, where sun and rain can meet;
Where I can sit in silence with a friend,
   Or stand in prayer with clouds beneath my feet.

BLANCHE W. SCHOONMAKER.

"Amen . . .

PRAYER FOR A MAY MORNING

Lord of the sweet new blossoming,
I ask today
That every woman may know spring
This May —

A spring that thaws the ice from lips
Locked for a time,
And warms the heart that knows no skips
Nor rhyme,

A spring that gives the hand a bloom
For winter's glove,
And makes the great wide world a room
For love.

HAZEL HARPER HARRIS.

" 'Faith is a fine invention' . . . in any season . . .

FLOWER-FAITH

When laying bulbs beneath the sod
For Winter sleep;
My faith, like quiet trust in God,
Is strong and deep.

The dark earth holds no thought of gloom
In hiding clay;
For I can see bright tulip-bloom
In far-off May.

ELIZABETH MAXWELL PHELPS.

"Her nails are coated scarlet and carefully lacquered . . . but under it she hides . . . 'a green thumb' . . .

SEEDING TIME

I

It it not the beets and the carrots,
   It is not the kale and the corn,
But something that stirred in my fathers
   Years before I was born.

I can buy for a shilling the carrots,
   The beets, and the curling kale,
But that which drives me to action
   Is something that's not for sale.

And the pleasure I feel in the garden
   Is not for the tasselled ears,
Nor plums nor yellow musk melon
   When the time of ripeness nears.

II

When the heat of August is heavy
   And the summer is on the wane
And the meager crop is ripening,
   I promise, "Never again!"

For the call of the road comes to me,
   I vision the redwoods' shade
And the granite cliffs in their bareness
   And the steep trail's toilsome grade.

And I say: "No more will I bind me
   To this barren patch of land
Where the trickles of water must finish
   The task I have in hand."

Then the parching drought of the autumn—
   "I will waste no labor here,
For the sparse returns of the tillage
   Are a meager crown for the year."

III

The rains fall in December
   And the showers drip from the eaves
And the flowers awake from their slumber
   And the roses put out new leaves.

The sprouting grasses a-quiver
   And the smell of the earth are a call,
The buds swell slow on the plum tree
   And the soft sun shines over all.

The book of verse loses flavor
   And the stories no longer bind—
The words that have chained my fancy
   Have vanished from my mind.

Something that stirred in my fathers
   Years before I was born
Like a slow fire smoulders within me,
   Flames up on a soft spring morn.

The ancient light glows within me
   With a heat I cannot withstand;
I set my foot on the terrace
   And a spade is in my hand.

                      I. D. PERRY.

"Pardon me . . . while I hum a little hum . . .

LOVE SONG

Like a lovely jasmine flower is my heart's dear,
Her silken garments white beneath moon-fire.
Her eyes are like two pools, serene and clear,
In whose deep depths I read my heart's desire.
And like a moon-laved fountain's spray
Is her blonde hair; her lips like crimson-bright
Pomegranate blooms. She's like a new spring day,
The beauty of a lovely scented night
When white gardenias spill their lush perfume,
And like music in the time of singing birds.
Her love is mystic as the ocean's spume—
She is a song—too wonderful for words.

BEATRICE PAYNE MORGAN.

To me the meanest flower that blows can give
Thoughts that do often lie too deep for tears.

WILLIAM WORDSWORTH.

"Some secrets are better when shared . . .

THE SECRET GARDEN

Now for a while we lock this door behind us,
   This garden door set in the moss-green wall,
Where only sun and flowers and trees could find us
   Who now must venture forth observed by all,
Part of a moving army bound toward places
   Beyond imagination and foretelling.
There will be knowledge of new names and faces
   When we return to our leaf-shadowed dwelling.

And when we do come back, I somehow feel
   We shall not lock the secret door against
Our new-found comrades. Danger may reveal
   That we have held our hearts too safely fenced
And that the world beyond the wall is one
   In friendship with our flowers and trees and sun.

ROBERT HILLYER.

"April showers . . .

RETURN

All the blue of the skies
In a puddle of rain;
And in the blue of your eyes
All of heaven again.

PAULINE STARKWEATHER.

There is no ancient gentlemen but gardeners . . .
They hold up Adam's profession.

WILLIAM SHAKESPEARE.

"The one in the magazine . . . with appropriate corrections . . .

GARDENER'S LAMENT

With grubby hands and sweaty brow
I've worked to make this lovesome spot.
Whose garden is this, anyhow?

I long to rest beneath the bough
And gloat on this fair scene, hard got
With grubby hands and sweaty brow.

A catbird slapped my face just now,
With swift and vicious wing, Great Scot,
Whose garden is this, anyhow?

From morn till even I've toiled, I vow,
In wind and weather, cold and hot.
With grubby hands and sweaty brow.

My hedge sustains the neighbor's cow;
His cat camps in my bergamot.
Whose garden is this, anyhow?

His dog with others holds pow wow,
Midst pansies and forget-me-not.
With grubby hands and sweaty brow,
Whose garden is this, anyhow?

FLORENCE HILLIARD.

"Nobody ever understood why . . . not even the lady herself . . . and yet the reason is obvious . . ."

THE LADY'S GARDEN

Disciplined by marriage,
She goes on mincing feet
And tends the primmest garden
On all the snobbish street.

There are patrician roses
And well-pruned English box,
And by her stately doorways
Austerest hollyhocks.

Serene, snow-white petunias
Are cramped in righteous rows
Where each capricious tendril
Is snipped off as it grows.

There are no tiger lilies
Nor jasmine—passion's own—
For she forbids exuberance
In scent or color tone.

How strange—her hopeless lover
Swears that one night she leaned,
Spring-mad, far out her window
By honey-suckle screened.

Flung seed of hardy zinnias
And cried with sobbing breath,
"Flame up, you lusty prodigals,
And bloom yourselves to death!"

JANIE SMITH RHYNE.

The world was sad, the garden was a wild,
And man, the hermit, sigh'd—till woman smiled.

THOMAS CAMPBELL.

" 'You are nearer God's heart in a garden than anywhere else on earth . . .'

REASSURANCE

I never knew the truth about my garden
Until the Spring you gently reappeared;
And then I learned that you had never left me,
And that untrue were all the things I'd feared.
"There is no death," you murmured through the crocus,
As yellow, purple heads peeped from the snow:
"I never went away at all," you whispered
From tulip cups that made a stately row.
"Dear heart, you never should be lonely,"
Blue Iris bore your words to me, so clear,
"I'm never far away, because I love you,
I couldn't leave you, don't you understand, my dear?"

But when the first red rose begins to open,
And lilies-of-the-valley haunt the air,
I hear the organ strains of bridal music,
And you are in my garden everywhere.

ELSYE TASH SATER.

Ye living flowers that skirt the eternal frost.

SAMUEL TAYLOR COLERIDGE.

" 'Humility, that low, sweet root . . . from which all heavenly virtues shoot' . . .

AT THE FLOWER SHOW

They sat with fingers locked, there on the bench.
No word was said, no sign was given. But here . . .
Before the throngs of people passing by;
The many rooms of heavy-scented flowers;
The splash of fountains playing in a mood
Of make-believe; the moss and fern that grew
In sanded pots, deep buried in cement
Along the garden walks with flagstone laid,
About a dusty wooden floor where soon
A Sportsman Show would flourish . . . here, a peace

They found, an earthly paradise complete.
But people, passing by and glancing, saw
Only his threadbare cuff . . . her thin black coat;
Nor guessed the heav'n of two shy hearts unlocked,
There by the fountain, at the Flower Show.

KATHRYN H. HALL.

A primrose by a river's brim
A yellow primrose was to him,
And it was nothing more.

WILLIAM WORDSWORTH.

"When a lad from Iowa is transplanted . . . he might take root in Trinidad . . . and like it . . ."

GARDEN IN THE TROPICS

My odd, exotic garden in the tropics
   Confounds me still with its lush mystery.
Although I see, my mind can scarcely credit
   The antics of my rooted banyan tree.

The shrimp flowers in their orange carapaces;
   The giant bamboo creaking in the sky;
The croton leaves, like tufts of parrot feathers;
   The bland hibiscus, scarlet as a cry;

"Delicious monster" and its leaves gigantic
   With holes to let the wind through; the bright gold
Papayas, melonlike, that grow on tree trunks;
   The travelers' palm with water in its hold;

All these, although I love them, still confuse me.
   I stand amazed at what each season brings,
As though a farmer, searching in the henhouse,
   Should see a phoenix hatch and spread his wings.

EUNICE TIETJENS.

"There's one flower missing . . . forget-me-not . . ."

THE BOUQUETS . . .

It was a wonderful bouquet! He said,
"Happy Birthday, Mother" and gave it to her arms to hold.
It was heavy with the giant marigold
That crowded perfect roses, white and red,
Tall, splendid gladioli, slim larkspur,
Proud, wax-faced lilies, and some were stranger-blooms—
Delicate, tender, nursed in hot-house rooms;
He told their long, bewildering names for her.
She sighed, "How lovely!" and she fixed them in a vase . . . .
"Now I must run—I'm glad they've pleased you so—"
She dropped her cheeks' pink roses. He must go—
His were important, hurried, business-days . . .
  There was a day he'd stayed: he was pride-flushed—
  He'd had a birthday gift for her. His small, brown fist
  Held ragged buttercups that were sun-kissed,
  And, in the center, one red clover crushed.
  He'd said, "Don't look until I fix 'em nice!"
  And in a jelly-glass they'd sprawled, and short ones drowned—
  And then they'd passed the birthday cake around—
  And laughed—and had two plates of cherry-ice!
It was a wonderful bouquet, but wasted price he'd paid!—
She looked right through it, seeing one red clover,
Warm, clenched buttercups, one small homed rover—
Who washed his hands for cake—and stayed and stayed!

RUTH E. LANCASTER.

    To see the world in a grain of sand,
    And a heaven in a wild flower;
    Hold infinity in the palm of your hand,
    And eternity in an hour.

WILLIAM BLAKE.

"Bubbles used to know how . . . but now she's eleven and getting older every day . . . while Happy is fast approaching seven . . . and learning a lot the hollyhock way . . .

HOLLYHOCK LADIES

There's a trick to making hollyhock ladies,
Of standing them straight in a dainty row,
Of arranging the flare of their skirts just so.
And when I was only slightly seven—
It's a wonderful age and close to heaven!—
I could make ladies to please a queen,
All pink and lavender, white and green . . .
So as I was passing a garden wall
The other day, and I saw there tall —
Nodding to me as I passed by—
Hollyhocks gay and laughing and shy,
I called to the auburn-haired mite who played
By the willow tree in the dappled shade,
And I said: "Hello. Have you ever made
Ladies out of these flowers?" They swayed
And bowed their rainbow-hued heads to me.
The child said, "No," and laughed with glee.
"I'm Susan," she said, "and I'm only seven"—
It's a wonderful age and close to Heaven!
So I picked a few that were dancing near,
To teach her the trick; but my dolls looked queer.
The child took one, and her fingers flew.
Astonished, I saw that Susan knew!

ELEANOR JOANNE BOESHAAR.

O'er folded blooms
   On swirls of musk,
The beetle booms adown the glooms
   And bumps along the dusk.

JAMES WHITCOMB RILEY.

"Here's another kind of Victory Garden . . .

APPLE TREES

Old apple trees atop a hill
   Write upon the sky
Words of wisdom and good will
   To passers-by.

In syllables of pink and white
   Their message tells in rhyme
That sweetness shared in spring delight
   Will fruit in time.

Green lettering on summer days
   Proclaims that nests have long
Been certain proof that patience pays
   In joyful song.

In fall, red lanterns signal out
   That plenty comes to bless
The trusting heart that knows no doubt
   Of Love's largess.

Bare limbs against a winter sky
   In tall, black script unfold
That bravery must tower high
   When winds are bold.

                HAZEL HARPER HARRIS.

" 'Wild orchids to you' . . .

ON PLANTING SEEDS

Nobody wants a cluster of wild mustard,
And no one a parcel of joe-pye weed;
Everybody wants florist's roses instead—
Gardenias, gladiolus, and a green orchid.

Nobody wants wild mustard, yellow
From a pure palette, or the purple joe-pye,
Done up in a bundle of fragrant sallow,
Sweet-in-death, and dragon's eye.

Everybody wants big tame red poppies;
Nobody wants the little wild white ones.
Everybody wants what everybody copies;
Nobody looks where the twinflower runs.

Nobody wants a bouquet of wild mustard
Or a sweet-smelling bunch of joe-pye weed,
Done up in dock leaves, the stems tied with worsted.
Nobody ever would plant that seed.

AUDREY WURDEMANN.

"Rosemary for remembrance . . .

GARDEN IN THE RAIN

Lashed by the white bombardment of the rain,
The amber warriors have left the field
To those sweet blossoms that forever yield
To their wild lips. But they shall come again,
Droning their battle songs like copper bells,
Climbing the bastions of the hollyhocks,
Charging the crimson turrets of the phlox,
Taking the larkspur's azure citadels.

And when the silence of the frost shall creep
To lull the victors and their slaves to sleep,
Let us remember in October's fires
Their songs, their colors, and their bright desires,
And we shall dream in warmth no ice removes,
Drunk with the honey of our earthen loves.

JAMES E. WARREN, JR.

" 'The world is so full of a number of things . . . I'm sure we should all be as happy' . . .

LARKSPUR

I planted some larkspur, but all of it was blue.
My old gardener smiled.
"I wouldn't worry. Enjoy it as it is—and wait.
Next year you'll be surprised."

Following the redbird and the robin
It came again this Spring.
This time I had no part in it,
Just the Springtime—and God.
There was blue larkspur as before,
But mingled with it white and pink, the color of tiny seashells,
A swaying flash of pastel shades above the green.
It might have been a fairy's scarf left fluttering on the grass.

My gardener was wise.
I didn't know that was the way of larkspur.
Since then I haven't worried about—oh, a lot of things.

Isla Paschal Richardson.

"A new slant on an old notion . . . I'll view a violet now with mixed emotion!"

VIOLETS

Who calls a violet a modest flower?
I have seen it wild, running
Across the spring meadow, through the damp wood,
Tempting the warm kiss of the sun,
Bending in the embrace of a shower,
Encouraging the first bee to buzz a serenade,
Beguiling the wind with its artful cunning.
A violet is hardly ever understood
By anyone.
It sows seeds everywhere
And spreads through a garden without shame,
Its life an escapade;
Yet like a hypocrite, it bows its head
Feigning the attitude of prayer.
Do not trust its innocence, instead
Inquire of wind or rain or passing bee
If violets have any other aim
Than coquetry.

Gertrude Ryder Bennett.

"Mistress Mary where have you been . . .? Off to a garden over the hill . . . And Mistress Mary what did you see . . .? All that was there . . . and I see it still . . .

BERRY PICKING

I made a slow contented pace
Up hillsides frail with Queen Anne's lace

And found a shadow-tangled way
Where gold streams trickled from the day;

I listened till I understood
The magic chat within the wood,

Then crossed a fence whose corners hinted
Black-eyed Susan gold was minted;

I stumbled where wild roses knew
The dainty footsteps of the ewe,

And sauntered one enchanted hour
Through jewel-weed and monkey-flower . . .

I left the place where I had found
A new-born moth upon the ground

And saw the shadows slanting tall
Across a brooklet waterfall;

Then from the hill I hurried down . . .
I saw the primness of the town,

And so to spare my lips a lie
I brought home berries for a pie.

FRANCES MORTON O'NEILL.

"Poem for a farmer who finds plowing pretty humdrum . . . especially when working on the vegetable patch . . .

PAN GOES PLOWING

I clambered up a redbud tree
And sat a flaming bough;
Then broke myself a sliver bright
To fashion me a plow.

I ran my furrow deep and long,
A wild, gay thing that whirled
A crazy, zig-zag running path
Around a stolid world.

And though it dervished free and mad
For men whose hearts run wild,
No human soul sang praise of it
Except a wee, lame child.

M. AGNES THOMPSON.

"Now we just take an aspirin . . . and keep on feeling terrible . . .

NAMES OF HERBS

The names of herbs are worth remembering:
Night shade and periwinkle, vervain and rue,
Each one medicinal, a precious thing,
By hedges of old gardens where they grew.

Physicians steeped with skill, to solace pain,
The purple marjoram with its sweet smell;
Ladies who lived in flowered Aquitaine,
Dipped their white hands in honeyed asphodel.

Hemlock and chickory, witches plucked apart,
Potions for grief, when powdered to a paste;
Who sought dim feverfew and its gold heart
For love, crushed on their tongues, its bitter taste.

CECILIA ELLERBE.

"Is everything taken care of . . .? The paper cancelled . . . the milk stopped . . . the telephone disconnected . . . oh, one thing more . . . write the seed catalogue company and give them the new address . . .

ON LEAVING

Take down the curtains, lock the door
    And give the key to someone new;
I'll see the jonquil buds once more
    And turn my back and go with you.

For little gardens everywhere
    Quicken to a loving hand,
And little houses just as fair
    Hug the highways of the land.

But there is only one of you
    To satisfy my spirit's need,
And home is anywhere we two
    Shall find a house and plant a seed.

HORTENSE ROBERTA ROBERTS.

"The lengthening shadows . . .

LATE SEPTEMBER

Here in this place the asters blow noiseless
In the warm wind. The leaves fall without sound.
Birds flit on the dry boughs, and motionless
The squirrels sit with curved tails and paws around
Acorns, but they do not eat nor stir
Nor talk. Among the gentians blue as sky
They sit staring as if the gentians were
Lights suddenly lit to startle the eye.
Nothing calls out here. Nothing will ever call
Perhaps, ever . . . nor bird, nor flower, nor leaf
Utter a faint heard syllable of fear
Though the incipient ruin of the fall
Haunts the bright branches like a dream of grief
Dimly remembered from a vanished year.

SISTER MARIS STELLA.

" 'He leadeth me beside the still waters' . . .

LITTLE LAKE

This little lake holds all the brooding stillness
    Of lonely mountain tops,
Upon its sun-warm surface of green water
    The burnished willow drops
Her pendant yellow boughs. It is so quiet
    A brown bird singing in a white birch tree
Seems to bring with it all the winds of wonder
    To brush tranquillity.

Here is a little lake set in the wildwood
    Of this green mountain hollow,
Known only to the bear and fox and badger,
    The kingfisher and swallow,
Having no need of men and their computing
    The greater with the less,
A secret, perfect thing, content, unconscious
    Of its own loneliness.

I must go far but shall not go forgetting.
    Henceforth in many an hour of doubt or pain
I shall be thinking of this silent water
    My eyes may never look upon again.
And I am taking with me peace to cherish,
    Solace that I have known,
A memory of green-rimmed, quiet beauty
    One hour has made forevermore my own.

LOUISE DRISCOLL.

Dear Diary

"Reno . . . At last it's over . . . the comic farce of convention . . . with all the rules meticulously observed. 'Incompatability' is a word big enough to include a number of people . . . and numberless things . . . Am I to blame because my heart, though empty, had no room for him?

THE REASON

There was eager love in his kisses,
    And passion and need;
Oh, I tried to give what he sought for
    His hunger to feed—
But I was as cold as a gravestone,
    As rigid as steel,
And he could not warm me to living,
    Nor rouse me to feel;
For ghosts of your kisses were haunting,
    And there in that place
Though he was as near me as breathing—
    Between us—you face!

MABEL NEWMAN.

Hope springs eternal in the human breast:
Man never is, but always to be, blest.

ALEXANDER POPE.

"Reno . . . It is a curious commentary on those of us who come here . . . that we imagine things will all be different . . . when it's over . . . only to realize that nothing is ever . . . very different . . .

POSSESSION

For these swift hours we spent together
(Words and stars and fingers' touch)
All the world is somehow altered . . .
Maybe not so very much.

So . . . though I forget your phrases
(Deathless truths and little lies)
Some small thing I'll keep forever
—Something . . . maybe . . . in your eyes.

LESLY RAINE.

"*Reno . . . The longer one waits for something . . . the harder it is to accept it casually when it comes . . .*

HARVEST

>Maybe I want to reap
>   Too much for what I sow;
>Maybe I sow too much—
>   I do not know.
>
>   MARY WISE WATTS.

"*Reno . . . It rained last night . . . I didn't know . . . I was sleeping . . . It's better that way, though . . . rain is too much a part of my day this season . . . and my memories last . . .*

REMEMBERING AN APRIL RAIN

There was so much I wanted to remember,
To hold close in my heart, washed bright by tears;
The words of a careless song, your voice made tender,
A thread of melody for lonely years.

But Oh, so much has gone; I seek in vain,
Comfort in things you loved, some word you said.
That day we walked bare-headed in the rain,
You said it showered blossoms on my head;
I laughed . . . Dear God, how could I know—
Remembering an April rain, would hurt me so.

                KAY FRANCE.

"*Reno . . . This morning I threw out all the old letters . . . but the maid did not know they were to be disposed of . . . so tonight, returning to my room in the hotel, I found them all on the dresser . . .*

DAWN DREAMS

>Last night I said I'd lay away all thoughts of you
>   Like some old wrap of woolen cloth
>Put back with moth balls, yet to keep a while,
>   Defying, confidently, man or moth.

Awoke today, to greet a bright new world
   Unveiling gray-pink misty dawn
Fading into rosy day and told myself
   That all I had of you was gone.

I busied me with foolish little chores
   Like dusting . . . baking apple tarts,
But, like a small bird slipping thru the trees,
   By night you nested in my heart.

Anne Moore McFarland.

"Reno . . . It is strange that two people may so much need each other . . . yet each have so little to fulfill the other's need . . .

LOVE

You wanted love—not love that I could give you,
But something that was fire and lightning flame;
And I had only lamplight for my windows,
And candleshine to greet you when you came.

A prairie fire held warmth that you were seeking,
That ruthless sweep, high challenge to the bold,
How could you know—when meteors flung red guidance—
That quiet hearths are best to keep the cold?

You wanted love . . . Somewhere perhaps you found it
And journey now with scorched heart cold and numb . . .
My candles burn a little every evening—
It may be they will last until you come.

Helen Welshimer.

"Reno . . . I have laughed twice today . . . once when I thought of the absurdity of the 'final decree' . . . the judge's solemn severing of something never quite united . . . and then again I laughed remembering two people who had said farewell . . .

FAREWELL

   For us farewell has proved a foolish word,
   Although we uttered it so earnestly.
   The heart, being trustful, valiant and absurd,
   Believed its sound of strict finality

But came to understand the syllables
Were impotent to call an end, were vain
Against a thousand tender miracles
Prolonging both the wonder and the pain.

For now you are the moonlight on my sill
And I the south wind soft against your cheek;
You are the rain at evening; I, the still
White words that February twilights speak;
You are the ache of music; I, the spell
Of stars. It was a futile word, farewell.

ADELAIDE LOVE.

Farewell! a word that must be, and hath been,—
A sound which makes us linger; yet—fairwell!

LORD BYRON.

"Reno . . . I had not realized until now, the complications involved in names . . . the problems of retaining my married name . . . the doubtful refuge of my maiden name . . . the taunting temptation of a third name . . . as close as life to me, although as distant as the stars . . .

TO THE ALMOST-FORGOTTEN

That I may never hear your name again,
Nor ever see your face, this is my hope.
'Tis said the wise shun poison; thus I wish
To have no further need to meet and cope
With that insane delight I found in you,
And nevermore to feel my pulses pound
With erstwhile quiet blood gone hot and mad,
Nor lose all thought in swirling fire and sound.
I want no more such whelming ecstasy,
No more such kisses, wild but bittersweet,
. . . Your lips I had; I could not reach your heart . . .
Therefore I pray that we may never meet
To rouse remembrance lulled with patient care
Into a slumbering ghost. And if I be
Harassed by haunting dreams, the matter lies
A secret issue 'twixt my dreams and me.

GEORGIE STARBUCK GALBRAITH.

"Reno . . 'What am I doing here . . . I've always led a well ordered life'?

RHYME TO A PRISSY LADY

Her speech and conduct were without flaw,
Her thoughts rested on the proper pegs;
She primly sipped at life through a straw,
And all she got was the dregs.

ENID BRYAN.

"Reno . . . It is so foolish writing these things in a diary . . . remembering . . . pretending . . . hoping . . . when there is so little to remember . . . when it is so futile, too . . . pretending . . . since there is nothing at all to hope for. Yet there is a measure of pleasure in winning . . . even at solitaire . . .

THE FLAME AND THE SMOKE

I think of you and the thought is flame,
But the flame will generate
The subtle, silver smoke of dreams,
And the dreams are opiate.

I think of you and the thought is fire,
But from the fire will rise
The pale, narcotic smoke of dreams,
And dreams are paradise.

GEORGIE STARBUCK GALRBAITH.

"Reno . . . There was a day when I could wait the time of your returning . . . knowing the hour would come . . . and bring its joy . . . Yet even then I was impatient . . . protesting . . .

ABSENCE

Your absence is a little hell
  That burns me with its fire;
And every day, with you away,
  The flame leaps high, and higher.

> But oh, when you come back to me,
> What bliss once more is given!
> Forgotten are the pangs of hell
> In the white light of heaven!
>
> CHARLES HANSON TOWNE.

"Reno . . . Strange that we are so far apart . . . that when you are in my mind . . . I'm quite sure I am out of it . . ."

CONVERSATIONAL GHOST

> At times,
> You are a myth;
> For many of our talks
> Are executed solely in
> My mind.
>
> SARAH LEEDS ASH.

"Reno . . . months later . . . Even my diary must hardly recognize me now . . . this book with which I have shared my most intimate hours . . . I have learned new words for it now . . . and have a new flourish with my pen . . . but I must not compare the writing with the early pages . . . there are names back there I might discover . . . and that's all over . . ."

CONCEALMENT

> I've learned to do my tasks quite well,
> At least the people say
> My gingerbread is fairly light,
> My music, sweet and gay.
>
> I call on shut-ins and I go
> To dinner and to shows;
> I laugh—oh, much more frequently—
> I'm sure nobody knows
> That now and then at people's teas
> I almost drop my cup,
> Because I am afraid I'll see
> Your face when I look up.
>
> HELEN WELSHIMER.

"Reno . . . I thought it might be difficult returning to these pages . . . the diary is so full of memories . . . but that's all past . . . all past . . . excepting when the book falls open to a certain page . . . Why won't ink fade . . . Why do dreams last?

I HAVE FORGOTTEN

I have forgotten you, my dear—
But not your eyes . . .
There are too many pulsing stars
Pinned to the skies.
I have forgotten Love, my dear—
But not its pain . . .
There are too many silver darts
In April rain!

ROSA ZAGNONI MARINONI.

"Reno . . . Laugh at me, Diary . . . the tall clock in the hall stopped this morning . . . and after all these months of winding it myself . . . it suddenly occurred to me that this was once his task each evening long ago . . .

SINCE YOU HAVE GONE

Since you have gone so far away
A curious thing I find;
The world is like a little clock
That God forgot to wind!

MARY CAROLYN DAVIES.

★ ★ ★ ★ ★ ★ ★ ★ ★

"New York . . . Brother Book . . . you are about to learn how a man acts when he is in love . . . stop me if I start penning 'woeful ballads made to my mistress's eyebrow' . . . but keep forever this cherished verse my lady made for me . . .

BLUE ON BLUE ON BLUE

Mountains have set their mark on me—
high horizons rising blue on blue on blue
compelling the lifted vision,
measuring all man can do.

Seas have set their mark on me—
sun-stippled and shadowed blue on blue on deep
surging with the long roll,
knowing what to keep.

Skies have set their mark on me—
clean rain-washed blue on blue on space
receding before the wing,
timing incidence and race.

One man has set his mark on me—
of all men, one—eyes blue in blue in blue
searching at the core of me,
believing me true.

GAYLEN SHANNON.

"New York . . . Diary, old man . . . I have reason to believe my lady speaks to her diary differently from the way she speaks to me . . . I saw a page today that spoke volumes . . . Ah that I might know her like her book . . .

LINES FROM A DIARY

So casual I was to you today—
And yesterday, and each remembered hour
We ever knew. Oh, there is more to say
Beyond white daylight, if one has the power!
But now, here in the quiet of my room,
Beside your picture in its honored place,

I press a switch, watching the sudden bloom
Of lamplight falling down across your face.
And I shall think of all you said to me,
Holding it close for just a little while,
Daring to greet those clear eyes tenderly,
And whisper "Darling!" to your slow, sweet smile.

Tomorrow when we meet, my heart will sing
"I love you!" . . . but I'll say—"It feels like spring."

Esther Baldwin York.

"New York . . . Diary, you old rascal, you wouldn't believe it! . . . but somebody else might . . . so I won't say a word . . . except . . . my lady is a poet.

NEVER UNLOVED LET ME GO

Give me your mouth for my kiss;
Give me your breast for my tears;
Love has meant nothing but this,
These years.

Love me and leave me for death;
Never unloved let me go
Chaste in my hour and unwished,
Below!

Kaye Huizing.

"New York . . . Don't say I didn't warn you . . . but I had to have a poem for her . . . and yesterday on the Avenue . . . the wind whipping around the corner almost pinned her against the building . . .

THE WIND BLOWS OVER YOU

The wind blows over you the way it blows
Over the sea when spring is coming down
To meet it on the beaches; when the town
Opens its windows and puts out its nose;
When daylight sticks her fingers into night;

When geese fly north, the meadows smell of rain,
The pussywillows feel a low, quick pain,
And fuzzy, soft gray buds come into sight.
That is the way the wind blows over you:
The way it blows when everything is dark
But the crystal flagons of the spilling dew
And the white birches sweetening their bark;
The way it blows on things it likes to touch
And wants to be with very, very much.

       THOMAS SUGRUE.

Unless you can dream that his faith is fast,
 Though behoving and unbehoving;
Unless you can die when the dream is past,
 Oh, never call it loving!

      ELIZABETH BARRETT BROWNING.

"New York . . . Relax, Diary, old fellow . . . it's late . . . and we're alone . . . let's talk together. There is a word I haven't introduced to you . . . 'marriage' . . . It is a state of . . . more or less uncertainty . . . created by dependence. Being in love . . . I dare all this . . . but being wise . . . I fear . . .

CRICKET IN THE HOUSE

Tentatively, soft and low,
A cricket somewhere starts to go
Under my flooring in the dark,
As cheerful as a golden spark.
He knows that he does not belong
In my house, but sings his song
With all the boldness he possesses,
With extra tender trills and stresses,
To lull that part of me called mind
And win me over to his kind.

He would like to make me think
That living is food and song and drink
And being in every limb as wise
And sightful as if made of eyes.

This little traitor of the night
Would have me think of wrong and right
As silence and a web of song,
Woven vibrant all night long.
He would have me join the choir
Whose only anthem is desire.

But he is of another world,
Where the flowers are uncurled
Like white angels to ensnare
Walkers on the dew and air,
To make them carry to a pod
The small and mighty bits of God.
He and I can never be
Dwellers in fraternity,
Save moments when I stand and face
Love lost in laws that govern space.

ROBERT P. TRISTRAM COFFIN.

★ ★ ★ ★ ★ ★ ★ ★ ★

"Omaha, Nebraska . . . May 10 . . . Dear Diary . . . Joe proposed to me today. All he could talk about was his money . . . as if I were afraid we'd starve . . . it was wonderful and awful . . . I told him no . . . I'm never going to marry . . . ever . . . especially anyone with money."

A GIRL REPLIES

My arms are slim,
My feet are bare,
I've a flicker feather
For my hair.

Chokecherry rouge
On my lips;
Windy scarves
About my hips.

I've mallow cheeses,
Buckwheat honey—
What more could I buy
With any man's money?
Ethel Romig Fuller.

"Omaha . . . May 24 . . . Dear Diary . . . Joe was here again tonight. This makes every night for two weeks . . . he won't take no for an answer . . . But if he thinks I don't know my own mind, he should hear what I told Marion today . . . She is so happy . . . but with a house like hers, who wouldn't be . . . with a house . . .

JIM AND MARION'S HOUSE

I've said I'd never marry, I—
    And still, and still, and still,
Since I've seen Jim and Marion's house,
    Perhaps, perhaps, I will!
It's such a quaintly modern place—
    Old English style, you know,
And, in the garden back of it,
    Old-fashioned posies grow.
And everything's just right inside—
    The living room, the hall,
The dining room, and kitchen, and
    The bedrooms; loved them all!

And Marion has a Persian rug,
    A waffle iron, a chair
Sent all the way from Belgium, and
    A set of Quimper ware.
And Marion has a sun porch hung
    With curtains, willowy green,
And all its windows look upon
    A neat suburban scene.
And Marion has her pantry shelves
    Lace-paper-edged and trim:
And Marion has a breakfast nook,
    And Marion has her Jim!
I've said I'd never marry—I—
    And still, and still, and still,
Since I've seen Jim and Marion's house,
    Perhaps—perhaps I will!

                      VIOLET ALLEYN STOREY.

They went to sea in a sieve, they did;
    In a sieve they went to sea;
    In spite of all their friends could say.

                      EDWARD LEAR.

"Omaha . . . June 1 . . . I guess Joe's hopeless . . . I've told him and told him again and again . . . maybe I'd better quit saying no . . . I'd die if he believed me. I told him about Marion's house . . . so . . .

DREAM HOUSE

When he comes tonight we will draw a plan,
    From chimney top to cellar sill,
Of the little house we mean to build
    Some day on a wooded hill.

A little house from the tales of Grimm,
    Quaint as the one that Gretel found,
With rocks and moss and a mirror-pool
    And dusky firs and pines around.

A zig-zag house like a crazy quilt,
    With panes as bright as pixy faces;
A roof made out of rainbow scraps,
    And doors in unexpected places.

We shall have the first dark violets
    Set in a yellow earthen bowl,
And burning logs on a spacious hearth
    For the ripening of the soul;

The friendship of a few old books
    With crystal words on every page,
And time for laughter, life and love—
    And live with them to a green old age.

                      MARION DOYLE.

And there is even a happiness
That makes the heart afraid.
                    THOMAS HOOD.

"Omaha . . . June 15 . . . Dear Diary . . . It's all settled!

FAMILIAR SETTING

The moon was silver, (which I know is trite)
The garden sweet with lilac, (a cliché!
This too is old, I fear . . .) soft velvet night
Hastening to a rendezvous with day . . .
Your lifted face, your hand within my hand . . .
Then revelation . . . wonder . . . reverence;
(And quite Victorian, I understand . . .
This hush of prayer at love's first imminence.)
A nightingale there by the garden wall
In sudden burst of song . . . (It well may be,
The dull mouthed platitudes . . . love after all
Is just a matter of biology.
Essence of all the bromides . . . this, I know . . .)
But God made Eden, just an hour ago!
                      CAROLYN ELLIS

"Omaha . . . No words tonight . . .

FUTILITY

How many times I strive to put my love
For you into a song—and always fail!
It is as if a little child had tried
To crowd the whole wide sea into his pail.

AELAIDE LOVE.

"Omaha . . . Dear Diary . . . All day I have been climbing stepladders . . . newspapers on the kitchen shelves . . . washing windows . . . ladders . . . all day . . . always . . .

LITTLE LADDERS

I know, now
that I have you near,
the love affairs that I once knew,
were simply little ladders, dear,
that I was climbing up to you!

KATHRYN KAY.

"Omaha . . . August . . . And I used to be so independent . . . why it seems as if I once said no . . . I can't believe it . . . and yet sometimes I almost wish . . .

LONELINESS

You took my face between your hands,
And held me with your eyes
Swift, shapely, comprehending hands,
Dear, earnest, hungry eyes.
You sang three words, then pressed your face
Against my vagrant hair . . . .
Till then there'd been no loneliness
Too vast for me to bear.

ELSYE TASH SATER.

"Omaha . . . Joe was the life of the party tonight . . . I don't see how he can be so funny . . . but I help . . . I laugh longer and applaud louder than anybody else . . . and he likes that too . . .

TURNABOUT

We're really equals,
don't you see,
in everything we do;
you say such lovely things to me,
but I think them of you!

KATHRYN KAY.

"Omaha . . . September . . . Dear Diary . . . He says I've changed in some ways . . . he says he likes me better . . . funny man . . . he doesn't seem to know why . . .

CONSUMMATION

Since I have tasted the forbidden wine
   Of this transcendent passion,
I cannot learn to love with quiet heart,
   And in a passive fashion,
Nor be content with less than what you gave to me,
Since I have known this bird-free, wind-wild ecstasy.

LISBETH WALLIS.

"Omaha . . . November . . . Dear Diary . . . Do you remember the house we planned? It's all built now . . . with everything we dreamed of . . . everything! . . . and one thing more the solemn architects forgot about . . .

SENTINEL

There hangs a little silver bell
   Above the doorway to my heart.
It tinkles, Oh, so tenderly . . .
   When you arrive . . . when you depart.

KATHERINE KELLY WOODLEY.

Once in the Dear Dead Days Beyond Recall

"I want to sleep late in the morning, my dear . . ."

SUN DIAL

I thank you that you do not chime the hours . . .
If it is "later than we think"
you do not shout it,
but exercising marvelous powers
of nice restraint and reticence about it
your silence is maintained.
You do not shrink
from truth:
if one is curious to know
how swiftly youth
and morning pass
the knowledge may be gained
quietly, the blow
be taken secretly . . . Clocks are for all
the blatant souls and crass
who wish to hear
the record of their days
proclaimed. But always some folk will recall
and hold a sun dial dear
for quiet ways.

B. Y. WILLIAMS.

"It is about half past ten according to the Rockies . . . the Alps are slow . . . while the Colorado River has wound down completely . . . the Grand Canyon . . ."

THE AGELESS

Only the jutting nothings
On the World's crust
Know of Time's passing
And turn to dust.
Nothing marks Time's passing
On the trackless blue . . .
The sky and the ocean
Are always NEW!

ROSA ZAGNONI MARINONI.

" 'The Old Order changeth' . . . but where there are children there is no order . . . so where there are children nothing changeth . . . no! . . . no!

SONG TO CHILDHOOD

Nothing is changed. Nothing is changed at all.
The white and purple lilacs smell as sweet
As they did yesterday. Beneath the swing
The grass is worn away by eager feet
Leaving the earth for cherry-buds and heaven.
The little girls still use the acorn-cup
When keeping house. The muted song of skates,
And pebbles of childish laughter still disrupt
The sun-stained air, to wing across the years
And touch my heart, for childhood's pink-white bough,
Still spills its blossoms on the golden wind . . .
God keep it so a hundred years from now!
Nothing, nothing is changed, my dear, I know . . .
Only the little children come and go!

EUNICE MILDRED LONCOSKE.

" . . . 'on the sands of time' . . .

QUESTION FROM A NEW MOTHER

Why should I need her footprint
On this official pad,
When every lovely feature
Proclaims her like her Dad?

NAOMI REYNOLDS HESS.

"No . . . not that . . . that's B . . . Higher . . . oh no . . . that's D . . . the other finger right there in the middle . . . see?

FIRST PIANO LESSON

Gay copper curls and a newly starched pinafore,
  Two little ribbons as bright as can be,
    Legs swinging merrily,
    Voice humming queerily,
Mary is searching to find middle C.

CHARLA M. BACKLUND.

"After all ... dates are vague ... in the dawn of history ..."

HALF-OF-ONE

Oh, today is very special!
We've declared a celebration!
For today is half-the-birthday
Of our youngest generation.

So her Daddy took her walking
In her ruffled blue sunbonnet,
And her Mommy baked a birthday
Cake with half a candle on it!

LISBETH WALLIS.

My mind lets go a thousand things,
Like dates of wars and deaths of kings ...

THOMAS BAILEY ALDRICH.

"Historians have a most difficult time telling their stories ... The best of heroes have some bad points ... the weakest, some good ... There are periods they might like to forget ... but it's all a part .. it is the story ... and the story is life ... and life is the adventure ..."

BIRTHDAY

At first I said: "I will not have, I think,
A cake this year. I'm much too old for it."
And then, "Perhaps a cake, but, oh! no pink
Candles for folks to count when they are lit."
Then I said later, "Well, perhaps a few
Small candles *would* make the affair more bright;
But the true number—it would never do!"
And yet today when I stood up to light
A candle flame for each year I have come,
I laughed, and how my spirit sang in me!
I was most proud (although my hands shook some)
As I held up the cake for all to see—
Years I have worked in, played in, and been sad,
Years I have loved in, lived in, and been glad!

ELAINE V. EMANS.

"If ever there lived a Yankee lad . . . wise or otherwise . . . good or bad . . . who, seeing the birds fly, didn't jump with flapping arms from stake or stump . . .

JIMMY

They dared Jimmy to take the jump
From the tower wall; so he did, of course,
And landed with a tremendous thump,
Covered with bruises and remorse.

But a bump upon a boy soon mends,
And tomorrow he will tell his story
In condescension to his friends,
Covered with liniment and glory!

May Richstone.

History is a fable agreed upon.
Napoleon.

" 'The hour of my departure has arrived . . . and we go our ways . . . I to die and you to live . . . which is better . . . God only knows' . . .

XANTHIPPE COMPLAINS TO A NEIGHBOR

No, he is not a handsome man, I grant,
My husband—lips too thick, an ugly nose,
And eyes—well—they do bulge. But that just shows
I married him for love. When I descant
On life's afflictions, when I rave and rant
About my lot, believe me it's not those—
Socrates' features—that I mourn as woes,
But his weird habits. And he's adamant.

Always the same old tunic—and no shoes—
Barefoot! My husband! He a sculptor once!
How happy I would be were he a dunce
If he'd go dressed like other folk, and pay
Our bills, and buy us food.
            What, lad? You've news?
Speak plainer, imbecile! *Hemlock? Today?*

Julia Boynton Green.

"If I were king . . . I'm afraid I would take a chance on being out of order . . . and ask for any convenient date she would arrange . . .

BELLE

She never placed world potentates
   In quite the proper order.
She could not bound the ancient states
   Or give their modern border.

The dates of battle she forgot,
   Old pacts did not disturb her;
Teachers agreed that she was not
   Prone to scholastic fervor.

But the lads found her fair and gay
   By all collegiate gauges.
And in her schoolgirl's eyes there lay
   The wisdom of the ages.

Eleanor Stanley Lockwood.

"But think what you both miss sitting there rubbing rosin on a fiddle string when you might be riding a fire engine . . . with sirens and whistles and water streaming everywhere . . .

APOLOGY TO NERO

Your fiddling has been stoned, for ages past,
As though no one but you had ever played
Bright notes above a burning city's roar . . .
But how shall we, the thrilled, the laughing, cast
A stone? What if it strike the barricade
We built against the crackling that would soar,
An angry hawk, into the lark-filled sky
Of our contentment? Such a fragile wall—
A song, a gifted word, a sunset glow;
Yet how impervious to the smoke and cry
Of all our Romes! Your pardon, Nero! Call
Us fellow artists of the callous bow.

Marguerite Steffan.

"Some fun . . . oh prodigal son!"

LITTLE BOY GROWN

Boy, come six years old today
Grandly giving your toys away,
Dealing out to the younger ones
Balls and whistles and wooden guns;
Oh, little boy grown too big to ride
The rocking horse, control your pride
And lay the teddy bear aside.

Give the littler ones your blocks,
Your rubber cat, and the duck that rocks;
And give the engine and cars instead
Of the teddy bear that you took to bed;
For you may find that nights will bring
Need of a friend to which to cling—
And teddy bears are comforting.

EDITH CHERRINGTON.

This is the place. Stand still, my steed,
  Let me review the scene,
And summon from the shadowy Past
  The forms that once have been.

HENRY WADSWORTH LONGFELLOW.

"So this is why money always burns in my pocket . . ."

TALISMAN AGAINST TOMORROW

Pick the fruit before it falls;
Beauty has need of taking,
Emptiness of being filled,
Bread of breaking.
The hungry mouse of time, unseen,
Is nibbling night and day—
Take your heart's desire now,
While you may.

IRENE WILDE.

"Man lived many centuries before the Golden Age ... and he's lived many centuries since ... come to think about it, it didn't last very long either ... maybe that's one reason it was Golden ...

TODAY

We may not have tomorrow,
And yesterday is past.
And our love is a lilting love,
Too gay, too sweet to last.

For steady love is calmer,
It runs a longer while
Than ecstasy that tilts the stars
And flames for half a mile.

But I would so much rather
Have had today with you
Than centuries with someone else—
Do you feel that way, too?

HELEN WELSHIMER.

"Lightning never strikes twice in the same place ... but they say history does repeat itself ...

PROGNOSIS: FAVORABLE

Remember the boy who didn't carry
Your books? The lad you yearned to marry
When you were ten? The captain of
The team, with whom you fell in love
Past consolation and belief—
Until you plunged to greater grief
One afternoon at a matinee?
(The times you've given your heart away!)
You thought you suffered, you thought you'd die,
You thought, "I'll never get over this."
You don't know whether to laugh or cry,
Looking back; but you cannot miss
The hope implicit: What happened then
Might—in a decade—happen again.

PATRICIA MARTIN.

"Once when I was a little boy . . . I saw a man digging and I asked him where he was going . . . 'To China' . . . he told me . . . Now I am big . . . America is starting in to dig . . . and it's almost for China . . . It's Japan . . .

A MAN MUST DIG

"A man must dig," he said. "A man must dig—
Small holes when he is little; when he's big,
Oil wells and tunnels and the like of that."
(The sunlight fell aslant his old straw hat.
He leaned indulgently upon his spade.)
"Now me, I dig for beauty. I have made
A sea of color from a spot of dirt."
(He flecked a spider from his flannel shirt
And tossed his gloves upon the garden bench.)
"In nineteen-seventeen I dug a trench.
I mind the night was cold and thick with stars—
Millions and millions of them—etched like scars
Upon the steel-blue sky. And then the roar
Of cannon broke. Say, mister, what's it for—
Night on the water, morning on a hill,
Church bells at sunset-time, and men that kill?
What is it all about? Though I am wise
With troubled years, it still gets in my eyes.
And I must dig, and I must cover up
With beauty something ugly in the cup
Of living. Somehow, somewhere, I must find,
To clothe the desolation of the mind,
Purple of pansies and the golden sheen
Of poppies drifting on a field of green.
And so I dig. My son and daughter scold:
'Dad, take it easy. Don't you know you're old?'
But I just smile and dig and let them rave.
A man must dig—a garden or a grave."

HELEN FRAZEE-BOWER.

Why so pale and wan, fond lover?
   Prithee, why so pale?
Will, when looking well can't move her,
   Looking ill prevail?

SIR JOHN SUCKLING.

"There isn't any way to turn back the years ... after a generation ... an old fashion is just a costume ... the new styles make all the past seem quaint ...

LOVER'S RETURN

My earliest lover called on me;
   Tremulous, I went to the door.
(Cis ran in as I poured the tea,
   Trailing her sand across the floor.)

My caller spoke of Robbin's farm—
   Bluebells blossoming in the wood!—
(Skippy shouted in alarm,
   "Mom, the pup's not feelin' good!")

We spoke of the agates we used to find—
   Treasured ring quite broken now—
(Cissy called, "Mom, Skip won't mind.
   He's throwing sticks at Evan's cow.")

We mentioned the rain in which he left—
   Night of anguish beyond belief!
(Suddenly, as he rose to go,
   I stifled a sigh of vast relief!)

HARRIET SEYMOUR POPOWSKI.

'Tis but the same rehearsal of the past ...
And History, with all her volumes vast,
Hath but one page.

LORD BYRON.

" 'Maud Muller on a summer's day ... raked the meadows sweet with hay' ... and not one wild oat fell her way ... but say!

PRACTICAL CERTAINTY

If I were only
  sweet sixteen
and hadn't seen the things I've seen
and hadn't done the things I've done
I'll bet you I'd be having fun!

KATHRYN KAY.

"Clean ... Clean ... Clean ... all night long ... How in the world does the place get so cluttered up ... what under the sun goes on around here ... a body would think ... but it hasn't time to ... clean ... clean ... clean ..."

WASTE

Late tonight, a cleaning woman
    Will find, on your office floor,
Scattered cigarette stubs, ashes,
    Dust of rainbows by the door—
Fragments of a dream like many
    She has swept away before.

ERNESTINE MERCER.

"Do historians ever fall in love with some far time ... and wish the world might wander back?"

CLASS REUNION

"The girls," we call each other,
    Overlooking added girth—
We who have dealt with death now—
    We who have given birth.
One white lie befits the occasion—
    "You haven't changed a bit!"
Noting grey locks, tired faces,
    We blithely bandy it.
We have put on insouciance
    As an outmoded dress,
Too tight to hook, absurd now
    Its one-time loveliness.
Day long, we keep the posture—
    But, when the night comes down
And lights are out on campus;
    Deserted, the small town,
Each finds the room assigned her;
    On some girl's cot, she lies.—
For her own girl-self, vanished,
    Tears flood a woman's eyes.

VIOLET ALLEYN STOREY.

"As a matter of record it won't really matter . . . a hundred years from now . . . but . . . Helen didn't fare so badly . . . and I understand there are still a few ships to be launched . . . so . . . What Ho! me hearty!

IN A HUNDRED YEARS

In after years, who will remember,
   And who will ever care,
That I was dark and beautiful?
   Or I was plain and fair?

And who will mark the closing
   Of a door in a dark, damp room?
Only these arms that enfold me,
   Someday, to be seed and dried bloom.

But the night-wind that sighs in the clover,
   And the dawn that bleeds on the hill,
And the sky with its stars, and the moon and the stones,
   And the sea, will be here still.

Who will then know of my going,
   By the fine, sharp sword of pain?
Only the rose with its roots in my heart
   And the crystal drops of rain.

                              EUNICE MILDRED LONCOSKE.

"There are certain dates that stick . . . 1066 . . . 1492 . . . 1776 . . . 1812 . . . 1865 . . . 1898 . . . 1914 . . . and Hallowe'en, 1925 . . .

TO A FIRST GRAY HAIR

I saw him square his shoulders, set his chin,
His quick, rebellious stare, and next a thin,
Slow smile that meant approval, and with grace
He brushed you to a swift and certain place.
He did not know I watched him in the mirror,
Nor why I kissed him twice and held him dearer.

                                GLADYS MCKEE.

"*An old, old custom . . . Flag Day . . . Memorial Day . . . Independence Day . . . Armistice . . . Thanksgiving . . . Christmas . . . Easter . . .*

THIS DAY

This day though ended I shall never fling
Into the basket of untreasured time,
Nor carelessly put by on some dark shelf
To lie unnoticed in the gray of grime.
This I shall save against a bitter need,
Safe-bottled in the cupboard of my heart
Upon the shelf of dear rememberings,
Labelled but briefly: "This balm set apart
For discontent." Some day I shall be tired
Of going and of coming. I shall need
A remedy to calm my spirit's core,
And nourishment on which its want may feed.
Then will this quiet peace flow through my veins.
The dark, wild waves of restless hours will fall
In final thunder on their barren beach.
There will be sun, still water, and the call
Of one shy bird, and you within my reach.

ISABELLE BRYANS LONGFELLOW.

"*'Requiescat in pace' . . . but definitely . . . ! but how . . . ?*

R. I. P.

Mary A. Linsley, according to your stone,
For ten years here you have slept alone.
(What was the earlier condition of your bed
I cannot say, who know you only dead.)
Did you listen to the preacher's remarks concerning dust?
I hope you got to paradise or purgatory just
Before they were abolished, for now there's only hell.
Is your last bed right for you? And are you sleeping well?
Do you ever pace the confines of your narrow little room
And wish you had a dust-pan and a crisp new broom
To sweep away the cobwebs and gather up the dirt?

Are you sometimes very lonely? Does the silence ever hurt?
Why don't you go a-calling on the lady next door?
Her name is Mrs. Bettencourt; if she should be a bore
Don't hesitate to look around—see on the other side,
A Mr. Perrault who was only twenty when he died.
Can you tell today is hot? Or hear my footstep's sound
Or see that in your flower-can a thirsty mouse has drowned?

JOHN PATERSON BRANTNER.

Sigh no more, ladies, sigh no more,
Men were deceivers ever;
One foot in sea and one on shore;
To one thing constant never.

WILLIAM SHAKESPEARE.

"That was the year the British burned Washington . . . oh, yes . . .
Judge Taney lived up in Frederick, Maryland, then . . . Frederick? . . .
A lawyer named Key lived there . . . Francis S. Key . . . Yes, moved
that year with his wife. Was he the one who wrote the poem . . . about
Fort McHenry? He was the one . . . and that was the year . . . It
begins, 'Oh say, can you see by the dawn's early light' . . .

LIFE TOGETHER

"Do you remember," my father says to my mother,
"That time we came—was it ten years ago?—the weather
Was better than this, hotter, but tiring, rather?
We sat by the gate, here, on an old log."
"Was that the day the bus was late?" says my mother.
But my father says: "No, no. That was another
Time we came, when I lost my stick in the heather.
Don't you remember the tramp and the black dog?"
"I think I remember," she says, and they smile at each other.
"That was the day—"
           Of such is their life together.

JOYCE HORNER.

"I have a wonderful clock at home . . . so lazy that though I jog it up every morning, it can never catch up with my watch . . . It is obviously embarrassed . . . its face in its hands every hour of the day . . . an unmitigated coward . . . Every morning at seven it gets alarmed over nothing . . . Some morning I fear it will give me the works . . .

TIME PIECES

I am not fond of clocks, they thrust
   Their vapid faces into view
Or strike the time, a kind of must
   Regarding things a man should do.
But watches have a friendly voice,
   Brought from the pocket where they cower,
They always let one make a choice:
   To know or not to know the hour.

LALIA MITCHELL THORNTON.

"'Thirty days hath September, April, June, and November . . . all the rest have thirty-one excepting February' . . . which has the lucky ring . . .

RELENTLESS TIME

Relentless time is never in retreat.
With sharp precision, measured moments run
In silent pageantry around the sun,
Unnoticed till a cycle is complete.
Elusive days are quickly shelved in neat,
Plain rows, red-lettered when a task is done
We would remember; and another one
Is check-marked where a memory was sweet.

We, who are riders on a carrousel,
Grasp for the lucky ring; strain to enlarge
One gay, exalted hour, only to yield
To time. No deft maneuvers can repel
The unseen force of minutes, set to charge
In swift battalions on our battlefield!

SARAH LEEDS ASH.

"The historian will ... and he will carefully list the number of votes cast in Arkansas ... the tides at Boston ... the name of the generals in the Boer War ... the cotton crop in Texas ... the automobile accidents in New York ... and a number of other vital statistics historians dwell on ..."

WHO WILL REMEMBER SPRING?

Who will remember Spring? Not the young,
Whose laughter will be echoed in the treble
Notes of many Springs; they know no tears
To greet the silver beat of April's rain;
The gay gold plush of many moons
Will glow against the velvet dark of sky ...
They will not know that dogwood on the hill
Has flamed and died within so brief an hour.

Who will remember Spring? Not the old,
Who count the endless chain of weary years
On tired fingers ... the melody of rain
Becomes a dirge for old forgotten things;
The gray geese echo with their lonely cries
The march of Spring across the summer fields ...
How can they remember April's kiss,
Who sit in lonely watch for winter's night?

Who will remember Spring? Will we two,
Whose hearts were broken by the loveliness
Of moonlight falling on the cherry trees,
Remember only April's fleeting glance?
What shall we say when winter's bitter snows
Have locked us close within her frozen spell?
Shall we remember then white mists of plum,
And blue forget-me-nots upon the hill?

EDYTHE HOPE GENEE.

For every sentence uttered, a million more are dumb:
Men's lives are chains of chances, and History their sum.

BAYARD TAYLOR.

"History has not salvaged much out of the billions of things that ha[ve] happened ... nor has it saved and handed down many of the millions of names ... but the heart is just as careless ... if this indifference is carelessness ... and both have saved enough ...

WHAT DOES THE HEART REMEMBER?

What does the heart remember, looking back
Along the years when one was very young?
Grandmother's shelf of fragile bric-a-brac;
Walks after violets; and being swung
In an old rope swing; long rainy afternoons
Up in the attic land of Make-Believe;
Fairy-tale books; and hurdy-gurdy tunes;
The starry, magic feel of Christmas Eve.

Running through rustling leaves and falling snow;
The sudden picnics on green slopes of spring;
A song that Mother sang nights long ago;
The heart remembers every lovely thing—
Like seeing sunlight through a window flowing,
And thinking, "This is what home is," and knowing!

ESTHER BALDWIN YORK.

Bliss in possession will not last;
Remembered joys are never past;
At once the fountain, steam, and sea,
They were, they are, they yet shall be.

JAMES MONTGOMERY.

"Wind up the clock ... roll up the ball ... purl one ... tick tock ... purl two ... that's all ...

REMEMBRANCES

Grandmother sits in her rocking chair,
And knits up her raveled days.
With a tranquil face and whitened hair,
Grandmother sits in her rocking chair;
And smiles at the wraiths that surround her there,
As she knits and dreams and prays.
Grandmother sits in her rocking chair,
And knits up her raveled days.

ETHEL B. CHENEY.

*...ote a poem about Paul Revere's ride and used the wrong
...o many more have learned the poem . . . than the
...ongfellow made history . . .*

GRANDMOTHER'S LILACS

Grandfather called them "laylock" trees,
Telling how Grandmother with pride
Planted small lilacs as a bride,
And never a chilling frost or freeze
Threatened their springtime bloom; they grew
In that stern country tall and true.

And "laylock" was, it seems to me,
A sweet old-word for lilac tree.

ETHEL B. CHENEY.

"I was there the day General Lee told his men goodbye . . . we hadn't eaten for two days . . . our shoes and ammunition were gone . . . but if he had said the word, we would have gone on fighting . . . in fact, we cried when he asked us to go home . . .

CONFEDERATE VETERAN

Alone there in the sun he grips his cane,
Hearing the First Manassas rumbling back,
The galloping clang of cavalry passing again
Toward Vicksburg in the night, the whistling crack
Of guns at Kennesaw. But, high and sweet,
And always louder comes the alien sound
Of bugles blowing beautifully Retreat
Across his spirit's withered battleground.

Who once was splendid as a bayonet
Sits crumpled, silent, where the slow wind blows.
Only his soldier's heart is marching yet
Whose shoulders bend beneath his ghostly gun
Which weary hands at last must ground upon
Some lovelier Appomattox than he knows.

JAMES E. WARREN, JR.

"Some of the things in history seemed so useless. I asked my teacher once if we couldn't change them . . . There was an odd expression on her face . . . then she laughed and said . . . 'Maybe . . . maybe you can . . . you're young' . . .

NOW BEGIN AGAIN

"Never forget, child," Grandmother said,
Lining the pan with waxy crust
And dumping in cherries, dripping red—
"You finish one thing"—she paused to dust
The sugar in—"then start right over
On something else; that's how you get
A good day's work done."

            She laid the cover
Marked with a fern, on the fruit, then set
The pan on her finger tips and sliced
It quickly around to a smooth, clean edge,
I liked that part, and the way she spliced
The crusts together and made a hedge
To keep the sweetened juice inside.

"What if I spoil it?" I had to ask:—
I had sewed my patchwork blocks too wide,
And tangled the thread, and wept over my task.
"You start again, child—start again
Just as if you had done it right;
If you must take out threads or stain,
That's your beginning." Tears dimmed her sight:—
"Be thankful if you can do it over."

The day she died, I asked if she
Had started Heaven like a child again;
But nobody knew, and I could not see,
And nothing has made the matter plain.
But at times, when I finish a task and stop,
Self-satisfied, with idle hands,
Or tangle my threads and let them drop . . .
A child, and a pie, and grandmother, stand
Before me, pictured invertedly
As a mirror turns everything about . . .

A little pig-tailed, shadowy me
Watching old hands roll pie-crust out
Upon the top of a clean, bare table,
With apples and cherries, green and red,
By a bowl of blackberries, gleaming sable,
For the Saturday pies.

        And an old voice said,
"Begin again, child—begin again" . . .
But it took living for me to discover
Why her kind eyes blurred with tears and pain . . .
"Be thankful if you can do it over."

AGNES L. PORTER.

Here the free spirit of mankind, at length,
Throws its last fetters off; and who shall place
A limit to the giant's unchained strength,
Or curb his swiftness in the forward race?

WILLIAM CULLEN BRYANT.

"Stages . . . of the dark ages . . . hold fond memories . . . when a lark ages . . .

LAMPLIGHTER

"The old order changeth"
  And that is good, and right;
And yet, somehow, things never seem
  So magical at night
As when lamplighters used to come
  With sticks to light the light!
I still can see the bent old man,
  Who, like a fairy story
Could touch the lamp before our house
  And give it sudden glory!

ELIZABETH DAWSON.

"It doesn't matter what the historians write ... when all is said and done ... just so they prove that life is good ... and that we all had fun ..."

ADMONITION

When I am gone and all my songs are sped
   Upbraid me in whatever tone you will,
Tell if you must, the foolish things I said,
   Rehearse the good, nor yet ignore the ill.
Say I was quick of temper and unwise,
   Prodigal, and the friend of knaves and those
Who prey on weaklings. In my brave disguise
   Show how I stalked, and mimic every pose.

Say that I had a hundred lies to tell
   And told them boldly, if you so recall;
Incredulous of heaven as of hell
   Cry how I mocked the wormwood and the gall.
Repeat I loved not wisely but too well
   But do not say I never loved at all!

                              SYDNEY KING RUSSELL.

Please Do Feed the Animals

"If the world is in a knot ... Freedom can untie it ... Freedom can do many things ...

YOU WOULD NOT THINK

You would not think
A chickadee
Could stir the branches
Of a tree.

You would not think
A little dog
Could shake a house
With his small jog.

You would not think
The step of man
Could dissipate
A bridge's span,

Or that his spirit
Could soar higher
Than bombers,
Pestilence, and fire.

RUTH LAMBERT JONES.

"Eggzactly ...

NEWS ITEM

The Redbreasts came to town today
  To their home in the tall elm tree.
They came the way they always come,
  Aeronautically.

The children are coming later on,
  Five or four or three.
They'll come the way they always come,
  Biologically.

BESSIE MARLIN MASON.

" 'Did you ever hear a blue-bell ring . . .'

SPRING'S GOLDEN BELLS

This morning I awakened
When dawn broke rosy red,
To the sweet sound of music
That blanketed my bed.

It drifted through the window—
A limpid litany;
And I arose in wonder
To seek its melody.

And lo, beneath my window
I spied a golden shower;
A carillon of gladness
Chiming the spring-tide hour.

And, silently, a robin
Stood on the nascent sod
Listening to gay forsythia—
The ringing voice of God.

SAMUEL J. ALLARD.

"For some unaccountable reason . . . I find no great amount of mercy in my heart . . . for a mouse . . . who seems bent on displacing us . . .

BROOD OF THE SPARROW

A sparrow has built in the house that we
Planned for a brown wren's family,
But motherhood always must be respected,
And never can babies be ejected,
And so the wings of the mother bird
Close to our alien heads have whirred,
Day after day, like a word repeated,
Day after day, like a prayer entreated
For the humble and homeless of every race
Who only ask for a nesting place.

DOROTHY P. ALBAUGH.

"When all of a sudden . . . one of the saintly artists laughed and called—'Look out below!'

THE BLUEBIRD

The angels are painting
The walls of Heaven;
They started this morning,
Long before seven.

My dear, they are using
A beautiful blue,
And just as the sun
Arose and threw

His golden glance
On the garden wall,
One of them let
A splash of it fall

Into the boughs
Of our apple tree—
It looks like a bluebird—
Come out and see!

MARION DOYLE.

"And a girl . . . and a boy who is bound to follow . . . are aptly named a nut and a swallow . . .

BIRD WORLD

Night is a raven
  Starry-eyed.
Dawn is a bluebird
  Heaven-dyed.

Day is a jay
  Full of blatant rush.
Evening a singing
  Hermit thrush.

RETTA SCOTT GARRETT.

"So this is what makes those meek souls . . . stroll blindly across Broadway . . . jaywalk across Times Square . . . driving traffic officers insane . . . and making taxi drivers die young . . . Someone should tell rabbits . . ."

LITTLE RABBITS

Little rabbits are about,
Hopping nimbly in and out
Of country roads within the span
Of the motors' caravan.
They do not pause to contemplate
The fate of rabbits who leapt too late,
They do not pause to ponder why
Their own sleek bodies do not lie
Beneath the grim, Gargantuan wheel
Of every passing automobile.
Little rabbits are abroad,
Leaving such affairs to God.

RUTH LAMBERT JONES.

"Feeding time for the lions . . . 12:00 and 6:00 . . . Please do not stand too near the cages . . . they are not vegetarians . . ."

KINDRED SOULS

We both are mothers, she and I,
And on the vine that dips
Across my kitchen window sill
She rests, between her trips
To satisfy her children's cries
With juicy bugs and butterflies.

She twitters wearily at me,
I answer with a sigh;
And as she drops to seize a worm
I hear her plaintive cry—
"If they keep clamoring this way,
I know they'll turn my feathers gray!"

JULIA REESE OSBORN.

"Fog comes in on little cat feet . . .

THE SILENCE

If I am very quiet
I can hear
the meaning
of my life
stir in the dark
like some
sure-footed beast
that takes the forest
in his stride
and leaves
the darkness
and the barriers
behind him.

JULIA B. COHAN.

"Canaries . . . I suppose . . . must be satisfied to be philosophers . . . sitting around in a library all day. Much like housewives . . . and yet . . .

EVEN A BIRD

Even a bird must fill its wings with sky
And put its breast against the sun to feel
The air pour into feather, wing, and thigh,
With heart as restless as a turning wheel.
A bird will track its dream into a cloud
And search the Infinite for what it may
Not find; a pale, lean, battling body, proud
To be a solitary thing away
From earth and sea and craving such
As it can find of something yet unknown.
A creature from God's hand, desiring much
And unafraid of seeking it alone,
A bird must willingly believe in things
Beyond the range of its aspiring wings.

C. FAYE BENNETT.

"I see your point, Bumble . . . but leave it be . . . lest in sitting down . . . you fumble . . . and leave it me . . .

INTERVIEW WITH A BUMBLE BEE

You rumble down
The crimson vortex of a rose
In avid haste—

Ecstatically,
You balance on your bull-dog nose,
Expertly placed.

Tell me, since I'm too huge
For calisthenics on a rose—
How did it taste?

Doris Barnett Roach

"Bubbles was telling me just last night . . . that Alec Templeton was born without sight, but did not learn he was different from others . . . until past eight years old . . . already he had found beauty . . . and he has never lost it . . . in the dark . .

REGARDING THE MOLE

Having no certain knowledge of the light,
He does not sense the terrors of the night.
Lured by the footsteps of the gallant spring,
The murmured voice of every burgeoned thing,
He goes adventuring: to darkly read
The hidden secrets of the buried seed,
To hear the whisper of the errant root.
And thus he ploughs his way in slow pursuit
Of beauty on a narrow, lampless trail
Beneath the cover of earth's emerald veil.
Marking his sightless, torturous track across
The ceilinged earth in tumbled sward and moss.
And shall we call him blind who charts serene
Through darkness, a path he has never seen?

Anne Southerne Tardy.

"Well, my word ... look what we have ... in the zoo ... a green-eyed monster ... and it looks like ..."

I AM NOT JEALOUS

I am not jealous of you.

I do not mind my seeing you
with dates occasionally.
I realize I'd be with you
If such a thing could be.

Always I smile, nod pleasantly,
and then endure their stare,
pretending to be nonchalant
so they'll not think I care.

But why select such awful frumps
to lunch and dine beside?
Their lack of charm appalls me, Dear ...
And rather hurts my pride!

KATHERINE KELLY WOODLEY.

I holde a mouses herte nat worth a leek.
That hath but oon hole for to sterte to.

GEOFFREY CHAUCER.

"But if he mentions the girl in green ... there'll be a scene ... So to keep the lion in the cage ... be your age ..."

FEMININE REACTION

When your glance strays
Over my head
And softly you praise
That girl in red,

If I demur,
It's jealousy;
If I concur,
It's hypocrisy!

MAY RICHSTONE.

"On the way to the park ... on the way to the zoo ... I had a rough ride ... Did you notice it too?"

DISCOVERY

The horse has a place on his back that is made
    Not cuddly and cushioned and plump,
But sticking right up, like a sharp little blade,
    Half-way from his neck to his rump.

It's some like an island, but most like a hill
    With acres of soft sand around it.
Not everyone knows that it's there ... but you will
    If you trot. That's the way that I found it!

HELEN FRAZEE-BOWER.

Here comes a pair of very strange beasts, which in all tongues are called fools.

WILLIAM SHAKESPEARE.

"Don't ever make the mistake of thinking you are insulting a man by calling him a brute ... it happens to be one of the highest compliments ..."

DARK VIGIL

There's fruit on the hangman's tree tonight—
    Heavy and cold and still;
The scaffold sycamore is gaunt
    And stern upon the hill ...
While down in the valley
    The human clan
Still mutters a curse
    On the swinging man.

There's fruit on the hangman's tree tonight—
    With none to pray him grace;
O, even the moon looks coldly down
    Upon the dead man's face;
But under his feet,
    On the righteous ground,
With a whine in her throat
    Lies the dead man's hound.

ELENORE LEE WHITE.

"A bowl of milk . . . a catnip mouse . . . and thou . . .

FRIGHTENED KITTENS

The world is a fishbowl
To dabble soft paws in,
And life is a tree trunk
To sharpen small claws in.
All corners are mouse holes,
Intriguing with mystery.
These concepts are part of
Each wee kitten's history.

But alas, the sad wonder
When real life discloses
That bugs often bite
Pink, inquisitive noses.
And oh, the despair
Upon small furry faces,
To find themselves stranded
In high, stairless places!

ESTHER BALDWIN YORK.

"Don't blame this on Me . . zee . . .

A TALE THAT'S TALL AND TEAS-Y

A baby beetle black and blue-y
  From out his winter home said "Phoo-ey,
I hear a hum so bumble-bees-y
  Across the field that's bright 'n breezy
And steps just like the centipedes,
  So many light 'n knee-zy.
It must be summer's come
  'N gone the winter cold 'n freez-y
With all its pesky sniffles
  So vexing and so sneez-y,
And I can leave my winter home
  So windy and so wheez-y
And gayly join the cats and dogs
  So happy and so fleas-y.

BELLE S. MOONEY.

" 'Up with me . . . up into the clouds . . . for thy song, Lark, is strong' . . .

THAN ONCE TO HEAR A SKY-LARK SING

No man could ask a greater thing
Than once to hear a Sky-lark sing,
Than once amid an English dawn
Along some hawthorn-scented lawn
To watch it soar and sweep on high
In some blue, rain-washed Summer sky.

No man could beg a greater gift
Than that some day his heart might lift
Along some far horizon's rim
And catch the music of that hymn;
To hear and know, and feel and see
That poet of eternity;
To know, at last, that Time is naught
When that great miracle is wrought!

WILLIAM L. STIDGER.

"A new tale . . . from an old wag . . .

THE DOG SALESMAN

"Ten bucks, he's yours. That dog," said he,
　"Has got a lot of pedigree.
Just watch the way he holds his head
　And how he sits and begs for bread.
His coat is soft, his eye is quick,
　And fast—just watch! Here, puppy, sic!
Day in, day out, though rich or poor,
　He'll watch your child and guard your door;
When day is done, right by your chair,
　No need to look, for he'll he there;
And should all others turn away,
　There'll be one friend you'll know will stay,
Through summer's heat, through winter's cold.
　Here's something you can't weigh in gold."

Meanwhile, the one who made the sale
　Just sat—just sat and wagged his tail.

J. HARVEY HAGGARD.

"Oh where . . . oh where . . .

A LITTLE DOG GOES ON

I brushed and brushed my best black coat today,
And tears fell fast because I brushed away
White hairs that said, as plain as plain could be:
"A white-haired little dog belongs to me!"

So many times I've brushed my clothes, annoyed
By those white hairs . . . if I could bridge the void
That hides Eternity, and see once more
A small white dog, trotting on Heaven's shore,
   Scratching up Heaven's flowers,
     Sniffing at Heaven's trees,
   Officiously barking at angels,
     And chasing heavenly bees . . .
I'd gather him into my arms, unmindful of stares,
And never again be annoyed . . . by small white hairs.

MARGARET RUSH.

"If cats would simply woo the muse . . . and cease to mew their woos . . .

PUSSY WANTS A CORNER

I've begged so long from door to door,
I guess I haven't any pride,
But it's so hard to forage any more
With such an empty place inside.
I wouldn't mind at all, you see,
About the garbage cans and such
Places where I eat—it isn't only me,
It's for the children that I care so much.
But you were generous, that was a lovely meal;
I feel genteel again. You were so nice
With bits of meat and milk, I feel
I can repay—your house is over-run with mice—
So please, kind lady, you could use a cat
Who won't be any earthly bother,
And six little kittens, sweet and fat,
Deserted by a roving father.

RUTH STEWART SCHENLEY.

"I knew a man once who lived in the city . . . and went for a walk every evening . . . Years ago he had a small dog . . . but he still goes for a walk . . . and whistles . .

A GOOD DOG NEVER DIES

A good dog never dies. He always stays;
He walks beside you, on crisp Autumn days,
When frost is on the fields, and when the year
Is ending, and the winter's drawing near.
And when it's summer, and the bees are humming,
He leaps ahead of you, and waits your coming.
And, anytime you're lonely, look, you'll see
His great eyes watching you, still solemnly.
Just call him in your heart, he'll cease his play,
His head within your hand, in his old way!

MARY CAROLYN DAVIES.

"It takes a big zoo for lions and tigers . . . but for a person . . . the winding stairway of a snail's shell . . . is adequate . . .

DESPAIR

Time was when a snail's slow passage around each
Blade of grass,
The glistening of a dewdrop on a gentian's purple
Face
Could make me ache in rapture
At such a perfect thing.

But now all that is over.
You never really cared!
I am alone again with pain,
Lost in the soft finality of rain.

I wish I could change places . . .
If only for a day . . .
And hide inside a snail's small house
And weep my heart away!

HILDA CONKLING.

"Classified Section of the newspaper . . . Lost . . . Reward . . . my house and property . . . my wife and family . . . myself . . .

LITTLE LOST DOG

Little lost dog, on the thoroughfare,
Worried black nose and the wire-stiff hair—
Some child is missing you, some tot will care—
Unhappy little lost dog!

Little lost dog, in the dusk and the rain—
Some youngster calling you, calls you in vain,
Baby nose snubbed to the windowpane—
Draggeldy little lost dog!

Little lost dog, on the avenue,
Blinded by headlights—he's searching for you,
Searching each face, all the wild dusk through—
Whimpery little lost dog!

Little lost dog, on the wheel-mad street,
Hungry small dog, but too frightened to eat,
Little wet dog, with uncertain feet—
Panicky little lost dog! . . .

Little limp dog—not so much for size!—
Little limp dog, with the death-dim eyes—
Some tot is missing you, some baby cries . . .
Waiting his little lost dog!

BLANCHE DeGOOD LOFTON.

"Whim . . . wham . . .

ZOO'S WHO

The dainty little bunny rabbit,
Multiplies from froce of habit.

The saucy little pekingese,
Leads a merry life of ease,
Chewing rugs and scratching fleas,
Sniffing bones and smelling trees.

JOHNNY McKINNEY.

"Is this poem about little boys saying pieces . . . little girls at recitals . . . business men in directors' meetings . . . or dogs?

TELL-TAIL

When friends tell us of their dogs' tricks,
How they can count from one to six,

And how they climb the stairway backward,
How cautious they are, bric-a-bracward,

How language feeling has increased
To such a point, the very least

Their owners can do is entrench
Themselves behind a wall of French—

We do not speak of our own pup,
Who lies down when we say "Sit up;"

Who, told to carry shoes to Mother,
Can't haul them fast enough to Brother;

Who welcomes thieves and burglars in,
Then bites policemen on the shin.

There isn't much that we dare say—
He grows more like us day by day,

Enjoying, too, the fine dementia
Of the great unintelligentsia!

ERNESTINE MERCER.

"Laugh . . . I thought I'd die . . .

CROCODILE TEARS

Never was a child sedater than the infant alligator,
Nor was there a meaner 'gater,
Than the baby 'gater's pater,
But the baby 'gather's mater was the greater alligator,
'Til the pater 'gater ate 'er.

JOHNNY McKINNEY.

281

"For the benefit of all New Yorkers brought up on the bottle . . . The Bronx Zoo has installed a cow . . . with spark plugs . . . horn and throttle . . .

ODE TO A JERSEY COW

Fragrant cow, on me take pity . . . . .
(I am from the big, big city
Where there dwelleth naught like thou,
Fragrant cow!)

I have bet a crisp new dollar
I could milk you . . . . . Now, don't holler—
Just be brave and patient, mate!
Cooperate!!

As I squeeze your spiggots, honey,
Turn your milk on good and runny—
(Or they'll joke me, long as I live!)—
Sweet cow, GIVE!

Please restrain your tail from wrapping
Round my neck while it is slapping . . . . .
Take your foot from out the pail,
Blonde female!

Noble critter, don't look baleful!
I must get a foaming pailful!
Squirt, cow, squirt! (I'm all a-jitter,
Noble critter!)
       ???!!!???!!!???!!!???!!!
Cow, you're just a four-foot fizzle
With your puny lactic drizzle!
I get sweat from off my brow
Faster than the milk from thou,
Cow!

                    MADELINE SLADE.

But thousands die without or this or that,
Die, and endow a college or a cat.

                    ALEXANDER POPE.

"And after the zoo is all closed for the night ... the keeper makes sure everything is all right ... with blankets and pillows all tucked into place ... and the thirsty young seal ... one last splash in the face ...

SHELTER THE LITTLE ONES

Winter, be very kind;
nature, be good,
and shelter the little ones
living in the wood.

O winter, wherever the snow
falls on the limb,
shelter each soft one there;
feed and warm him.

O winter—the lovely and wise—
wherever they plod,
shelter the small ones, furred
and feathered by God.

JOSEPH JOEL KEITH.

So, naturalists observe, a flea
Has smaller fleas that on him prey;
And these have smaller fleas to bite 'em;
And so proceed *ad infinitum.*

JONATHAN SWIFT.

From a Purely Philosophical Standpoint

" 'In the Spring a young man's fancy' . . .

NURSERY NOTE

Out of the mouths of babes
Great truths are said to come,
Along with cigarette butts,
Lost pins, and last week's gum.

THELMA IRELAND.

"Why, Marion, how could you? Everybody knows it means the lives of a cat!

A STITCH IN TIME SAVES NINE

"A stitch in time saves nine,"
  Grandmother said,
Holding her needle up
  To catch the thread.

Peering at me above
  The quaint steel rim
Of spectacles as bright
  As seraphim,

"A stitch, you know, my dear,
  If done in time,
Will serve as well—or better—
  Than will nine."

"Yes, Ma'am," I'd say politely,
  (As all good children should.)
Nor drop the smallest word to hint
  I had not understood—

"A stitch in time saves nine,"
  She'd say, and tie a knot;
While I, a wriggling question mark,
  Was wondering: Nine what?

MARION DOYLE.

"I've been sitting here half an hour trying to think of something to say about this poem ... still can't seem to find the words ..."

THE TEMPO

The words must go their hasty way,
though conversation strikes no sparks:
what brilliant things we'd think to say
with half an hour between remarks!

KEITH THOMAS.

"One may choose a Colonial mansion ... a thatched cottage ... a castle in Spain ... it doesn't matter ... as long as the roof doesn't leak ..."

HOUSE OF HAPPINESS

Take what God gives, O heart of mine,
   And build your House of Happiness.
Perchance some have been given more,
   But many have been given less.
The treasure lying at your feet,
   Whose value you but faintly guess,
Another builder, looking on,
   Would barter heaven to possess.

Have you found work that you can do?
   Is there a heart that loves you best?
Is there a spot somewhere called home
   Where, spent and worn, your soul may rest?
A book? A tree? A friend that's true?
   A dog that loves your hand's caress?
A store of health to meet life's needs?
   Oh, build your House of Happiness!

Trust not tomorrow's dawn to bring
   The dreamed-of joy for which you wait;
You have enough of pleasant things
   To house your soul in goodly state.
Tomorrow Time's relentless stream
   May bear what you have now away—
Take what God gives, O heart, and build
   Your House of Happiness today!

B. Y. WILLIAMS.

"All you do unto others . . . you'll find due unto you . . ."

LOST LOVE

You cannot hold your love and so you sigh?
You ask a reason? I will tell you why:
Love is a credit, not a debt;
Your love is what you give, not what you get;
You cannot lose true love, when love is true
You do not hold your love, your love holds you!

MARIE MEDORA.

For truth has such a face and such a mein,
As to be loved needs only to be seen.

JOHN DRYDEN.

"Do you suppose it was a purely philosophical gesture then . . . Jill's tumbling after . . . was it merely to save Jack's pride . . . or did the wise lassie come along for the ride?"

JILL

For ages the wisemen have studied strange things,
Including the sphinxes and signets on rings;
But with all of their wisdom, adroitness and skill,
Much more sagacious is Jack's little Jill.

It was she who discovered that love has a salt
Which takes the insipidness out of each fault;
And induces a thirst for an endless brigade
Of cherubs bespeckled with peach marmalade.

She can shatter the broker's esteemed confidence
In landscapes . . . by praising a white picket fence;
And can rival such wealth as from goldmines or mints
By use of pink thumbtacks and clouds of blue chintz.

It might be disputed by Solomon's ghost—
The Quiz Kids, Mr. Gallup, or Emily Post;
But when Jack drops a moon in the Reverend's purse,
Jill becomes sage of the whole universe.

REBA PETERS MATHENY.

" 'Whether 'tis nobler in the mind . . . to suffer the slings and arrows of outrageous fortune, or to take arms against a sea of troubles and by opposing, end them' . . .

AND IF I SAY

And if I say to you, "Now let me die;
It is not sad to end this present life."
I do not mean that I am tired of strife
Or that I fail to thrill to sunset sky.
The sky was dark the day that Paris fell
But Love will rise above such wordly hate.
So, knowing this, I do not curse my fate
Or think my Age a living Hell.
But, having looked abroad, I know my need;
I see the incompleteness of my dream,—
The wished-for goals that are not, merely seem,
Since all my cherished hopes were only greed.
It's for myself and not the world I sigh;
I have not found my place; so let me die.

ALBERT WARNER DOWLING.

I have no other but a woman's reason:
I think him so, because I think him so.

WILLIAM SHAKESPEARE.

"Why not . . . the tailor has to live doesn't he? . . . What would the doctors do, if everybody were well? . . . Pity the policeman in the perfect city . . . Thread your needle, seamstress . . . with a philosophical stitch . . .

GAIN

"A stitch in time,"
   They always warn
Before the thing
   Is even torn—
And yet a heart
   Might be enriched,
Embroidered well
   To hide where stitched!

KATHRYN WRIGHT.

"Shsh-sh-sh!

LET US BE SILENT

Then do not try to think of words, Beloved;
One has not yet been born to meet this moment.
Let us be quiet, holding heartbeats lightly
As on a dry green blade before the coming
Of one inimitable globe of dew
There is no sound to mark a snowflake falling;
Let us be silent as a turning star.

MAUDE BURBANK HARDING.

"Suitable for framing . . .

LIVE TODAY

LIVE TODAY FULLY! It alone,
From all the treasury of time, is yours.
Your yesterdays are like the embers of
Forgotten fires that cannot cheer you now;
And you may never see tomorrow's sun.
Give joyful thanks for dear, familiar things.
Gather transient beauty while you may;
And clasp it to your needy heart today.

RUTH INSCHO.

"A gentleman named Swift once casually remarked . . . 'Vision is the art of seeing things invisible' . . .

CIRCLE OF A TEAR

The polished lens to which we fit
Our eye, to view what distance bars,
Is small in scope, but will permit
The boundless miracle of stars.

But smaller yet and wondrous clear
(And magnifying quite as well)
Is that pale circle of a tear
Through which we look on Heaven or Hell.

JOHN RICHARD MORELAND.

"But isn't the line ... 'Great Scot, perhaps I am!' ..."

RATHER!

I'd rather be
A menace than a hero.
I'd rather be
A fire, than be a Nero.

I'd rather be
A skunk, than be a rabbit.
I'd rather be
A nuisance than a habit.

MARY BUIRGY.

Who harkens to the gods, the gods give ear.

HOMER.

"Tomorrow I think I will try this old fellow's philosophy ... it appeals to me ..."

PROCRASTINATOR

He always said, Tomorrow
I will do thus and so—
Tomorrow ..."

He lived in mediocrity for sixty years,
Self-confident and proud,
Happy in the deeds he would be
When tomorrow came.

One day he reached a feeble hand
From underneath the cover of his bed;
He patted his wife's wet cheek;
He smiled cheerfully and told her,
"Don't worry, Ma. I'll be well—tomorrow."
And he was ... he died.

Teach me your wisdom
Oh wise, wise foolish one!

ADRIAN F. NADER.

"Six and eight are fourteen to a mathematician . . . but to a philosopher . . . almost anything . . ."

COLD AS SNOW

I said that sonnets were too cold, precise
As scales and formal as geometry;
That beauty frozen into blocks of ice
Could never stir the pulse to ecstacy,
But now my thoughts are not so young and small.
They know that beauty, tamed, finds ways to sing
And lines may run and have no grace at all
That might have shone like steel for tempering.
A sonnet has a coldness like the snow,
A mingling of austerity and peace,
And like the snow that blankets Autumn's flow
Of burnished color with its frosty fleece,
It chastens beauty, but it does not kill,
For fire, beneath the cold, is living still!

ALICE MOSER.

He knew what's what, and that's as high
As metaphysic wit can fly.

SAMUEL BUTLER.

" 'Grow old along with me . . . the best is yet to be' . . ."

IF WE HAVE CLIMBED

Oh, have you stood upon the mountain's crest
To watch the sun sink in the west
And noted how it turns gray clouds to gold;
Fills valleys with its glory, fold on fold;
Drapes distant, somber peaks with veils of rose
Before they fade to darkness and repose?

So it can be with us, ere comes the night,
If we have climbed life's steep paths to the height
Where we can let the spirit rest and know
That God will touch our souls with afterglow.

EDITH TATUM.

" 'Let me live in a house by the side of the road ... without the rest ...

MAN THINKS MORE OF HIS HEART

Man thinks more of his heart than of anything else—
More than of earth and sky, or the sleep of September,
The sensuous whirl of the silken and slumberous waltz,
Voices that plead and sing, or the cool and limber
Boughs of the maple. Man cannot bear to miss
The music of the summer; but he stands
Safe in the doorway of his heart's dark house
To count the stars and listen to the winds.

And, while the winter calls, he is content
To read beside a fire of his own making
Deep in the inmost room till it is spent.
And, when the house grows chill, he rises, liking
To pause at last with poems in his head,
And, closing his book, go decently to bed.

JAMES E. WARREN, JR.

"I know a lady who kept a small bundle of letters ... tied in blue ribbon ... On her sixtieth birthday her granddaughter found them ... and read them ... She asked, "Granny, who was Paul?' But Granny couldn't remember his last name!

We put our souls into the things called things,
The fashioned wood and fabric to our use,
That through the years have heard our inmost muse,
Our secret weeping and the voice that sings.
A thought forgotten long ago still clings
To the worn broidery that can not lose
The fingers' touch. The drawer that keeps the news
Of love's first coming holds our spirit-wings.

The key-closed drawer that holds love's tidings dear,
That keeps the very words as does my heart,
It too my heart's own tenderness must prove.
I feel it in soft silence, hark to hear
The sweet, incessant murmur that may start
But never end: I love you—love you—love ....

LULU W. CHITTENDEN.

"Inexperience is the best preacher ... unless the church is empty ..."

LIP WISDOM

When I was one and twenty,
   Concerned with much undone,
I criticized aplenty
   The ways of everyone.

I cried of change and nettled
   My kin with verbal storms;
And, in my mind, I settled
   The world with my reforms.

But folks went un unheeding ....
   At thirty, I could see
The change the world was needing
   Began, somehow, with me.

JANE SAYRE.

"The whole is equal to the sum of its parts ..."

LIFE'S SYMPHONY

"O Master, I would play the violin!
Pray try me! I am really not unskilled!"
The master with a patient gesture stilled
The ardent voice. "The music must begin—
Seest thou for violins I have no need.
Back to the wood-winds; take thine own bassoon
And play thy part." The strings were all in tune,
The brasses ready. Still the voice did plead
"O Master, I play only three short bars!"
"Thou playest the bassoon well—no more entreat—
Thy three short bars are needed to complete
The music that shall lift men to the stars!"

O Soul, play well the few notes given thee—
The Master needs them for Life's Symphony.

B. Y. WILLIAMS.

"December 6, 1941 . . .

SLEEP WELL

Sleep well, dear heart,
I will withhold the sorrow,
So you may better bear it
On tomorrow.

Dream happy dreams,
For at the coming dawn
You'll wake to find
All dreams have gone.

NELLIE S. RICHARDSON.

Even the worthy Homer sometimes nods.

HORACE.

"But in spite of it all . . . 'The play's the thing' . . .

FOOTNOTE TO SHAKESPEARE

All the world's a stage, etc.
But when the hero or the heroine walks out and leaves the cast,
The play goes on. Always, the play goes on.
Sometimes they find a new hero or a new heroine;
Or the villain takes the hero's part
Or they get along without a hero or a heroine;
The cast can always improvise.
Sometimes the costumes are torn and draggled
And there is no time for repairs between performances.
Sometimes they have the wrong props, or no props at all
And the wrong scenery, and no curtains;
Only a bare floor and a bare wall.
Sometimes the heat is off, and the call for lights
Unheeded. So they stumble through it some way
In the dark. Perhaps the ending
Isn't always as snappy as the playwright's version,
But it's just as final.

HELEN PEAVY WASHBURN.

"Dedicated to a man in service I knew ... and to a little girl in Texas who went upstairs to bed in the dark for the very first time ... and to you at the dentist's ...

COURAGE

Courage is armor
A blind man wears;
The calloused scar
Of outlived despairs:
Courage is Fear
That has said its prayers.

KARLE WILSON BAKER.

"There was a man once in Sing Sing ... who liked philosophy ... the last night he was there he said he was a philosopher ... but in the morning ... he wasn't ...

JUST FOR TODAY

Just for today, O heart of mine, be brave—
  The passing day is such a little while,
Your courage surely can endure so long!
  Perhaps tomorrow at your fears you'll smile.
    Just for today be brave.

Just for today, O heart of mine, be true,
  True to the things that you have counted best.
The heart that lives its high ideals today
  Can hardly fail to meet tomorrow's test!
    Just for today be true.

Just for today, O heart of mine, be glad—
  Be good to live with; smile; put by your care;
Love life and friends and joy. If there's a cloud
  Still trust tomorrow's skies to be more fair.
    Just for today be glad.

Just for today, O heart of mine, be kind—
  Have patience, nor refuse the helping hand;
Forbear to judge your brother's error now;
  Tomorrow you may better understand.
    Just for today be kind.

B. Y. WILLIAMS.

"Maybe it wasn't the pipers who were pied ... the rats ..."

INCIDENTAL EXPENSE

How many pipers must I pay
To cancel off the score?
A dozen now have sent their bills.
Dear heaven are there more?
How many pipers played the tune
To which we had our dance?
I think a wood-wind orchestra
Accompanied our romance!

GEORGIE STARBUCK GALBRAITH.

"But Central Park is full of signs shouting hoarsely ... 'Keep Off the Grass' ..."

POSSESSION

I own these lands,
And yonder hill and valley
Know that they are mine ...
For did I not as late as yesterday
Brand paths with foot-pressed signs,
And touch, with ceremonious hands,
The rock and pine!

These wide-spread fields
Leapt into life
From seeds I scattered in the Spring.
For their rich yields
I gave as price
A sinewy offering.

The cricket and the bird I claim ...
For every sound or song that's heard
On ground or tree in my domain
Belongs to me.

MILDRED CARTWRIGHT JOBSON.

" 'Man shall not live by bread alone' ..."

THE DREAM-BEARER

Where weary folk toil, black with smoke,
   And hear but whistles scream,
I went, all fresh from dawn and dew,
   To carry them a dream.

I went to bitter lanes and dark,
   Who once had known the sky,
To carry them a dream—and found
   They had more dreams than I.

MARY CAROLYN DAVIES.

" 'Man proposes ... God disposes' ..."

CYNICISMS

Man is a slave, a chattel,
   A dupe, and a siren's tool,
Man is the kin of cattle
   With the earmarks of the mule.

Love is a trap, a trouble,
   The gist of a liar's joke,
Love is, at best, a bubble,
   Or a squealing pig in a poke.

Life is a scourge, a sorrow,
   The butt of a jester's wit,
A futile and frail tomorrow,
   With death at the end of it.

But I who am slave and chattel,
   And I who am named for death
Shall trumpet and bray and prattle
   Their worth till my dying breath.

FAYE CHILCOTE WALKER.

"Some people study philosophy . . . some teach it . . . some talk it . . . some try it . . . but only once in a while do you find one of those rare souls who live it . . ."

MY SECRET

I lie propped snugly in my poster bed
And watch my quiet company come and go.
I smile indulgently at what they say,
"You'll soon be up and well again, we know."
Meaningless phrases, all meant well,
Every last one thinking, as his eyelids fill,
"Poor soul, knowing that she'll never walk again,"
With only me knowing that I will.

ELIZABETH S. KUNKLE.

"When the lion shall lie down with the lamb' . . .

TIGERS WITHOUT MERCY LEAP

Tigers without mercy leap,
But not upon their own asleep.
The sharp-winged falcons plunge like rock,
But not upon the falcon flock.
Alone of all the things on earth
Man torments his own from birth.

As a steel shark beneath the deep,
As a steel hawk across the sky,
Man's enemy, the heroes sweep—
Loud for blood the sages cry:
Dread the faggot-bearing mob,
Dread the martyr in his pride—
Dread the great demand of love
(Dread the fire of love denied).
Alone of all the things on earth
Man torments his own from birth.

TOM BOGGS.

"Anticipation is often more satisfactory than realization . . . and much easier, too . . ."

AUTOBIOGRAPHY

From poverty
I fashioned wealth,
In gnawing pain
I wrote of health.

My very lack
Became a store
To borrow from—
And not deplore

With courage
For accompanist,
I sang the beauty
I had missed.

LOUISE CRENSHAW RAY.

" 'Let not the marriage of true minds admit impediment . . .'

WINDOW WASHING

Today we two wash windows, he without
Upon a ladder and myself within,
Facing him through the pane. With friendly shout,
He points to where my cheesecloth has not been,
And I point back where he has left a blur,
Till bright between us gleams the spotless pane.
Then suddenly I turn philosopher,
Thinking: This is the way two hearts maintain
The long-unblemished vision, eye to eye—
The willingness of each to see the cloud
Upon his side, to clear and rectify
That film which forms for love the fatal shroud.
Today we two wash windows till they shine,
Till not one blur deflects his eyes from mine!

ISABELLE BRYANS LONGFELLOW.

"For whose philosophy is so strong . . . that he would hunt the whole night long, for just a sliver . . . for his quiver . . .

HOW WOULD YOU HANDLE IT

If you shoot an arrow into the air,
And it falls to earth you know not where,
There's not much left to do but swear.

JOE A. NOBLE.

"Some philosophies have a most casual introduction . . . and an interesting progression . . . and a climax . . . Well, here is an example . . . and a powerful one . . .

CONQUEROR

Once upon a time
A green cell became lazy
And so—
Instead of using its chlorophyl
To manufacture starch
From sunshine and water
(A tedious process, I assure you)
It ate another cell.

Thus was born,
All unheralded by newspapermen,
The shorter working day
Dependent upon
A carnivorous society
Which at present
Has so advanced
That certain nations attempt
To devour other nations,
Hoping ultimately to achieve
For the "chosen races"
An even shorter working day
Than the first lazy cell enjoyed—
Until eaten by
An unprincipled neighbor—
The copycat!

ADRIAN F. NADER.

*"A man named Lindsay saw Abraham Lincoln a few years ago . . .
'It is portentous and a thing of state . . . that here at midnight . . .
in our little town . . . a mourning figure walks . . . and will not rest . . .
near the old courthouse . . . pacing up and down . . .'*

LINES FOR A DEAD LIBERAL

Now that he stands upon a steeper hill
Than any mountain he has ever trod,
Even as he stands face to face with God
His heart is heavy with our human ill,
His great heart broods upon the mystery still
Of bruitish fears that grind man to the clod,
Of greed that breaks his back, the savage rod
That mutilates the mind it cannot kill.

As long as men are hounded by stark hate,
He cannot rest; as long as men deny
The stars and bread, he grapples with grim fate;
As long as women weep and children cry,
Attorney for the inarticulate,
He is our trumpet to eternity.

JOSEPH AUSLANDER.

"And forget?

HOW WE FORGIVE THE OLD IMMENSITIES

How we forgive the old Immensities
The wrongs they heap upon us! We forget
Their vast transgressions, cherish them as though,
Our creditors, they held us in their debt.

The Earth . . . what have we not forgiven Earth?
She has repaid our faithful reverence
With famine, earthquake, drought, and burning heat,
With freezing cold and endless pestilence.
But yet we have acquitted her of these
Because of . . . April nights and lilac trees.

And we have pardoned Love for broken vows,
For shattered hopes, and pleas that fail their mark,
Because . . . we can remember having felt
Warm hands stretched out to ours across the dark.

And Man . . . with what forbearance have we seen
His cruelties and killings which defile
The name he bears! And why? Well, one of us
Has chanced to see a toothless baby smile;
And one of us recalls he has a mother;
And each of us, among the hosts of men,
Has sometime claimed some other man for brother.

For wanton tricks and baleful knaveries
How we forgive the old Immensities!
For that we may have courage left to live,
We take their little bribes and . . . we forgive.
GEORGIE STARBUCK GALBRAITH.

"It is the grand paradox that while a straight line is the shortest distance . . . it is not at all . . . because there is no end to an infinitely straight line . . .

CREDO OF UNREST

Something in me feels
That half a fulfillment is better than the whole.
In this geometry of living,
I choose the arc, and I fear the circle . . .
The lust for life unsated remains a lust,
The pinnacle unscaled remains a height desired,
And landmarks are fairer than destinations . . .
My heart is not a trophy room for old glories
But a camp beside the roadside
Of new high hopes, the quest unfinished,
And the endless, resistless urge of the Almost.
LOLLY WILLIAMS.

The Mystery Deepens

"The most blood-chilling element . . . in any mystery . . . is suspense . . .

THE LONGEST HOUR

"Be good enough to wait below,"
The doctor brushed me as he hurried by.
"There's nothing you can do, you know . . ."
Nothing but wait down there while you might die.

The autumn sun, already cool,
Cast purple shadows in the darkening hall;
Your battered hat hung tipsy on the newel,
And, thrown upon the table by the wall,
Your old tweed coat lay, with its smell
Of earth, and burning leaves, and rainy walks—
The odor that brought back the spell
Of all our days together and the talks
We used to have before the fire at night.
The shadows deepened. I could scarcely see
My way back to the hall to lay my head
Against your coat and wait there in the gloom,
That long, still hour. At last the doctor said
I might come up. I stumbled to your room.

"I told you I was tough." A laugh caught in your throat.
Your hand found mine. I could not say the things I should.
"It was so lonely down there by your coat—"
A foolish thing to say, and yet you understood.

ELIZABETH GREY STEWART.

"All the time I was thinking about the little boy . . . but the villain was her husband . . .

FIRST LOVE

He scrubbed his ears this morning,
The old shirt would not do,
He combed his hair full half an hour
And stopped to tie his shoe.

We could not understand it—
This quite mysterious change
But when we saw them up the street
I did not think it strange—

For there she walked beside him,
He carried all her books.
The mystery had been revealed,
'Twas she who changed his looks!

His father seems bewildered
But tries to understand—
(I fear he has forgotten
That he used to hold my hand.)

LAUFA M. LOCKWOOD.

"Spilt milk . . .

WE HAVE WEPT

Oh, we have wept together,
Guinivere and I.
Her man wore mail of metal,
Mine a striped tie.
Centuries between us,
Arthurs lived and died.
But, this we have in common:
We both have loved and cried.

We have wept together,
Guinivere and I,
For love that shook our being,
And wrung our spirits dry.
Sisters in our sadness,
Kin in sorrow's sigh.
We have wept together,
Guinivere and I.

MARY-SCOTT WILLOUR.

"This is surely a mystery all right . . . Now, who will solve it?

AND WHAT THEN

Beware the stuff that's made of sun and shadows—
Remember once another lonely god
Took dust and dreamed a dream and breathed upon it
But never wholly captured it from sod,
Always the dream he dreamed returned to nothing—
Always he must create anew . . . Beware!
Your shadow-dreams may walk out from their shadows
To melt again and leave you lonely there.
Always the substance of the shadow passes,
The sun goes down and leaves a silvered trail;
Only the memory of a dream is constant,
The substance of a dream is far too frail.
The world is peopled with the ghosts of dream-kin . . .
Nothing is real except the vain desire
To reach out into air and pluck a shadow
As capable as you of feeling fire.
But always as we touch the cherished image,
Within our very hands it disappears—
Unless one has the courage of the first God
He quenches his own fire with his own tears.
Unless you have the courage to dream over
And over once again and yet again,
Beware the stuff that's made of sun and shadows,
For you will surely lose it—and what then?

GRACE PHILLIPS.

"Who murdered that sweet old song . . . in four parts . . .

MALE QUARTETTE

The funniest men I've seen as yet
Are the ones that sing in a male quartette—
Perhaps the music synchronizes
Better in assorted sizes.

PAULINE STARKWEATHER.

"There isn't one single clue to this mystery . . . and I am not at all sure the author has any right to her conclusion . . . There is no iota of proof . . .

RIDDLE FOR THE PRACTICAL MAN

A frivolous fluff of filmy nothingness
Provocatively perched upon your hair;
Mysteriously defying gravitation;
Beyond the scope of male imagination;
Decidedly a feminine affair;
Flirtatious, but assertive, none the less;

A puff of nonsense, lighter than a feather,
A cloud of mist, like breath in frosty weather.

Come now!
    Is that
    A hat?

SARAH LEEDS ASH.

There was an awful rainbow once in heaven;
We know her woof, her texture; she is given
In the dull catalogue of common things.
Philosophy will clip an angel's wings.

JOHN KEATS.

"And the body was found . . . all cut up in one-hundred-pound pieces . . . and stuffed into a closet . . .

A DILEMMA

The elephant took his vacuum cleaner
And swept up peanuts out of my hand.
A handy gadget he'd be, if leaner
To rid apartments of dust and sand.
He'd sweep the carpets in manner stately
And not use any electric juice,
But one small item concerns me greatly,
WHERE WOULD I STORE HIM WHEN NOT IN USE?

CATHARINE WILLIAMS.

" 'Elementary . . . my dear Watson' . . .

PERSPECTIVES

The laws of optics don't explain
   Why fruit atop the tree
Looms larger, fairer to the sight
   Than what is hard alee;

Nor why a salesgirl—save for some
   Whose tact is superhuman—
Can always spot a distant man
   Before a present woman!

                               ERNESTINE MERCER.

I feel my sinews slacken with the fright,
And a cold sweat thrills down o'er all my limbs,
As if I were dissolving into water.

                               JOHN DRYDEN.

"Junior Miss-tery . . .

LARGE SIGHS

What happens to the gals who wear a twenty
   When dresses all are twelves?
For cute tricks there are coverings a-plenty.
   For poppets, pigmies, elves.

They say that Cleopatra once was rolled
   In rugs, to call on Caesar;
Perhaps she shopped where only tens were sold—
   It took eighteen to please 'er

So bring a tent, a toga at my call.
   Or else find standing there
A daughter of the gods, divinely tall
   And most divinely bare.

                               ERNESTINE MERCER.

"There is a mystery ... even behind rich, yellow, clotted cream ... You try to figure it out next time you skim cream ... while the clot thickens ..."

WHY COWS FEED ONE WAY

I wonder if all you can say
Why cows at pasture feed one way.
They always do. Don't trust just me—
Go up to the pasture bars and see.
Every last sleek heifer's daughter
Crops the grass, her mouth a-water,
The same direction as her friends.
There must be some good law that tends
To such matters, for cows at feasts
Are most law-abiding of all beasts.

My theory is that it is smell:
Look at the cows, and you can tell
What way the wind is, without fail.
A well-conducted cow's long tail
Hangs to leeward of each breeze.
A cow smells daisies rather than sees
What is going to be sleek cow,
Not daisies, ten short minutes from now,
And so she eats her dinner twice.
I think my theory cuts most ice.

There is a fairly largish school
Who bar cows from the Golden Rule.
They hold that cows feed that position
Purely out of competition.
They say there is no natural need
To feed one way; it is sheer greed—
Each cows thinks each sees clovers fatter
And has her eye on something better.
And so falls into the sin of sheep.
But I think cows are much too deep.

ROBERT P. TRISTRAM COFFIN.

"*Whodunnit? . . .*

SONNET

So you declare your love, yet here I stand,
  Helpless against the worship in your eyes,
Eager to comfort you with little lies,
  I cannot even take you by the hand,
Because it would be wantonly unwise,
  To let your dream of love take shape and rise,
Only to die upon the cold gray sand
  Of disillusion in some desolate land.

And what is love so pitiless and cold,
  That you should fashion all your dreams in me?
And who am I whose heart too soon is old
  Because I sorrow for lost ecstasy?
So we stand spellbound looking down the years,
  Too lonely to find solace in our tears!

CAROL SCOTT.

Like one that on a lonesome road
Doth walk in fear and dread,
And having once turned round, walks on,
And turns no more his head;
Because he knows a frightful fiend
Doth close behind him tread.

SAMUEL TAYLOR COLERIDGE.

"*The place is haunted . . . with everything she wanted . . .*

MIDNIGHT IN AN EMPTY HOUSE

Strange voices and old music
Climbed the wall . . .
The world was white with silence
And all creatures unheard of
Crept the unearthly stair.
I woke . . .
You were not there!

JULIA B. COHAN.

"A problem for the Bureau of Missing Persons . . .

TO YOU

At times you seem so tangible, though you
Are but a dream, a quaint composite wrought
Of one child's laugh, another's hair, the blue
Of some small neighbor's eyes, an image caught
And lost again.   Still, since there is a place
Where souls shall meet, perhaps, too, God will give
A bit of room within the azure space
Of heaven to the little dreams that live,
Throughout the meager years, a vital part
Of every childless woman's wistful heart.

DOROTHY P. ALBAUGH.

My soul is full of whispered song—
  My blindness is my sight;
The shadows that I feared so long
  Are full of life and light.

ALICE CARY.

"The night was so black . . . that you couldn't see your hand before your face . . . and, suddenly . . .

A BLIND GIRL SPEAKS

I would not have you always pity me,
Nor think of me as being only blind.
'Tis true I walk in darkness, but I see
Such beauty that I do not wholly mind;
Such joy in rains, such joy in dewy flowers,
And pure content from seeing with my hands.
There is an understanding in the hours
That only one in darkness understands.
In rooms alone I do not ever dread;
It is as if God, too, were in my home
Of walls, with loving arms so gently spread
To guard me from the little fears that come.
I have the wind, the songs of wren and lark,
And I have learned from listening in the dark.

HELEN LOOMIS LINHAM.

"There was a ghost ship once . . . that sailormen called 'The Flying Dutchman' . . . a ship doomed never to reach port . . . but to sail on and on . . . and on . . . forever . . .

TO A WRECKED AUTOMOBILE

A ghost of laughter floats above the hill;
A phantom of gay talk rides on the wind;
A snatch of silver song hangs, echo-thinned;
These prove that once they lived, who now are still.
What treacherous honor, ill-timed pride in skill . . .
What misspent courage on a vain course pinned . . .
What dangerous love of speed . . . what demons grinned . . .
And lured them here to rob them, maim them,
A father's shining hope . . . a mother's care . . .
A stalwart young man's strong and lissome grace,
A sweetheart's promise of a life to share . . .
The unfilled beauty of a girlish face,
A joyous song of love, an answered prayer
Lie in this twisted tin . . . this roadside place.

ALICE MORREY BAILEY.

"At the trial . . . I kept wondering . . . about the feelings of the big, stolid cop who had been first at the scene of the crime . . . and about the judge . . . who seemed so bored . . . so remote . . .

SURVIVORS

What does the great whale think
In his ocean lane,
Seeing the ships that sink
To the dark domain . . .

These are his ancient foes
Pursuing each other . . .
Mounting the crest, he blows
To the moon, his brother.

SAMUEL SCHIERLOH.

"Sometimes I think the best mystery stories are those in which you cannot really guess the solution . . . but in which the clues make you suspect . . . that the solution will be . . . tremendous . . .

GIFTS

O, time, when your swift hours of toil are spun,
My homing heart turns to its dwelling-place,
And as the gate clicks, in the window space
Is framed my glad and golden-hearted one
Who peers into the night so chill and dun.
I turn the key and swift with childish grace
He runs to me, lifting a joy-lit face,
And cries, "What have you brought your little son?"
O sweet expectancy, O dear suprise!
Within the house of years I watch and wait;
Night's golden gondola skims western skies,
And soon a hand will fumble at life's gate,
And I impatient, call with eager breath,
"Come in," and then . . . "What have you brought me, Death?"

JOHN RICHARD MORELAND.

Is there beyond the silent night
  An endless day?
Is death a door that leads to light?
  We cannot say.

ROBERT GREEN INGERSOLL.

"And then there is the greatest mystery of all . . . 'O grave, where is thy victory . . . Death, where is thy sting' . . .

GOING AWAY

Death doesn't scare me . . . when I die
God will look down some place up, high,
And say: "You liked lilacs, didn't you?
Apple-wood fires, you see I knew:

"Wild plum trees on a very green lawn,
Very blue windows to hold the dawn!
I have such a house . . . and I want you to see
What the wind has done to my cherry tree!"

HELEN WELSHIMER.

"People who are used to mysteries know . . . that the answer which seems impossible, beyond suspicion . . . is often the right one . . .

WHERE DOES LAUGHTER GO?

Do they allow laughter in heaven?
Not polite laughter, walking on tip-toes,
Tripping out of corners, a dainty child,
Leaving behind the petals of a rose.

I mean the noisy laughter, loud and shrill,
Striding upon its heels, from place to place,
The giggly kind, that rises to a shriek,
Then looks around the room and hides its face.

I fear their lack of dignity would mar
The cool, white halls of heaven, and if so,
(Since laughter has no place in hell), then where
Will yours and mine and others have to go?

ELVA A. SMITH.

"Where were you . . . on the night of June 13th . . . my small one? . . .

SMALL ROOM

This little room was always full of song,
And laughter rang within it all day long.
Here was the haven of the smallest one,
Herself a shining fragment of the sun.
Within its walls, amid its sweet confusion,
She and her toys found refuge and seclusion.
So full of life, tight-braided pigtails flying,
She flaunted tidiness without half-trying—
Her petticoat a circle on the floor,
A foolish sun hat tossed behind a door,
A shoe without a mate upon a chair,
A tangle of bright ribbons for her hair,
Sometimes, nose pressed against the window pane,
She marveled at the silver of the rain,
Or, having seen the flowers come and go,

Cried out with ecstasy to see the snow.
Such memories leave little space for tears
As days march after days, years after years.
The warm spring rain again slants toward the hill;
The little room is orderly and still.

      DOROTHY ASHBY POWNALL.

  Ere sin could blight or sorrow fade,
   Death came with friendly care;
  The opening bud to heaven conveyed,
   And bade it blossom there.

     SAMUEL TAYLOR COLERIDGE.

"Cherchez . . . La Femme . . .

THE MOTHER OF AN ANGEL SPEAKS

I think I'll go to Heaven when I die,
 Just for a little while;
I may not remain long, but just enough
 To see my God's kind smile.
I'll seat myself outside the Golden Gate
 Upon the star-wet grass,
And I shall watch for Mary day and night
 Until I see her pass.
And when I do, I'll call her softly, so:
 "Mother!" (One word will do.)
And when she turns, I'll say in a low tone:
 "Please, may I speak to you,
I have not called Saint Peter, being a man,
 He might not understand.
But you, being a mother, will not scorn
 To take me by the hand.
Please, lead me into Heaven for a while—
 One small gold hour, just one,
That I may see my Angel baby safe
 Near to your Son . . ."

     ROSA ZAGNONI MARINONI.

"This is a mystery . . . dating back to the Civil War . . . back to the shadows of Libby Prison . . . and men are still trying to discover . . . why Thaddeus had to die . . .

FOOTPRINTS

Through the bleak years she kept them there—
Little black footprints on the stair.
Thaddeus, last of her little ones,
Bold with the knowledge that youngest sons
Do no wrong in a mother's sight,
Thaddeus stepped in new paint one night,
And wilfully marked the steep stairway.
There were the prints, long after the day
That Thaddeus died in Libby's grim
Prison of hate. She spoke of him
Always as though he were still alive
And close to her as the other five.
Thaddeus, just the dimming track
Of those small scuffed boots could bring him back,
Far more real than the pictured form
Of a tall, gaunt man in a uniform.
Footprints climbing a narrow stair,
And Thaddeus just ahead—somewhere.

Dorothy P. Albaugh.

"A mystery solved . . . by the process of deduction . . .

AWAKENING

Gentle and sweet, I'm sure, was her awakening.
I hope she did not feel too great surprise.
I wonder if she knew how long, how long I waited
For her to open once again her eyes.

She had been smiling with a tender laughter,
Our tiny son—"His darling little head,"
Her hand in mine, it seemed my love must hold her—
"I think—I'll sleep—a little while," she said.

Sometimes I think I hear her laughter, sweeter
Among the bird notes of a golden morn.
I know the angels have found life completer,
Since she awoke, new-born.

ETHEL B. CHENEY.

"The denouement to end all denouements . . .

CHILDREN OF EARTH

Space was their coverlet,
Time was their bed,
Years were their pillows
(Not soft, they said).

Life was their slumber,
Dreams were their breath,
Then—the surprising thing!—
Waking was death.

JEANNETTE SEWELL DAVIS.

" 'What are the wild waves saying' . . . What is the answer beached in foam . . . What, I always ask, in praying . . . is the mystery of home . . .

RETURNING

Hang out the moon on a silver string—
The moon with a turned-up-corner smile!
Polish the curving crescent! Swing
The golden lantern! The last long mile
Of his journey home must be full of shine
And expectant joy—and remembering!
Hang the big dipper over the pine!
Let the stars blossom; let them sing
Over his head as he hurries home
Through the wistful and all-fragrant spring!

White be the clouds and the lifting foam
On the jagged rocks where the waters fling
Their turbulent greetings to the shore!

Set all the high hills echoing
Softly to melodies heard before!
Bring all the boughs to their blossoming;
Circle the clouds with a rainbow ring;
Call on the birds for a wild, glad cry!
Stir all the leaves to a whispering
Song of the soul as he passes by!

      ETHEL BRADLEY MEYER.

"The only clue is in a letter she wrote once . . . 'I'll never leave you, darling' . . . and she always keeps her word . . .

LAUGHTER—AFTER

I'll be back before you know it, dear—
O, even before you know I've gone—
And together we'll laugh in the dark, we two,
At the way I've got my halo on!

And because you love to touch my gowns
And always finger the silken things,
I'll willingly bend to your eager hand,
Loving your touch on my stylish wings.

Ah don't, my dearest! Show me your smile,
And give me your word that you will try
To mange a grin—a "really" grin—
At the funny, peculiar way I fly,

And laugh out loud if a bit of cloud
Should catch on your dark and somber tie,
And solemnly tell the laundress that
It must be heavenly lipstick dye.

O, we shall have fun, my darling one,
No sorrowing loss, no elegy;
Before you know it, the same dear you
Will have a lovelier, brand-new me.

      LOLITA L. GILPIN.

"He would have been there that night . . . like the other suspects . . . but he had a perfect alibi . . ."

DEATH IS THE DREAM

Death is the day I cannot see your face,
Nor take your arm, nor walk along with you,
Nor ever, looking in your eyes, may trace
The little warm emotions passing through.
Death is the loneliness of your lost touch
In all the places of our dearest speaking.
It is the prophecy of losing much
In flesh's comfort and in music's seeking.

Death is the dream of how we stood and talked
On much-loved corners of remembered streets
Or some park angle where I often walked,
And death will be the verse that gently treats
Of how sleep came at last with cool caress
And smoothed our hearts into forgetfulness.

JAMES E. WARREN, JR.

"'Ah . . . sweet mystery of life' . . ."

PLEDGE

When that day comes when I shall sit and drowse
   Before a dreaming fire, and stir, and nod,
Winking at death—call me, and I shall rouse,
   Pierced by that sound as by a glance from God;
Or if some ghost of you be passing near,
   Having in memory what this day has done,
Come close and touch me then, and you shall hear
   My heart's last words, "Good-night, my lovely one."

DOROTHY KISSLING.

"'Wherefore art thou, Romeo?' . . ."

AS SWIFT SEASONS ROLL

Your features fade in cumulous mists of years,
Your voice no longer stills nor wakes my heart:
No subtle phrase disturbs, nor yet endears
Responses checked with sophomoric art.

Though enchantment of those days delights me still—
A proud aloofness is my secret boast:
New dreams and deeds have challenged me until
You have become a satisfactory ghost!

GRACE D. LECKLITER.

"Presto ... chango ... I can't figure it out ... but they say ... that it's sometimes done ... with mirrors ...

PAGAN

You may bind my hair with ribbon
Or flowers, but do not weep.
You may dress me in a gown of blue—
When I take my final sleep.
You may even pray a little,
(But do not pray too long)
For as soon as I lay me down to sleep
I'll turn into a song

HAZEL E. MELAMEDE.

"Fingerprints on a heart ... are not evidence for experts ... but experts don't know all the answers ...

MY HEART WILL KNOW

When I am dead, and over me
The cool night wind is blowing,
Touching with soft fingers
The grasses growing there—
I shall nestle closely in my bed
So long and narrow,
Dreaming that your fingers
Have touched my loosened hair.

When lilac trees spill fragrance
In the rain-sweet April morning,
And trail their heavy blossoms
Where I slumber quietly—

I shall feel their scented breath
Upon my throat and eyelids,
And dream that in my long sleep
You are lying close to me.

When I have rested years on years
Within the dear earth's dampness,
When in your heart I have become
A dream of long ago—
Stoop softly by my gravestone
And whisper that you love me,
And though your voice I cannot hear
My listening heart will know.

MABEL NEWMAN.

Right as an aspen leaf she gan to quake.
GEOFFREY CHAUCER.

"It was midnight by the library clock . . . the doors and windows were shut tight . . . but the hangings in the doorway stirred . . . as if there were a little wind . . .

RETURN

Over and over, around and around,
She circled the house without a sound.

The watch-dog that patrolled the dark
Let her pass with never a bark;
Her stabled pony shied, and then
Snuffed at his scattered oats again.

A well-remembered creak was still
As she eagerly passed the wide door-sill
And saw the cat's unwinking gaze
Welcome her back without amaze.

Flopping his tail, the terrier fat
Stretched at ease on his fireside mat;
Her bird, as she neared on soundless feet,
Fluttering begged for its wonted sweet;

And old, familiar, friendly things,
Breathing the comfort that custom brings,
Wrapped her close in their silent spell;
"Home!" she whispered, "All must be well!"

But the human heart she had held most dear
Never knew she was bending near,
Never heard as she wildly wept,
Never woke but, untroubled, slept.

"Oh," she sobbed as she turned and fled,
"Now I know I am really dead!"

MARY COLES CARRINGTON.

St. Agnes' Eve—Ah, bitter chill it was!
The owl, for all his feathers, was a-cold.

JOHN KEATS.

"I don't know who it was ... but I think ... perhaps ... it was somebody I had seen before ... somewhere ...

ALL-SAINTS' EVE

Look!...   There, beyond the window-pane!
Through the withered and rattling vine!
A wee face spangled with silver rain,
Lovely and wan, stares in at mine!

White as a shell upon the sands
Where the black billows break and pass,
Something is pressing tiny hands
Against the barrier of the glass.

Something eerie and fey and pale
Is peering in from the haunted night,
At our small room snug from the angry gale
Where faces glow in the firelight.

Slant, strange eyes under sea-green hair
Look wistfully in through the window-pane....
Quick!...   Open the casement!... What is there
That cries in the wind and the streaming rain?

It has gone, it has gone—there is nothing there
Blown by the storm to our window-pane!
Only the night and the chill sea-air,
And the voice of the sorrowful rain.

LEAH BODINE DRAKE.

"From the world's best-selling Book of Mysteries . . . 'What is a man profited, if he shall gain the whole world and lose his own soul?' . . .

BROOKLYN BRIDGE ON A FOGGY NIGHT

Here where the sordid streets becomes a maze,
Time seems to end. A cloud of fog comes drifting
Like incense from an altar. Dampness sprays
The blackened shadows night has spread, and shifting
Mist obscures the proud expanse of arch.
Beyond the fog, a Dark Unknown.
But corridors of night still feel the march
Of towering cities linked by steel and stone.
Men know the dreams, both drudge and artisan,
That count not lengthening years they toil and plod.
Man does not build a monumental span
To lead to Nothing . . . Nor does God!

MARTHA LYMAN SHILLITO.

"So few people know the second verse that answers one oft-repeated question . . . that it is really a mystery too: . . . 'Who is Sylvia? . . . What is she?' . . .

OMNIA VINCIT AMOR

Farspent, my dust may blow along
The thundering centuries, and Song
May gather what is left of you
And gently blend the best of two
Who dreamed and met with dreams' defeat;
Thus it may be we yet shall meet,
Not lip to lip, not heart to heart
As lovers meet and grieve and part—

I cannot tell you when nor how,
Perhaps a thousand years from now
Some singer's sensing heart and brain
May hear and voice our lost refrain:
Invincible we still may be,
In deathless song our victory!

FRANCES ELEANORE SCHLUNEGER.

Why is this thus? What is the reason of this thusness?

ARTEMUS WARD.

"It was dark as midnight . . . I couldn't see anything . . . I couldn't hear anything . . . but . . . somehow I knew . . . that . . . something . . . was standing beside me . . .

RETURN TO SOMERSET FARM

There are spots that a ghost would as soon forget,
   And paths that his feet would spurn,
But when April is greening at Somerset
   I shall know—and I shall return.

And ever at golding of daffodil,
   Be the season early or late,
They shall hear my whistle beside the hill,
   My hand on the pasture gate.

The sumach will stir by the dairy door,
   The trout will leap by the falls,
The horses stamp on the stable floor
   Whinnying in their stalls.

And men will whisper, turning their heads
   To peer down the meadow track,
"It's time to be spading the garden beds—
   The ghost of Richard is back."

KATHARINE BURT.

"Sometimes ghosts come clothed in living flesh . . .

MISS AGATHA SEES A GHOST

There underneath the elms, the small white house
my father had described time out of mind
stood in the drip of April rain.
The shabby path was lined
with boxwood tangled deep in matted grass,
and lilac twigs tapped weirdly on the pane.
An elfin air possessed the wayward eaves—
all seemed as legendary as last year's leaves,
as lost to human meaning. But a thin
wisp of domestic smoke rose from the red
stack of one tottery chimney in the ell.
I would have thought to find a witch within
mumbling an incantation by the hearth,
brewing some spell,
and a black cat with slanting eyes of jade
stalking the kitchen slowly back and forth.

When I had asked the road, a villager said,
"The Simmons place? First turn, then straight ahead . . .
a couple of miles or so;
family's all gone, I don't know where.
Some crazy spinster that they used to know—
an old Miss Agatha is living there;
no means for rent, so they just let her stay—
nobody else would live there, anyway."
She opened when I rapped the knocker . . . . "Well! . . . .
It's Lemuel . . . . Lemuel!
At last you're here," she whispered, "really you!"—
searching my features with half-frightened eyes.
With a faint smile
I made pretence to cover my surprise;
Lemuel? . . . . That was father's name . . . . not mine.
And then, emboldened, old Miss Agatha set
a hand on either shoulder. "Lem," she said,
"I always knew. . . .

I've known for all this endless while
you never were the kind that could forget . . . .
I *knew* that you'd be coming back again . . . .
Living or dead," she murmured, "living or dead . . . . "
And suddenly she crumpled in a heap
upon the floor.
I lifted the figure in its poplin dress
onto the sofa, like a child asleep;
and then, in whimsical tenderness,
I kissed the drawn pathetic mouth before
I closed the door.

           KATHARINE BURT.

"Blue Print for the Perfect Crime . . .

"Murder will out ... in the very last chapter of all ..."

THE TENANTS

Among the black trees spider-webbed
  Against a red and wintry dusk,
I leaned upon the sagging gate
  And looked up at the evil husk

Of that old house, remote from town
  And haunted, so the farm-folk said,
By brother-ghosts—the victim stabbed,
  The killer hanged 'til he was dead.

"How does it feel," I asked the pair
  Of farmers lounging in the door,
"To live within a haunted house?
  You must have nerves of steel and more!"

A hoot-owl cried within the wood;
  The sky above was red as sin;
The shadows deepened; side by side,
  Each figure eyed me with a grin.

Then one replied, "We have to stay—
  This is our home, the land we tilled—
For I'm the one they hanged," he said,
  "And he's the one I killed."

LEAH BODINE DRAKE.

That blessed mood,
In which the burden of the mystery,
In which the heavy and the weary weight
Of all this unintelligible world,
Is lightened.

WILLIAM WORDSWORTH.

To Make a Long Story Short

"Bedtime story . . . it's up to you to read between the lines . . .

TELL US A STORY, GRANDMOTHER

An amber cat, an aspen tree,
And a little white house belong to me!
A silver spoon, a pewter pot,
A hive of bees, and a garden plot,
A Wedgwood plate and a luster cup
And time for dreams when the moon comes up.

Once, long ago, when I was young,
I had jade and opals strung
On a silver chain, a gown of silk,
A Watteau fan—and a skin like milk!
And besides all these, over and over,
I had a heart of a handsome lover.

An amber cat, an aspen tree,
And a little white house belong to me,
And time to dream, when the sun goes down,
Of a flashing smile in a face of brown
And time to think, when the moon has set,
Of somber eyes like polished jet.

A silver spoon and a pewter pot,
A hive of bees and a garden plot,
A Wedgwood plate and a luster cup—
And times for dreams when the moon comes up.

But there's something more to this story, too:
Now, my darlings, I *have you.*

MARION DOYLE.

And so from hour to hour we ripe and ripe,
And then from hour to hour we rot and rot;
And thereby hangs a tale.

WILLIAM SHAKESPEARE.

"Chapter one . . . the beginning and the end of the sweetest story ever told . . .

FIRST LOVE

Here is the stuff of legends,
The hallowed hour,
Gold-fraught and echoless,
The voiceless bower.

Here is the awkward gesture,
The shining eyes,
The blinding edge of fire
Of love's bright guise.

Boy, the fumbling explorer—
Girl, tender guile—
Fused and sparked to explosion,
In passion's first trial.

Spurred by the urgent flesh,
Once I was here,
Caught in this aching wonder,
This timeless year.
PVT. EVERETT A. GILLIS.

Story! God bless you! I have none to tell, sir.
GEORGE CANNING.

"Truth is stranger than the cinema . . . and wiser too . . .

TEARS

Alice and Betty and Eva Jo
Wept great tears at the picture show;

Father swallowed behind his tie
And Mother mopped her lashes dry;

But Grandmother had no tears to fall
Because she had already used them all.
FRANCES ALEXANDER.

"You never can tell a book by its cover . . ."

COUNTERPANE

"She's made her bed; now let her lie in it!"
  When Nan took Pete, 'twas this her elders said;
But I—I knew she'd disappoint their scorn.
  I'd watched Nan make her narrow, white iron bed!

She never stopped to smooth the pillow out
  Or shake the sheets and blankets where she'd lain.
She simply gave the lot a yank, a toss,
  And then, on top, she'd spread the counterpane.

But, if the product proved uncomfortable,
  None heard, and not the sharpest eye could tell
How lumpy was that bed that Nan had made—
  She smoothed its gay-flowered counterpane so well!

                    VIOLET ALLEYN STOREY.

"To be continued in the next installment . . ."

BRENDA PASSES

She came like morning—
Eager, blue-gold, tender,
Breathing glad light—
Unconscious of her splendor.

Young love she met along an April way
Where rolls the greening earth from night to day,

And at the imploring magic of his smile,
She walked with him a lovely lilac mile.

When suddenly bespoken for some noon
Beyond the by-way of the earth and moon,

Wanting to stay, reluctant to surrender—
She went away, unconscious of her splendor.

                    MARY WHITE SLATER.

"Why a lending library is more satisfying than a bookstore . . .

IN A GREEN GARDEN

I had a silver penny
   I brought to town to spend,
But passed it to a ragged man
   Who walked without a friend.

I cut a flute of willow,
   Green willow in the spring,
Then gave it to a crippled child
   And taught it how to sing.

Mine was a heart for loving,
   As tender as the rain.
I lost it to a whistling boy
   Who sailed away to Spain.

I live in a green garden
   Where birds sing every day.
But all the things which bring me joy
   Are those I gave away.

                    BEULAH MAY.

"A good policy . . . in spite of the liability . . . and yet fire and theft might be cheaper . . .

WIVES ARE SO UNSELFISH

If I did not stay trim and smart,
Somebody else might steal your heart—
Some selfish little creature who
Would probably be mean to you.

So when I spend your money for
A saucy hat, a mink coat, or
A fabulously pretty dress—
I just insure your happiness!

                    MAY RICHSTONE.

"It happened on March 11, 1888 . . .

OLD JOSIAH PREDICTS

"It looks like snow," Josiah said to us
As he tipped his fine, old head 'way over back
To peer upward at a swiftly fading sky;
A sky that had been blue an hour before—
A blue it seemed our fingertips could touch.

He said he felt it 'close' and as he spoke
He raised his arm and pressed his open palm
Against the coldness of the morning air;
Finding there some unseen guarantee—
That meant to him his prophecy was good.

"It looks like snow," Josiah said again;
And as we smiled at his repeated words,
The shrouded sky let down a chilly veil
That settled on the ground like dewdrop mist—
A mist that quickly whitened as we watched.

"Winter's apt to start its stay like this;
This snow a-siftin' down . . . slow-like and fine:
But . . . I wouldn't doubt, before the night sets in
That you will wade through drifts, wind-piled and deep."
He looked around, "I wouldn't doubt," he said.

ESTHER HOUGHTALING.

That's another story . . .
LAURENCE STERNE.

"Did somebody mention Scarlett O'Hara—oh, excuse me, it must have been Belle Watling . . .

MISS JULIE

Poor Miss Julie lived alone,
She whose life was black with sin,
Just outside the Southern town
Where no sunlight entered in.

336

Townfolk whispered of drawn blinds,
And loud music that was played
By her friends late in the night
When she plied her shameful trade.

Once they stoned Miss Julie's house,
Counting it a Christian deed;
They demanded she leave town,
But she laughed, and paid no heed.

Women mocked her painted cheeks,
Hennaed hair, mascaraed eyes;
Said no good would come of one
Flaunting plumes of paradise.

But they did not know last fall,
When the Widow Brown was ill,
Lying, penniless, alone,
That Miss Julie paid the bill.

They would mock me if I told
How one day upon the street
She had helped a poor blind man
Who lay crippled at her feet.

They would laugh with bitter scorn
That her heart could hold good will,
And that once I saw her kneel
At a new grave on a hill.

On that great and fearful morn,
When God bids the saints come in,—
Will Miss Julie join that throng—
She whose heart is black with sin?

     WILLIAM ARNETTE WOFFORD.

I cannot tell how the truth may be;
I say the tale as 'twas said to me.
     SIR WALTER SCOTT.

"Melody in 4 F . . .

A 'CATCH' IN TIME

According to the ancient saws
I need not land you yet because
Some big and better fish await
The rearranging of my bait.

But I am hauling in my line
Well satisfied that you are mine
For I have heard too many say
"You should have seen what got away!"

MARCIA NICHOLS HOLDEN.

"Mystery story . . .

THE SILVER STIRRUP

Upon the mantelpiece a portrait rests—
A girl's face fringed with bangs
Of purple-glinted black. Beside this face
A silver stirrup hangs.

I took it down and handled it and said,
"A silver stirrup's rare."
"Unusual, indeed," the slow reply
Of him who hung it there.

"A trophy, or did some proud artisan
Find you a willing buyer?"
"I neither won nor bought it," he replied,
And gazed into the fire.

"Where is the other stirrup?" A gust of sleet
Stung the dark casement pane.
He answered, "There's only one." And then
We talked of storm and rain.

MARGUERITE MCCREARY.

"And oh my! They could have lived happily ever after . . ."

DISAPPOINTMENT

She polished plate and sugar bowl
And made the china teacups shine.
She polished laughter, smoothed her soul,
For Evan was to come at nine.

Her waiting heart, so lifted up,
Her eager dreamed-warmed eyes so bright,
Gleamed like the Dresdan china cup
Or candles glowing in the night.

The swaying coach wheeled down the moor.
It stopped. The cumbrous doors swung wide.
An old man, pallid faced and dour,
The only passenger inside.

DOROTHY MOORE GARRISON.

"Some books are better when read the second time . . ."

AFTER ABSENCE

Two years had passed; and once again we came
Into the room so often known before.
Unchanged, the green fringed rug upon the floor;
Unchanged, the bronze lamp with the amber flame.
The smiles with which you met us were the same,
And, after your first nod, the evening bore
The jesting, friendly air old evenings wore,
As though time had no chasms to reclaim.

Two years had vanished like a fleck of foam
When hand reached out to hand, and mind to mind!
So that I wonder if, through vaster deeps,
When the loosed spirit flees from kin and home,
One may revive lost comradeship, and find
That love which seems forgotten only sleeps.

STANTON A. COBLENTZ.

"And your eyes spoke volumes ..."

MOMENTS

The moon was falling into our street
  Out of a tree,
And we walked slow, and the night was sweet,
  And there were three
Stars huddled together in the space
That is the sky, and in your face
Was a little laughing, a little pain
And the fear that there could not be again
A night so dear as this night had been.
And we said Good-by, and I went in.
And you walked away; and the church clock spoke.
And the moon fell into our street and broke.

MARY CAROLYN DAVIES.

"A half remembered tale ... of the eternal male ... who mourned his fate ... too late ..."

THE PUMPKIN EATER'S WIFE

Old Peter's wife, a madcap bagatelle,
Tossed her young head and vowed she would not stay
At home; sometimes, moonstruck, she was away
All night—until he shut her in a shell.

There through long years he kept her very well;
Nor from her pumpkin-prison could she stray;
Nor could she now be restless, eager, gay ...
With her horizon but a yellow cell.

And when at last it happened that she died,
He hardly missed her: she had grown to be
So quiet, self-effacing, calm, and slow.
This wifely paragon he brushed aside
To cherish in his aching memory
The truant bride who left him long ago.

IRENE TAYLOR.

"To make a short story long . . . the things we say . . . the quick remarks . . . have been so slow in forming . . .

ECHOES

Strange how such long-ago moments
Still return to stir me
And goad me into action:

My saying: "I can't . . . I've got to quit;"
You standing there, wise and successful,
Answering steadily
"The first school I taught was a failure."

I said, "I felt I had to speak out
And say what I thought."
You smiled,
"Sometimes it's a good idea
To let people wonder what you are thinking."

The inscription in a book:
"To my little girl
Who went to church on a rainy Sunday—
From her Father who believes in going to church."

Even in those later years when, tired,
You spoke to me sharply of my own parenthood:
"They don't know the first thing about minding!"
Even that comes back and has come back through the years
In a realization of your love and concern.

All of the things you used to say to me
Lie here in my heart today,
Echoing.

HARRIET SEYMOUR POPOWSKI.

So geographers, in Afric maps,
With savage pictures fill their gaps,
And o'er unhabitable downs
Place elephants for want of towns.

JONATHAN SWIFT.

"Once upon a time . . . and once was enough . . ."

FIFTH READER

"Fifth readers are for them that want to teach!
You're schooled enough," my harassed mother said.
"Stop wishing now for things beyond your reach!
In two years you and Henry will be wed,
If study hasn't spoiled your rosy looks.
When you're plumped out, my purple watered silk
Should fit you well. Now say no more of books,
But take your lantern, child, and go and milk."

That night a turkey-egg hatched out that I
Had found and given to a clucking hen.
That gobbler grew until he stood this high,
Which made it hard to hide him now and then.
I sold him in the fall, and bought my new
Fifth Reader—but I wished I had him, too.

II

One morning while we scraped potato bugs
From vines to cans, I burst right out at Ma:
"I don't mind pitching hay, and hauling lugs
Of windfalls to the pigs, for you and Pa—
But that is what I'd have to do, and more,
For Henry, when I'm married—and I won't!"
"Why, child! You never talked like that before!
You like him, don't you?"
                "No, I don't! I don't!"
Ma looked across the fields. From far away
Her eyes and voice came, as she said, real slow:
"There'll be no wedding, then, until the day
You set, yourself—there, child, I know, I know . . .
His ma and I made foolish plans, I guess.
But we'll find uses for that purple dress."

IRENE STANLEY.

He left the name at which the world grew pale,
To point a moral, or adorn a tale.

SAMUEL JOHNSON.

One of Mabel's fables ... Moral ... be artistic ... but not oral ....

FIRST LOVE?

You vowed I was your first love
Your first taste of passion's fire;
But I shrugged laughingly away,
Your kiss proved you a liar.

MARY WISE WATTS.

That best portion of a good man's life,—
His little, nameless, unremembered acts
Of kindness and of love.

WILLIAM WORDSWORTH.

"This is the life and these are the letters ... misunderstandings that bound like fetters ...

LOVE LETTERS IN AN ATTIC

Untie the strings, and let us read together;
Here is the record! Oh, those turbulent days!
See how we veered; how, twisting like a feather,
Our thoughts blew up, blew down. After that phase,
Came the wild joy of knowing, this was real;
We loved, we longed. And, ignorantly, married;
You never knew my absolute ideal;
Nor I, the load you shouldered, and have carried;
Infrequent letters, written on short vacation,
Mentioned the babies' health, the gathering debts,
Our struggles ... how we hated separation ...
Then comes the gap. Life spread its worrisome nets;
You loathed me more, for nagging words you faced;
For every drop you drank, my tears were ten;
The nights apart, the walls, the wicked waste!
"Enclosed find check."
               Those were your letters, then.
Forget it, now. Here on an attic landing,
Two grayheads, having learned their mutual need,
Open in love, in loyal understanding,
The heart's own missives no one else could read.

DOROTHY COWLES PINKNEY.

"Some stories are all action . . . some description . . .

PARK AVENUE, LOOKING SOUTH

The doormen on Park Avenue
    Are standing at their doors;
They help the tenants sortie
    To concerts and to stores;
They whistle for the taxis
    And call the cars by scores.

In wintertime the doormen
    Can watch the ladies fold
Their silver foxes round them
    Before they risk the cold,
And watch the rich, like others,
    Grow tired and bored and old.

The doormen greet each evening
    The great who come to feast;
They bow in bridal couples;
    They bow out the deceased.
And of all who grace Park Avenue
    I do not like them least.

                      IRWIN EDMAN.

"Now is the time to memorize this story . . .

PRAYER OF THANKS

Lord of my life, can life be bare
With beauty springing everywhere?
Can I forlorn and lonely be
With sweet bird-song from every tree?
Can I succumb to doubt and fear
With tasks to do and friends to cheer?
What matters it that I am poor,
With roses blooming at my door!
Can I complain, by sorrow pent,
Knowing I have the boon, content?
Trouble shall flee and fear take wing,
For life still brings me songs to sing.
Lord of my days, how thankful I
For a thankful heart, as life goes by!

                      THOMAS CURTIS CLARK.

"Weekend short story . . . 'Friday's child is full of woe . . . Saturday's child has far to go . . . But the child that is born on the Sabbath-day . . . is brave and bonny, and good and gay' . . .

PROMISE

If I live 'til Sunday,
(Heart torn in two)
Here is what I promise . . .
This is what I'll do:

Leave your cage door open . . .
Let you fly about;
(If I live 'til Sunday,
Which I doubt.)

Sunday is tomorrow;
If I live 'til then
I'll restore the freedom
Of your wings again;

Loving you I'll leave you
To the winds, and bliss.
(If I live 'til Sunday,
Lost like this.)

FRANCES BOAL MEHLEK.

"The story that continues . . .

ON LINCOLN'S BIRTHDAY

Let us not mourn him now, but follow him,
Complete the work his master-life began.
Ours is a tragic time, truth's light is dim,
Men are still slaves. God calls to every man:
Go forth and spend your lives for all men's good,
Build me a world of brotherhood.

THOMAS CURTIS CLARK.

"This is a great war story . . . there will be longer stories written . . . but few will sing as this one does . . . of that last measure of devotion . . .

THE CONVOY PASSES

Two of them were dead of thirst and one was raving mad,
And there they sat, the four of them, and him, poor lad . . .
Adrift upon a churning sea and far from any shore,
A sunken ship behind them and Eternity before.

Sure, they thought they all were mad when softly in the gloom,
Soft and slow and stately and as silent as the tomb,
Came a cautious convoy, treading light—ah, light!—
The mine-infested waters and the Death-infested night.

Fever, fear and famine, or mirage of troubled brain?
No, 'twas there before them, shadowy but plain,
Troopship after troopship, half the nation's pride,
And they a little row-boat, drifting with the tide!

"Light a flare!" they babbled, "Daybreak they'll be gone!"
Lapsing into silence, weighing pro and con:
Mine-infested waters, Death-infested night,
And the faint and fitful flicker of a too-revealing light.

Could be, 'twixt the convoy and the unimportant tub,
A sneaky little, slinky little, slimy little sub,
Cuddling in its covert, lurking in its lair,
Asking for its single purpose no more than . . . a flare.

Soft and slow and stately, silent as the tomb,
Troopship after troopship, vanishing in gloom,
Small and mute and motionless, with all a nation's pride,
One little row-boat drifting wide . . . wide.

NORMA JEAN BUNTING.

"And you ... and you ... and you ... would probably do the same thing too ..."

KNOWING

It was wild grape time when poor Ebb Lowe
Came to live there at the old Josh Place.
There was no other place for Ebb to go.
He bought it cheap—deep horizons in his face.
Neighbors thought Ebb just a 'onery cuss'
Who hardly had one stick of wood ahead.
Somehow he lived through all the winter fuss
And never bothered much in what they said.
Then blades of grass revived, peach trees stood pink.
(What lovely things can spring from soil)
That early summer Ebb tried hard to sink
A well. Eighty feet were dug and they struck oil.

Now neighbors sit around and tell
How they knew that oil was in that well.

JOHN B. CRUISE.

"The best remark I ever heard was made by a woman gently told that her best friend had just died. She smiled and said—'My, how interested Ann will be!'"

GREEN STREET

All of Green Street will be
Up in heaven, presently,
For in the rain and in the snowing,
I have seen them going, going, ...

When Mrs. Jones arrives today,
Will someone hurry up and say,
"You come from Green Street, Faragay?"
And beg her for the news she knows,
Of how the world of Green Street goes,
And will there be a little stir
In heaven when they welcome her?

EDITH HORTON.

"Classified ads . . . real estate section . . . Sunday paper . . .

SALE

A tangled path, a spring-fed pond—
A little handkerchief of pond
Embroidered with forget-me-not—
A little, crooked brook beyond,
An orchard, bent in memory of storm;
On half a lot,
A sleeping house that may not keep us warm:
All these we found.
The house is old, the spring runs cold,
And russet apples crowd the ground.

EUGENIE CARVER.

"Courage . . . has very small beginnings . . . as you must have discovered . . . but that, Sheherezade, is another story . . .

TO MY DAUGHTER

The darkness frightened me when I was small;
  The last, long flight of stairs without a light,
The gloomy angle of the upper hall,
  Where strange and solid shadows tricked my sight.

But now my eyes that once were frightened wide
  By this, can recognize the ghosts upon
The friendly walls; and night steps in beside
  The hearth, through windows where no shades are drawn.

My little love, the dark's not worth your tears:
  The night's a sleepy sister to the day.
A little while you'll come to bolder years
  And scorn the little girl who felt that way.
A little longer while, you'll hear one call
  And, rising, say, "It's nothing, dear, at all."

EUGENIE CARVER.

"There was an author once in Greenwich Village . . . who might have written The Great American Novel . . . and maybe he did . . . he was a 'ghost writer' . . .

THE MOON MENDER

Old Enoch Wright was six feet three
And just as lean as he was tall,
But his deft fingers certainly
Could bud a tree, repair a wall.

The easy task or intricate
Delighted him: a stubborn lock,
A wayward gun, a fretful gate,
A tipsy sill or sleepy clock.

He would walk miles if one but ask
His aid, and every hard pressed neighbor
Knew just the man to do his task:
He spent his days at "thank you" labor.

Even the gossips would confess
And lay a wager Enoch Wright
Could mend the moon, and ladderless,
If it went dark some windy night.

While he repaired his neighbor's house,
Helped drain a bit of sodden field,
Made traps to catch the mole, the mouse,
Or stored some widow's autumn yield,

His own house tottered, board and brick,
His land went hungry begging seed,
And where crops once grew green and thick,
Flourished the dock and jimson weed.

Across his fenceless, unkept lands
Strange cattle roamed and grazed at will,
And waiting for his truant hands,
His plows grew rusty on the hill.

JOHN RICHARD MORELAND.

"You'll take what you beget . . .

"FIFTH FLOOR, CHILDREN'S"

"Is someone helping you?" she asked. I smiled
And touched the little party dress of blue.
"I'll look around," I said, and was beguiled
By heaps of small girls' frocks in every hue.
"They come with socks to match," the salesgirl beamed,
  "And here are ribbon bows already tied."
I touched them with a longing hand and dreamed
  I had a daughter shopping at my side.
"These just came in." She smoothed a tiny muff
  And brought a bonnet trimmed with bits of fur.
I stroked the minute gloves just big enough
  To hold and warm the soft pink hands of her.
"This what you want?" she asked. I shook my head.
"Some sturdy overalls for boys," I said.

EUGENIA GERLACH STEIN.

"And no one knows just what the author has in mind . . . for tomorrow . . .

INTERRUPTION

In strange, imagined lands that ever glow
With beauty and adventure, my small son
Will often wander far and never know
That as he reads, the hours pass one by one.
I warn him gently; but he hears me not.
I lift his face to mine: unseeing eyes
Look vaguely past my own to realms of thought,
Then straightway, deaf to his protesting cries,
I close the book and lead him off to bed.
Absorbed in life, like him, we little heed,
Until we have to go, good-byes unsaid.
Then, "One more chapter—one more page," we plead.
God firmly shuts the book, puts out the light.
"Some other day," He says, "No more tonight."

MARGARET BAILEY MILES.

"*R. F. D. . . . A fantasy . . .*

LATE REPAIRING

Red moon on the hill's dark rim:
pool of yellow lantern glow
beside the barn below,
where, at his pump, farmer Lenson is work-bent.

Under moon the lanternlight seems almost spent,
lies pale, lies dim;
no sound but clink of tool
on steel, and the wind's voice, cool
in the corn.   He has come late
to this repair,
and the moon late,
too, to make its glowing in midsummer evening air,
and he works there alone,
with the faint breath of cattle in their stalls,
and the sky-coasting nighthawk's high, thin
cry for company—but something is here
    that is his own—
as if the moon's glow and lanternlight constructed walls
to keep him safe within.

AUGUST DERLETH.

"Scenario for the perfect picture the world lives for . . . and the critics score. One . . . for the money . . . Two . . . for the show . . . Three . . . to get ready . . . and . . . Four . . . Oh No!

SO WE ARE THREE

So we are three:
    My darling, and my darling's darling,
        And, humbly, me . . . .
And where, before,
We thought there were no more
To add to Happiness,
'Tis only now we know
What life . . . and love . . . are for.

DAVID O. SELZNICK.

"Factual essay ... in black and white ... but mostly in the red ..."

ARISTOCRAT

Poetry is delicate,
Seldom ever brash—
 Seldom ever contacts
Hard, cold cash.

HALLIE PHILIPS.

And give to dust that is a little gilt,
More laud than gilt o'er dusted.

SHAKESPEARE.

"'Dear to my heart are the scenes of my childhood' ..."

STORY HOUR FOR REFUGEES

It is the witching time again: the day
 Burns out in purple twilight. On the grass
Strange shadows somersault, and who can say
 What may, or may not, wake and come to pass?

Fairies or goblins? In a moment now
 Angela and Pierre will come to me,
Unsmilingly, and pause and gravely bow.
 "Madame, the story—it is time, you see."

What does one tell to children who have seen
 The stark sky splintered with a blazing hell
Of bursting bombs, whose feet, along the green,
 Have stumbled over death? What does one tell?

How does one start the words and watch them grow—
 Unfolding into life, and love, and laughter?
How does one end the tale for two, who know
 There is no "living happy ever after?"

HELEN FRAZEE-BOWER.

"Some stories you have to finish for yourself . . . but some stories you can . . ."

SARAH'S HEAVEN

I aways think of Sarah
  When I see a red dress.
Red she wore and rouge she wore,
  So nobody should guess.

Lipstick and quick laughter
  And a pain in her side.
I think I was with her
  The only time she cried.

Cried for what had never been
  And now could never be—
A baby at her bosom
  And a son beside her knee.

"That would be my heaven—
  But there's only earth," she said.
"And so there's nothing left to do
  But laugh and wear red."

But I think there is a heaven,
  And I think Sarah's there
In a blue, crumpled housecoat
  And smooth-braided hair;

Without any laughter
  Or ever any pain
Or need to wear bright lipstick
  Or scarlet frocks again;

Grave and still and happy,
  As any girl would be,
With a baby at her bosom
  And a son beside her knee.

                Margaret Widdemer.

"Story of glory . . .

THE DREAM SHINES ON

One weary night when dark was not yet gone
I waked and said, as though the words were given,
   "But still the dream shines on."

Day was not near; no star looked through the gloom;
But courage suddenly was with me, like
   An angel in the room.

And now, whenever sorrow waits with dawn
In other years, I shall not be afraid,
   Knowing the dream shines on.
NANCY BYRD TURNER.

If all the world and love were young,
   And truth in every shepherd's tongue,
   These pretty pleasures might me move
   To live with thee, and be thy love.
SIR WALTER RALEIGH.

"Continued in our next . . .

SONG FOR EVENING

This night, whatever day has brought of shadow,
Comes peace, with healing dew and quiet, long,
Slow weaving of lavender dusk on hill and meadow,
   And one late robin's song.

The evening star will take its watch and stand
In pure, still loveliness. As sure as Heaven,
As sure as love, unto a weary land
   That blessing will be given.

Today's distress, the burden of tomorrow,
Will dim like dreams. The thought of God will keep
Such old and faithful guard that even Sorrow
   Must fold her hands and sleep.
NANCY BYRD TURNER.

"The question that's never, ever quite asked . . . and never, ever quite answered . . .

EVEN GOD WANTED A SON

It's all right—somehow—dear God,
(All-loving, Omnipotent One),
But even You felt a need of Him,
Your Galilean Son.

Even You wanted to live through Him,
To feel His childish love,
You wanted to laugh and grow through Him
And rise, "On wings like a dove."

It's all right—somehow—dear God,
But I, too, needed a child
To make me look outside of myself
To be more calm, more mild.

You even wanted to share with Him
Suffering on the Cross,
You hovered over Him, gave Him strength,
Buoyed Him up in loss.

You know of my hunger, dear God?
How I'd feathered the secret nest?
And now—how things have no power to help
Or heal the ache in the breast?

Then, be gentle with me, dear God,
When because of my lack I rebel—
For even You wanted Your son so much
You left Heaven itself for Hell,

So that we might be shown Your Way,
(All-loving, Omnipotent Light),
I cannot quite understand, dear God,
But somehow, it must be right.

VICTORIA ADELAIDE HARVEY.

"Why in the world does it have to stop here . . . just when it's getting interesting . . .

LADY CONSOLED

My lady loved a king's son
who kissed and rode away.
She watched from her high casement
and wept a bitter day.

Some say a careless minstrel,
who chanced to stroll along,
devised a brittle ladder
of laughter and a song.

ANNETTE PATTON CORNELL.

"The End . . .

LAST LEAVE

Tonight the moon is gray, and leaves
Go drifting down the bay like silver coins—
You smile at me above the gleaming candlelight,
And yet I know your heart is storing memories
Against another day—another hour—
We fight so to be casual, for this
Must be no time for tears, no place for grief,
And yet the silence is desperate
Above the heart's slow breaking sound;
The waiter hovers near, impatient with the time—
"Something more madame?" he says;
Something more? No, there can be nothing more
Than this I hold tonight; for eyes that strive
To meet my own through a frightened veil
Of loneliness; for strong brown hands to clasp
Against my heart for one last star-swept time;
There must be no tomorrow—no wind
Must ever stir these latent shadows from their sleep—
The hour is late; the candles flicker and burn low,
And out across the bay a thin ghost-moon
Slips below the water behind a bridge of stars.

EDYTHE HOPE GENEE.

"There isn't any such thing as a complete story . . . they all begin before any beginning . . . they all go on after the end . . .

IN THE WAKE OF LOVE

You go
And take the love-filled night
And leave me empty dawns and tear-filled sight.
You take the only heart that could combine
And make forever whole this heart of mine.
You go
And leave a shell that hides a dying thing,
And how can the smileless eyes laugh once again
Or the songless lips attempt to sing?
Even your parting shadow that fell across the floor
Could not be mine, for it returns no more.
You took my only solace, sleep,
And strangled dreams of love now form a lifeless heap.
You brought the life and love that in me stirred
And left a death that has interred
My soul beneath the weightless dearth
Of all deserted souls.

You go,
And all I know
Of life and love and laughter
Follows after.

RUTH CARROLL.

COUNSEL FOR DREAMERS

Guard well the dream. Let no conspiring day,
No hour of triumph quench the hesitant spark
Of beauty within the mind that seeks its way
Like a slow flame hard-struggling out of dark.
Cherish the dream. Hold to that nameless joy
That children capture on a sunlit hill.
A thousand hands are striving to destroy;
Defend each path with all your strength and will.
Remember, all the glory, all the power
Some day shall be as chaff within the hand.
Guard well the vision. Then, some distant hour
When fools, bewildered, empty-hearted, stand
Before the closing casements of the night,
Poems shall be your latchkeys, songs your light.

ANDERSON SCRUGGS.

Index

INDEX

A

A BARD	Sydney King Russell	77
A BLIND GIRL SPEAKS	Helen Loomis Linham	313
A 'CATCH' IN TIME	Marcia Nichols Holden	338
A CURIOUS LADY	Jeannette Sewell Davis	89
A DILEMMA	Catharine Williams	309
A GIRL REPLIES	Ethel Romig Fuller	239
A GOOD DOG NEVER DIES	Mary Carolyn Davies	279
A GRACE	Mary Carolyn Davies	204
A LETTER FOR YOU	Louise Driscoll	117
A LETTER FROM NORWAY	Margot Manseau	120
A LITTLE BOY OUT WALKING	Helen Dahle	135
A LITTLE DOG GOES ON	Margaret Rush	278
A MAN MUST DIG	Helen Frazee-Bower	253
A MOTHER PRAYS	Goldie Capers Smith	140
A PERSEVERING LITTLE OLD LADY	Claude George Wilson	85
A PERSONAL MATTER	Patricia Martin	133
A POET TO HIS DAUGHTER	Anderson M. Scruggs	137
A SHIRT TALE	Alice Morrey Bailey	82
A SOLDIER'S MOTHER WRITES TO A FRIEND	Maurice Hill	121
A SON AT SEA	Margery Ruebush Shank	176
A STITCH IN TIME SAVES NINE	Marion Doyle	286
A TALE THAT'S TALL AND TEAS-Y	Belle S. Mooney	276
A WEDDING PRAYER	Helen Welshimer	96
ABDICATION	Katherine Kelly Woodley	107
ABSENCE	Charles Hanson Towne	232
ADAM WAS HAPPIER THAN WE	Mabel Posegate	14
ADMONITION	Sydney King Russell	265
AFTER ABSENCE	Stanton A. Coblentz	339
AFTER BATAAN	Edna Mead	186
ALIEN CHILD	Myrtle G. Burger	78
ALL-SAINTS' EVE	Leah Bodine Drake	324
ALONG ABOUT NOW	Jane Sayre	201
AN OLD CUSTOM	Erica May Brooks	169
ANANIAS	Sydney King Russell	15
ANATOMIST	Aldona Bauser	147
ANCESTORS	Eleanor Glenn Wallis	71
AND AFTER THIS	Francisca Vallejo	192
AND IF I SAY	Albert Warner Dowling	289
AND SO RESTRAINT	Margery Parvis	160
"AND THIS I ASK—"	Mayhoward Austin McEachern	19
AND WHAT THEN	Grace Phillips	308
ANGELING UP	Ruth Averitte	179
APARTMENT-HOUSE CROONING	Jane Sayre	129
APOLOGY TO NERO	Marguerite Steffan	250

INDEX—Continued

APOLOGY WITHOUT WORDS	Louise Owen	203
APOSTROPHE TO YOUTH	Frances Davis Adams-Moore	174
APPEASEMENT POLICY	Mary Keith Cox	161
APPLE TREES	Hazel Harper Harris	219
ARISTOCRAT	Hallie Philips	352
AS I WALKED INTO LONDON TOWN	Mabel Posegate	43
AS SWIFT SEASONS ROLL	Grace D. Leckliter	321
AT MIDNIGHT I REMEMBERED	Mary Brennan Clapp	128
AT SIXTEEN	Irene McDermott	139
AT THE FLOWER SHOW	Kathryn H. Hall	215
AURORA	Claude George Wilson	60
AUTOBIOGRAPHY	Louise Crenshaw Ray	300
AUTOBIOGRAPHY	Mary Willis Shuey	84
AUTOBIOGRAPHY	Juliet Wilbor Tompkins	85
AUTUMN	Marion Doyle	63
AWAKENING	Ethel B. Cheney	318

B

BASEMENT CAFETERIA	Antoinette Willsod	91
BEATITUDES	Mary White Slater	24
BELLE	Eleanor Stanley Lockwood	250
BELOVED	Mabel Posegate	55
BERRY PICKING	Frances Morton O'Neill	222
BIOGRAPHY	Virginia Scott Miner	83
BIRD WORLD	Retta Scott Garrett	270
BIRTHDAY	Elaine V. Emans	248
BITTER HERITAGE	Billie Marie Crabb	143
BLIND CHILD	Violet Alleyn Storey	21
BLUE ON BLUE ON BLUE	Gaylen Shannon	235
BOY ETERNAL	Barton Rees Pogue	131
BOY RUNNING	Sarah Litsey	130
BREAKFAST	Isabelle Bryans Longfellow	196
BRENDA PASSES	Mary White Slater	334
BRIDE'S HOUSE	Lida Wilson Turner	103
BRIDES	Isabelle Bryans Longfellow	97
BROOD OF THE SPARROW	Dorothy P. Albaugh	269
BROOKLYN BRIDGE ON A FOGGY NIGHT	Martha Lyman Shillito	325
BROTHERS	Beulah Ridgeway Winans	88

C

CANTEEN WORKER	Esther Baldwin York	184
CENTURY OF NO PROGRESS	Martha Lee Lorenz	142
CHANGELING	Florence Hartman Townsend	50
CHARITY WARD	Esther Weakley	156

INDEX—Continued

CHILDREN OF EARTH	Jeannette Sewell Davis	319
CHILDREN'S WARD	Mary Lanigan Healy	131
CHRISTMAS LETTER FROM MY SON	Blanche DeGood Lofton	121
CIRCLE OF A TEAR	John Richard Moreland	290
CITY WIND	Gilean Douglas	51
CLASS REUNION	Violet Alleyn Storey	255
COLD AS SNOW	Alice Moser	292
COLD SHOWER	W. E. Farbstein	154
COMFORTING THOUGHT	May Richstone	102
COMPENSATION	John Gallinari Whidding	58
CONCEALMENT	Helen Welshimer	233
CONFEDERATE VETERAN	James E. Warren, Jr.	262
CONQUEROR	Adrian F. Nader	301
CONSOLATION	Anne Murry Movius	140
CONSUMMATION	Lisbeth Wallis	243
CONTENTMENT	Rosalie Garrett Peters	130
CONVERSATIONAL GHOST	Sarah Leeds Ash	233
CONVINCED	Hazel Harper Harris	163
CONVOY	Dorothy Curran	191
COUNSEL FOR DREAMERS	Anderson M. Scruggs	357
COUNTERPANE	Violet Alleyn Storey	334
COUNTRY SCHOOLHOUSE	Harvey Wagner Flink	138
COURAGE	Karle Wilson Baker	296
CRACKER BOY	Isabel Tudeen	74
CREDO OF UNREST	Lolly Williams	303
CRICKET IN A CYCLONE	Rosa Zagnoni Marinoni	56
CRICKET IN THE HOUSE	Robert P. Tristram Coffin	237
CRIPPLED CHILD	Ethel Romig Fuller	140
CROCODILE TEARS	Johnny McKinney	281
CROSSROADS	Ruth Bassett	178
CYNICISMS	Faye Chilcote Walker	298
CYNTHIE-ANN	Genevieve Atwood	81

D

DARK VIGIL	Eleanor Lee White	275
DAWN DREAMS	Anne Moore McFarland	229
DAYTIME STARLIGHT	Dixie Willson	128
DEATH IS THE DREAM	James E. Warren, Jr.	321
DESIGN FOR A LAST LETTER	Gladys McKee	113
DESIGN FOR ENCHANTMENT	Elaine V. Emans	106
DESIRABLE MALE	Kaye Huizing	102
DESPAIR	Hilda Conkling	279
DISAPPOINTMENT	Dorothy Moore Garrison	339
DISCOVERED	Dorothy Burnham Eaton	61
DISCOVERY	Helen Frazee-Bower	275
DIVERGENCE	Helen Darby Berning	42

INDEX—Continued

DOING DISHES	*Ethel Romig Fuller*	199
DOMESTICITY	*Albert Horlings*	104
DOUBLE DUTY	*W. E. Farbstein*	168
DRAW THE VEIL	*W. E. Farbstein*	196
DREAM HOUSE	*Marion Doyle*	240
DUSK	*Harriet Seymour Popowski*	59
DUSTING	*Louise Rhoads*	177

E

ECHOES	*Harriet Seymour Popowski*	341
EFFICIENCY EXPERT	*Jane Harris*	73
END OF SUMMER	*Margaret E. Sangster*	59
ENGINE TROUBLE	*Jill Christopher*	149
EPITAPH FOR A LOST ADVENTURER	*Marion Doyle*	44
ETERNAL TRIANGLE	*Violet Alleyn Storey*	103
EVEN A BIRD	*C. Faye Bennett*	272
EVEN GOD WANTED A SON	*Victoria Adelaide Harvey*	355
EVEN IN DREAMS	*Irma Wassall*	45

F

FABLE FOR SPRING	*Irene Wilde*	53
FAMILIAR SETTING	*Carolyn Ellis*	241
FAREWELL	*Adelaide Love*	230
FARMER'S TWILIGHT	*Margaret J. E. Brown*	58
FEMININE MATHEMATICS	*May Richstone*	165
FEMININE REACTION	*May Richstone*	274
"FIFTH FLOOR, CHILDREN'S"	*Eugenia Gerlach Stein*	350
FIFTH READER	*Irene Stanley*	342
FIRESIDE WEATHER	*Inez Culver Corbin*	64
FIRST DAY AT SCHOOL	*Jessie Corrigan Pegis*	135
FIRST LOVE	*Pvt. Everett A. Gillis*	333
FIRST LOVE	*Laufa M. Lockwood*	306
FIRST LOVE?	*Mary Wise Watts*	343
FIRST PIANO LESSON	*Charla M. Backlund*	247
FIVE BARE BOYS	*Robert P. Tristram Coffin*	54
FLOWER-FAITH	*Elizabeth Maxwell Phelps*	210
FOOTNOTE TO SHAKESPEARE	*Helen Peavy Washburn*	295
FOOTPRINTS	*Dorothy P. Albaugh*	318
FOR A LITTLE GIRL	*Eunice Mildred LonCoske*	20
FOR A NEW WEDDING RING	*Gladys McKee*	96
FOUR-FOOT ORATORS	*Robert P. Tristram Coffin*	72
FREEDOM	*Alicia Kay Smith*	46
FRIGHTENED KITTENS	*Esther Baldwin York*	276
FROM SOMEWHERE IN THE PACIFIC	*Rachel Lumpkin Wyly*	118

INDEX—Continued

FROST IN THE NIGHT	Elizabeth-Ellen Long	67
FULFILLMENT	Charlotte Wise	164
FULL CONFESSION	Adelaide Love	165
FUTILITY	Adelaide Love	242

G

GAIN	Kathryn Wright	289
GALLANT ONES	Dorothy Quick	187
GARDEN IN THE RAIN	James E. Warren, Jr.	220
GARDEN IN THE TROPICS	Eunice Tietjens	216
GARDENER'S LAMENT	Florence Hilliard	213
GIFT	Mary Ellen Buckingham	115
GIFTS	John Richard Moreland	314
GOING AWAY	Helen Welshimer	315
GOOD MEN	Jesse Stuart	185
GRACE BEFORE SUMMER	Witter Bynner	54
GRANDFATHER SAID	Marion Doyle	141
GRANDMAMA	Beth Conley	132
GRANDMOTHER'S LILACS	Ethel B. Cheney	262
GREEN STREET	Edith Horton	347

H

HALF-OF-ONE	Lisbeth Wallis	248
HALO FOR A HUSBAND	Gladys McKee	106
HAND HIM A HALO	Addison H. Hallock	107
HARVEST	Mary Wise Watts	229
HEAVEN ISN'T ONE PLACE	Helen Welshimer	36
HEAVEN'S BOUNDARY	John Richard Moreland	21
HIGH FLIGHT	John Gillespie Magee, Jr.	119
HOLLYHOCK LADIES	Eleanor Joanne Boeshaar	218
HOUSE OF HAPPINESS	B. Y. Williams	287
HOW WE FORGIVE THE OLD IMMENSITIES	Georgie Starbuck Galbraith	302
HOW WOULD YOU HANDLE IT	Joe A. Noble	301
HUNGER	Ruth L. F. Barnett	198
HUSTLING WITH HERRICK	Keith Thomas	150
HYBRID	Neeta Marquis	75

I

I AM NOT JEALOUS	Katherine Kelly Woodley	274
I HAVE FORGOTTEN	Rosa Zagnoni Marinoni	234
I LIKE MUD	Marel Schwartz	133
I WOULD NOT HAVE YOUR MEALS ON TIME	Helen Welshimer	204
IF WE HAVE CLIMBED	Edith Tatum	292

INDEX—Continued

I'LL BET A BUTTON	Frances Rockwell	202
IN A GREEN GARDEN	Beulah May	335
IN A HUNDRED YEARS	Eunice Mildred LonCoske	256
IN CHURCH	Helen Loomis Linham	24
IN THE WAKE OF LOVE	Ruth Carroll	355
INCENDIARY	Kathryn Kay	167
INCIDENT AFTER INDUCTION	Janet Gerard	179
INCIDENTAL EXPENSE	Georgie Starbuck Galbraith	297
INNER LOOKING	Virginia Brasier	190
INTERRUPTION	Margaret Bailey Miles	350
INTERVIEW WITH A BUMBLE BEE	Doris Barnett Roach	273
INVADER	Gertrude Ryder Bennett	67
IT IS STILL GOD'S WORLD	Eunice Mildred LonCoske	29
IT'S A PROMISE!	Margaret Fishback	126
I'VE NEVER BEEN IN ENGLAND	Florence Wightman Rowland	181

J

JENNIFER JEAN	Janice Blanchard	198
JILL	Reba Peters Matheny	288
JIM AND MARION'S HOUSE	Violet Alleyn Storey	239
JIMMY	May Richstone	249
JUST FOR TODAY	B. Y. Williams	296

K

KEEP KNITTING	Margaret Eaton	189
KILLED IN ACTION	Esther Griffin White	189
KINDRED SOULS	Julia Reese Osborn	271
KNITTED SHAWL	Margaret Widdemer	20
KNOWING	John B. Cruise	347

L

LADY CONSOLED	Annette Patton Cornell	354
LADY IN A SPOT	Kathleen Sutton	160
LADY OF DESIGN	Annette Patton Cornell	161
LAMPLIGHTER	Elizabeth Dawson	264
LARGE SIGHS	Ernestine Mercer	310
LARKSPUR	Isla Paschal Richardson	220
LAST LEAVE	Edythe Hope Genee	354
LATE LOVE	Isabelle Bryans Longfellow	166
LATE REPAIRING	August Derleth	351
LATE SEPTEMBER	Sister Maris Stella	224
LATE SUMMER DUSK	Quincy Guy Burris	57
LAUGHTER—AFTER	Lolita L. Gilpin	320
LETTER	Isabel Fiske Conant	120
LETTER FROM LONDON	Marion Lipscomb Miller	116

INDEX—Continued

LETTER OF CONDOLENCE	John Robert Quinn	118
LETTER TO JIM	Ellis P. Legler	114
LETTER TO MANY	James E. Warren, Jr.	40
LETTERS	Florence M. Bennell	114
LET US BE SILENT	Maude Burbank Harding	290
LIFE HISTORY	Gail Brook Burket	36
LIFE TOGETHER	Joyce Horner	258
LIFE'S SYMPHONY	B. Y. Williams	294
LILLIPUT	Virginia French	37
LINES FOR A DEAD LIBERAL	Joseph Auslander	302
LINES FROM A DIARY	Esther Baldwin York	235
LIP WISDOM	Jane Sayre	294
LITTLE BOY GROWN	Edith Cherrington	251
LITTLE LADDERS	Kathryn Kay	242
LITTLE LAKE	Louise Driscoll	225
LITTLE LOST DOG	Blanche DeGood Lofton	280
LITTLE RABBITS	Ruth Lambert Jones	271
LIVE TODAY	Ruth Inscho	290
LONELINESS	Elsye Tash Sater	242
LOST LEAVE	Roena Burger	115
LOST LOVE	Marie Medora	288
LOVE	Helen Welshimer	230
LOVE LETTER	Cy Lance	113
LOVE LETTERS IN AN ATTIC	Dorothy Cowles Pinkney	343
LOVE SONG	Marguerite Janvrin Adams	101
LOVE SONG	Beatrice Payne Morgan	212
LOVE STORY	Mildred Goff	76
LOVE'S BOUNTY	Archibald Rutledge	143
LOVER'S RETURN	Harriet Seymour Popowski	254
LOVERS IN WARTIME	Alma Roberts Giordan	183
LULLABY FOR A YOUNG MOTHER	Edna Becker	127

M

MALE QUARTETTE	Pauline Starkweather	308
MAN THINKS MORE OF HIS HEART	James E. Warren, Jr.	293
MARRIAGE	Mary Carolyn Davies	98
MARY LOVED LILACS	Lulita Crawford Pritchett	86
MIDNIGHT IN AN EMPTY HOUSE	Julia B. Cohan	312
MISS AGATHA SEES A GHOST	Katharine Burt	327
MISS JULIE	William Arnette Wofford	337
MOMENTS	Mary Carolyn Davies	340
MONDAY IN APRIL	Aimée B. Andresen	52
MORE FITTING, I THINK	Berniece Graham	136
MOTHER FEELS A DRAFT	Louise Shaw	176
MOTHERHOOD	Edith Cherrington	14
MY COUNTY, 'TIS OF THEE	Dudley B. Madden	174

INDEX—Continued

MY FATHER AND I	Kathrine H. Williams	26
MY HEART	Blanche DeGood Lofton	152
MY HEART WILL KNOW	Mabel Newman	322
MY MOTHER	Anne Zuker	134
MY SECRET	Elizabeth S. Kunkle	299

N

NAMES OF HERBS	Cecilia Ellerbe	223
NAZARETH'S BOY	Jessie Wilmore Murton	17
NEVER TELL THE WHOLE OF IT	Mary Willis Shelburne	164
NEVER UNLOVED LET ME GO	Kaye Huizing	236
NEW POSTMAN	Isabel Fiske Conant	120
NEWS ITEM	Bessie Marlin Mason	268
"NO HELP WANTED"	Mildred Bresee Osterhout	104
NOTE TO AMERICA	Elaine V. Emans	193
NOTE TO THE POSTMASTER	Barbara A. Jones	112
NOW BEGIN AGAIN	Agnes L. Porter	263
"NOW IS THE TIME FOR ALL GOOD MEN TO—"	Angelo Lane	180
NURSE'S DAY OUT	Margaret Fishback	127
NURSERY NOTE	Thelma Ireland	286

O

O, THE LONG WAITING FOR THE WANTED WORD	Florence Hamilton	112
OCCUPATIONAL THERAPY	Sprague O. Smith	146
OCCUPATION: HOUSEWIFE	May Richstone	202
OCTOBER EVENING	Faith Baldwin	63
ODE TO A BREAKFAST EGG	Madeline Slade	201
ODE TO A JERSEY COW	Madeline Slade	282
OFFICE WOMAN SPEAKS	Marvel Barrow	152
OH, ABRAHAM	Cecile Bonham	16
OLD JOSIAH PREDICTS	Esther Houghtaling	336
OMNIA VINCIT AMOR	Frances Eleanor Schluneger	325
ON CLEANING CUPBOARDS	Mabel George Haig	199
ON LINCOLN'S BIRTHDAY	Thomas Curtis Clark	345
ON LEAVING	Hortense Roberta Roberts	224
ON PLANTING SEEDS	Audrey Wurdemann	219
ONE REBEL	Grace W. Lippincott	74
OUTMANEUVERED	Evantha Caldwell	34

P

PAGAN	Hazel E. Melamede	322
PAN GOES PLOWING	M. Agnes Thompson	223
PARADOX IN SOX	Lenore Eversole Fisher	162

INDEX—*Continued*

PARK AVENUE, LOOKING SOUTH	*Irwin Edman*	344
PATIENCE, PATIENCE	*W. E. Farbstein*	166
PATTERN FOR LOVE	*May Richstone*	107
PERSPECTIVES	*Ernestine Mercer*	310
PINEY WOODS GRIEVING	*Evantha Caldwell*	148
PINEY WOODS KINSHIP	*Evantha Caldwell*	79
PIONEER WOMAN	*May Frink Converse*	70
PLANKTON	*Harold Willard Gleason*	93
PLEDGE	*Dorothy Kissling*	321
PONTIUS PILATE SPEAKS	*Mabel Freer Loveridge*	23
PORTRAIT	*Billy B. Cooper*	86
PORTRAIT	*Sydney King Russell*	147
PORTRAIT OF MY MOTHER	*Margaret E. Bruner*	80
POSSESSION	*Mildred Cartwright Jobson*	297
POSSESSION	*Lesly Raine*	228
PRACTICAL CERTAINTY	*Kathryn Kay*	254
PRAIRIE SONG	*Charla M. Backlund*	38
PRAYER	*Kathryn Kay*	101
PRAYER	*Edith Haskell Tappen*	26
PRAYER AT EVENING'S END	*Adelaide Love*	105
PRAYER BY A VERY NEW DOCTOR	*Blanche DeGood Lofton*	150
PRAYER FOR A MAY MORNING	*Hazel Harper Harris*	209
PRAYER FOR POETS	*Joyce Marshall*	90
PRAYER OF THANKS	*Thomas Curtis Clark*	344
PRIVATE LIVES	*May Richstone*	80
PROCRASTINATOR	*Adrian F. Nader*	291
PROGNOSIS: FAVORABLE	*Patricia Martin*	252
PROMISE	*Frances Boal Mehlek*	345
PROTEST	*Marvel Barrow*	154
PUPPY LOVE	*Eloise Wade Hackett*	141
PURE IN HEART	*Kathryn Kay*	155
PUSSY WANTS A CORNER	*Ruth Stewart Schenley*	278

Q

QUERY	*Jessie Wilmore Murton*	46
QUESTION BEFORE THE HOUSE	*Mayhoward Austin McEachern*	22
QUESTION FROM A NEW MOTHER	*Naomi Reynolds Hess*	247
QUESTION ON LOT'S WIFE	*Mildred Shacklett*	15
QUIET PURITANS	*Isabel Fiske Conant*	27

R

RAIN AT MIDNIGHT	*Julia B. Cohan*	53
RATHER	*Mary Buirgy*	291
REASSURANCE	*Elsye Tash Sater*	215
RECOMPENSE	*Louise Shaw*	104
RECONCILED	*Pauline Havard*	88

INDEX—Continued

RECORDS FROM A CLOTHES-LINE	Agnes L. Porter	62
RED FOR MOURNING	Evantha Caldwell	153
REFUGEE	Bee Forsyth Wolverton	87
REGARDING THE MOLE	Anne Southerne Tardy	273
RELENTLESS TIME	Sarah Leeds Ash	259
REMEMBERING AN APRIL RAIN	Kay France	229
REMEMBRANCES	Ethel B. Cheney	261
REMINDER	Sydney King Russell	42
RETURN	Mary Coles Carrington	323
RETURN	Gertrude Perry Stanton	18
RETURN	Pauline Starkweather	213
RETURN TO SOMERSET FARM	Katherine Burt	326
RETURNING	Ethel Bradley Meyer	319
RHYME TO A PRISSY LADY	Enid Bryan	232
RIDDLE FOR THE PRACTICAL MAN	Sarah Leeds Ash	309
R. I. P.	John Paterson Brantner	257

S

SALE	Eugenie Carver	348
SARAH'S HEAVEN	Margaret Widdemer	353
SCULPTURED HANDS	Agnes Stewart Beck	76
SEEDING TIME	I. D. Perry	210
SELF-PRESERVATION	May Richstone	168
SENTINEL	Katherine Kelly Woodley	243
SEVENTY AND FIVE	Salibelle Royster	75
SHARING	Cecile Houghton Stury	28
SHELTER THE LITTLE ONES	Joseph Joel Keith	283
SILENT NIGHT	May Ward	181
SIMILITUDE	Helen Hooper	154
SINCE YOU HAVE GONE	Mary Carolyn Davies	234
SLEEP WELL	Nellie S. Richardson	295
SMALL GARDENS	Blanche W. Schoonmaker	209
SMALL GENTLEMEN PREFER MOMS	Susie Lee Cummings	129
SMALL ROOM	Dorothy Ashby Pownall	316
SO WE ARE THREE	David O. Selznick	351
SOFT CONQUEST	Anderson M. Scruggs	97
SOLDIERS' FAREWELL AT DAWN	Fay P. LeCompte	183
SOME OTHER TIME	Ellis P. Legler	61
SONG	Florence Hamilton	191
SONG FOR A CHILD	W. H. McCreary	197
SONG FOR EVENING	Nancy Byrd Turner	354
SONG OF FUTILITY	Ethel W. Wegert	151
SONG TO CHILDHOOD	Eunice Mildred LonCoske	247
SONNET	Carol Scott	312
SPIRIT	Louise Driscoll	39
SPRING SATURNALIA	Elsie-Jean	148

INDEX—Continued

SPRING WISDOM	Jessie Farnham	149
SPRING'S GOLDEN BELLS	Samuel J. Allard	269
STAR FROM AN APARTMENT	Myrtle Adams	205
STARSHINE AND SAWDUST	Blythe Cleave Bretz	70
STILL WATER	Polly Price Madden	79
STORY HOUR FOR REFUGEES	Helen Frazee-Bower	352
STRANGE COMFORTING	Katharine Washburn Harding	71
SUBSTITUTE	Elaine V. Emans	16
SUMMER OF ST. LUKE	Carrie Chase Sheridan	29
SUMMER STORM	Eugenie Carver	56
SUNDAY NIGHT SERVICE	Louise Lounsbury	19
SUNDAY SERVICE	Ethel Romig Fuller	39
SUNDAY SONG	Violet Alleyn Storey	171
SUN DIAL	B. Y. Williams	246
SURE THING	W. E. Farbstein	200
SURREALISTIC REACTION	Maude Barnes Miller	155
SURVIVORS	Samuel Schierloh	314

T

TALISMAN AGAINST TOMORROW	Irene Wilde	251
TEARS	Frances Alexander	333
TECHNIQUE	Jessie Farnham	146
TELL US A STORY, GRANDMOTHER	Marion Doyle	332
TELLING THE NEWS	Virginia Taylor McCormick	27
TELL-TAIL	Ernestine Mercer	281
THAN ONCE TO HEAR A SKYLARK SING	William L. Stidger	277
THE AGELESS	Rosa Zagnoni Marinoni	246
THE AWAKENING	Hallie Philips	105
THE BLUEBIRD	Marion Doyle	270
THE BOUQUETS	Ruth E. Lancaster	217
THE CALL	Elizabeth Virginia Raplee	45
THE CONVOY PASSES	Norma Jean Bunting	346
THE DANGER	Francesca	182
THE DESOLATE COUNTRY	Adelaide Love	47
THE DOG SALESMAN	J. Harvey Haggard	277
THE DREAM-BEARER	Mary Carolyn Davies	298
THE DREAMER	Katherine M. Hadden	162
THE DREAM SHINES ON	Nancy Byrd Turner	354
THE EMINENT GUEST	C. Faye Bennett	11
THE FALLEN WARRIOR	H. Ford Oglesby	186
THE FLAME AND THE SMOKE	Georgie Starbuck Galbraith	232
THE FOURTH COAT	Myrtle Adams	188
The Heart Grows Faint at Many Things	Dale Fisher	182
THE HEART IS A STRANGE THING	Minnie Case Hopkins	151
THE HEART OF HOME	Ethel Romig Fuller	200
THE HOUSE REJOICES	May Carleton Lord	192

INDEX—Continued

Title	Author	Page
THE LADY'S GARDEN	Janie Smith Rhyne	214
THE LAST SUPPER	Helen Welshimer	25
THE LITTLE ROAD	Minnie Case Hopkins	44
THE LONGEST HOUR	Elizabeth Grey Stewart	306
THE MAN OF IT	Marcia Nichols Holden	187
THE MISSES THING	Dorothy Ann Blank	90
THE MOON MENDER	John Richard Moreland	349
THE MOTHER	Ethel Barnett de Vito	175
THE MOTHER	Nell Griffith Wilson	109
THE MOTHER OF AN ANGEL SPEAKS	Rosa Zagnoni Marinoni	317
THE OLD FARM SLEEPS	Irene Stanley	60
THE POET	Adrian F. Nader	84
THE POET TO HIS DAUGHTER	Thomas Sugrue	136
THE PUMPKIN EATER'S WIFE	Irene Taylor	340
THE RACE	Helen Bickel	51
THE REASON	Mabel Newman	228
THE SCHOOL BUS TAKES MY YOUNGEST	Hazel M. Kerr	137
THE SECRET GARDEN	Robert Hillyer	212
THE SERVING MAID	Ethel B. Cheney	167
THE SILENCE	Julia B. Cohan	272
THE SILVER STIRRUP	Marguerite McCreary	338
THE TEMPO	Keith Thomas	287
THE TENANTS	Leah Bodine Drake	329
THE TOWN WATCH	Keith Thomas	64
THE WANDERER	Mary White Slater	33
THE WEATHERCOCK	Julia Anne Rogers	55
THE WIND BLOWS OVER YOU	Thomas Sugrue	236
THE WISH	Eunice Mildred LonCoske	208
THE WOMAN OF IT	Marcia Nichols Holden	142
THERE WERE TWO ROADS	Irene McDermott	35
THESE ARE THE EYES	Sarah Litsey	153
THEY SHALL COME BACK	Anderson M. Scruggs	193
THIS DAY	Isabelle Bryans Longfellow	257
THREAT	Nellie S. Richardson	77
THRESHOLD	Katherine van der Veer	50
TIED	Mabel Freer Loveridge	92
TIGERS WITHOUT MERCY LEAP	Tom Boggs	299
TIMBER LINE	Dorothy Garrison	32
TIME PIECES	Lalia Mitchell Thornton	259
TO A CERTAIN POET	Hazel E. Melamede	91
TO A FIRST GRAY HAIR	Gladys McKee	256
TO A LOVELY YOUNG LADY TEACHING GEOMETRY	Anderson M. Scruggs	116
TO A WRECKED AUTOMOBILE	Alice Morrey Bailey	314
TO A YOUNG WIFE	John Paul Seiberling	108
TO MY BROTHER	Helen Welshimer	177

INDEX—Continued

TO MY DAUGHTER	Eugenie Carver	348
TO SUSAN, REGARDING FRECKLES	Keith Thomas	170
TO THE ALMOST-FORGOTTEN	Georgie Starbuck Galbraith	231
TO YOU	Dorothy P. Albaugh	313
TODAY	Helen Welshimer	252
TRANQUILLITY	Grace Noll Crowell	41
TRAVELERS	Mabel Tuttle Craig	47
TROOP TRAIN FOR DOVER	Kaye Starbird	180
TURNABOUT	Kathryn Kay	243
TWO WORDS	Ethel Romig Fuller	108
TWO YEARS OLD	Nancy Moore	171

U

UNCLE JERRY	Adrian F. Nader	92

V

VALUES	Geraldine Ross	119
VERITY	Virginia Laura Smith	157
VIOLETS	Gertrude Ryder Bennett	221

W

WAITRESS	Elias Lieberman	89
WASHERWOMAN'S PRAYER	Helen Frazee-Bower	28
WASTE	Ernestine Mercer	255
WE HAVE WEPT	Mary-Scott Willour	307
We Put Our Souls Into the Things Called Things	Lulu W. Chittenden	293
WE WHO WAIT	Mary Cherry Phelps	178
WHAT DOES THE HEART REMEMBER?	Esther Baldwin York	261
WHEATEN INTERVAL	Ethel Romig Fuller	197
WHEN I AM OLD AND FULL OF YEARS	Julia Clay Barron Webb	17
WHERE DOES LAUGHTER GO?	Elva A. Smith	316
WHO WILL REMEMBER SPRING?	Edythe Hope Genee	260
WHY COWS FEED ONE WAY	Robert P. Tristram Coffin	311
WIND IN THE CITY	Harriet Lundgaard	65
WINDOW WASHING	Isabelle Bryans Longfellow	300
WIVES ARE SO UNSELFISH	May Richstone	335
WOMAN IN SPRING	Isabelle Bryans Longfellow	52
WOMAN'S SACRAMENT	Anna M. Priestley	22
WORDS FOR A DAUGHTER	Elizabeth Grey Stewart	34

INDEX—*Continued*

X

XANTHIPPE COMPLAINS TO A NEIGHBOR	*Julia Boynton Green*	249

Y

YES SURREALISM	*Johnny McKinney*	38
You Are So Economical of Love	*Ruth Carroll*	168
YOU CAN ALWAYS TELL WHERE A FAMILY LIVES	*Helen Welshimer*	132
YOU DIDN'T KNOW	*Eva Sparks Taylor*	82
YOU WOULD NOT THINK	*Ruth Lambert Jones*	268
YOUNG AMERICA—FIRST	*Billie Marie Crabb*	126
YOUNG CLERK	*Louise Liebhardt*	78
YOUNG FISHERMAN ON THE GULF	*Edith Tatum*	18
YOUNG MAN'S FANCY	*Thelma Ireland*	170
YOUNG MARINER	*Lois Snelling*	32

Z

ZOO'S WHO	*Johnny McKinney*	280